Perpetual Peace

Perpetual Peace

Essays on Kant's Cosmopolitan Ideal

edited by James Bohman and Matthias Lutz-Bachmann

The MIT Press
Cambridge, Massachusetts
London, England

Set in New Baskerville by The MIT Press.
Printed and bound in the United States of America.

Library of Congress Cataloging-in-Publication Data

Perpetual peace : essays on Kant's cosmopolitan ideal / edited by James Bohman and Matthias Lutz-Bachmann.
    p.   cm. — (Studies in contemporary German social thought)
    Includes bibliographical references and index.
    ISBN 0-262-02428-4 (hard : alk. paper). — ISBN 0-262-52235-7 (pbk. : alk. paper)
    1. Kant, Immanual, 1724–1804—Views on peace.   2. Kant, Immanuel, 1724–1804 —Criticism and interpretation.   3. Peace—Philosophy.   4. International organization—Philosophy.   5. Rule of law—Philosophy. I. Bohman, James. II. Lutz-Bachmann, Matthias. III. Series.
JX1946.P47   1997
327.1′72′092—dc21

96-37739
CIP

Contents

Perpetual Peace

Introduction

James Bohman and Matthias Lutz-Bachmann

Written in 1795 and slightly revised in 1796, Immanuel Kant's essay "Toward Perpetual Peace: A Philosophical Sketch" begins with a remark about the irony of its title. A peace can become "perpetual" in one of two ways. Humanity can find perpetual peace "in a vast grave where all the horrors of violence and those responsible for them would be buried."[1] Understood more optimistically, "perpetual peace" means that human beings can solve the problem of violence for a second time and emerge from the state of nature among nations with a new form of cosmopolitan law and "a peaceful federation among all the peoples of the earth." This cosmopolitan ideal is not only necessary for survival but also a requirement of practical reason. "Reason," Kant writes, "absolutely condemns war" and sets the achievement of peace as an "immediate duty."[2] Accordingly, the moral progress of humankind has only one yardstick: whether or not it can solve the problem of war and enter into a universal community of all peoples governed by the rule of law.

The immediate occasion for Kant's essay was the March 1795 signing of the Treaty of Basel by Prussia and revolutionary France. In this treaty, Prussia ceded to France all territory west of the Rhine, in exchange for which Prussia expected to be allowed to join Russia and Austria in partitioning Poland to the East. It is just this sort of strategic treaty that Kant condemns as illegitimate: it is only "the suspension of hostilities, not a *peace*." The "pure illusion" of the balance of power does nothing to change existing conditions between states or to create a new condition that would permit peace to become more than the temporary silence of weapons. Here Kant returns to Charles Irenée Castel de Saint-Pierre's "Projet pour rendre la paix perpétuelle en Europe," to which he owes not only the title of his essay but also its form: like other proposals for genuine peace throughout the eighteenth and nineteenth centuries, he adopts the convention of imitating the structure of a peace treaty with its articles and clauses.[3] Already in 1713, the Abbé de Saint-Pierre had proposed that peace could be brought about only by an "eternal peace treaty" that established a permanent congress of the states of Europe. Kant generalizes this proposal to include all peoples in a universal, cosmopolitan peace. Unlike the Abbé, however, Kant addresses his treatise not to the princes and rulers of Europe but to a public of all enlightened citizens of the world who see the necessity of establishing genuine peace. Kant's ill-ease at the political implications of such an audience compelled him to add a "Secret Article of Perpetual Peace" to the essay's second printing in 1796; the article asserts the secret permission of kings and state authorities that would allow philosophers "to speak freely and publicly on the universal maxims of warfare and peacemaking."[4]

There have been many other occasions in the 200 years since the publication of Kant's "Toward Perpetual Peace" for moral persons to give public voice to their condemnation of war and the horrors of organized political violence. The essay's anniversary year, 1995, also marked the fiftieth anniversary of the end of World War II and of the establishment of the United Nations Charter. The essays in this volume were written for a conference held at the Johann Wolfgang Goethe Universität in Frankfurt in May 1995 to commemorate all these anniversaries.[5] Taken together, they argue for the continued theoretical and practical relevance of the cosmopolitan ideals of Kant's "Toward Perpetual Peace." They also show that history has both confirmed and outstripped Kant's prognoses. Above all, the recent history of political violence has shown again and again that we have hardly solved the problem of the state of nature among states.

Long held to be a mere occasional essay, "Toward Perpetual Peace" is now widely accepted as a central work of Kant's political and legal philosophy, and as in many respects his most innovative work in this area. The pacifying effects of law [*Recht*] is its basic theme. Kant argues that a peaceful global order can be created only by a cosmopolitan law [*Weltbürgerrecht*] that enshrines the rights of world citizens and replaces classical law among nations [*Völkerrecht*].[6] Global peace is not only the goal of Kant's universal and progressive philosophy of history, which is explicitly written "from the perspective of the cosmopolitan citizen"; it is also an achievable goal. Kant proposes specific practical mechanisms (made efficacious by historical trends) by which the abolition of "the practice of war" becomes a feasible goal for future generations rather than an abstract moral demand or a utopian ideal. In "On the Common Saying, 'This may be true in theory but it does not apply in practice,'"[7] Kant had argued that "a world state" would represent the perfection of a republican constitution, but later he came to fear it as a potentially "soulless despotism." In "Toward Perpetual Peace" Kant admits that a world republic is "the one rational way to achieve peace," but he maintains that peace will be attained through the inevitable spread of the institutional and legal structure of a "peaceable federation" among independent republican states, each of which respects the basic rights of its citizens and establishes a public sphere in which people can regard themselves and others as free and equal "citizens of the world."

The end of the Cold War has brought hopes for new levels of political integration and for new regional and international institutions. At the same time, massive inequalities in the distribution of resources seem to undermine prospects for political order. Arguments concerning global justice and peace now seem to involve issues much broader than the costs Kant saw in "the constant preparations for war" entailed by the Westphalian model of peace among the nations of Europe. The very process of globalization that Kant made so central to "Toward Perpetual Peace" has continued unabated, with new and far-reaching consequences. On the one hand, increasing economic interdependence has changed the nature of international relations in ways that Kant could not have anticipated. As many of the contributors to this volume point out, some of the traditional issues of power and security are less important and others now have entirely different meanings.[8] The liberal hope of Kant and Mill that "the spirit of commerce" would create a harmony of interests on a world scale has faded.

Recent history has also increased the awareness of the value of the diversity of human communities. This emphasis on cultural pluralism, coupled with the negative consequences of resurgent nationalism, ethnic separatism, and religious fundamentalism, makes it more difficult to imagine a political solution to global conflicts based on principles and procedures that all can agree are fair. The very nature of war and armed conflict seems to have changed. At the end of a century that has seen unlimited wars against whole populations and the invention of weapons capable of previously unimaginable destruction, armed conflict now takes the form of genocidal civil wars that existing international organizations exhibit no capability or will to prevent. These "post-Westphalian" developments are the themes of many of the essays that make up the second half of this book, giving Kant's call for a basic shift from an international to a cosmopolitan order a new meaning.[9] While altering the assumptions that inform Kant's practical proposals, this new historical context actually makes the normative side of those proposals more, rather than less, interesting. (The same cannot be said for the descriptive side: with the benefit of 200 years' hindsight, many of our contributors revise or jettison Kant's progressive philosophy of history.)

Peace is in fact one of the central concepts in modern political philosophy, particularly in social contract theory. Widely agreed to be necessary for human flourishing and for a just political order, the peace of political order stands in sharp contrast with the violence of the state of nature. In "Toward Perpetual Peace," Kant shares the modern abhorrence of the violent consequences of "savage and lawless liberty." His cosmopolitan approach, however, stands in opposition to the predominant view of international relations since World War II: the "realistic" approach inspired by Thomas Hobbes.[10] According to the Hobbesian approach, violence is a necessary feature of all politics; because it is an ineliminable part of international politics, to eschew the acquisition of power is to forfeit the interests of one's national community. The logical consequence is that peace can be secured only through a credible balance of threats and the power to carry them out. Thus, the solution to the problem of international peace approximates the state of nature in Hobbes, where each sovereign state has the right to enforce its agreements with other states.

For Kant, even if such a balance of power is temporarily peaceful, it is not a true peace. A just peace can be achieved only if we leave this state of nature, since the continued threat of war promises to annihilate "civilization and all cultural progress through barbarous devastation."[11] Abolishing the practice of war is not merely a moral ought for Kant, since, as he notoriously argued, the problem of leaving the state of nature and entering civil society can be solved even by a "nation of devils."[12] Rather than rely on the coercion of the external Hobbesian sovereign, however, Kant seeks to achieve peace by instituting a new sort of public law. Compliance among states is not only a matter of survival and well-being (and thus of enlightened self-interest); it also requires a new sort of institutional setting for global political order in which the rights of the world citizens and the social conditions for peace are protected by both public law and world opinion. Most of all, Kant rejects the negative and temporary characterizations of peace that are the common coin of the realist tradition and of all international law in the usual sense of the term.

Kant develops his positive ideal of a "perpetual peace" on two different levels. First, it must offer an explanation of the causal mechanisms operating in human history that are sufficient to bring about global peace, even as nations are reluctant to surrender their "right" to protect their interests by war. Following the political economists of the Scottish Enlightenment, Kant's analysis of these trends depends on an invisible hand, which he calls "providential" but which we might today call dialectical. Despite, and indeed because of, human inclinations to aggressiveness and acquisitiveness, the spread and interconnection of peoples across the face of the earth will create the conditions of peace. Thus, *globalization* is the process by which the conditions for positive peace come about. Second, Kant argues that a positive and multidimensional conception of peace requires new institutions of *cosmopolitan law* [*Weltbürgerrecht*] above the level of the nation state. Civil law does not end the violent state of nature, since it is possible for a state to be internally peaceful and externally bellicose. These new legal institutions might simply replace the previous ones: just as republics have replaced the older constitutions, cosmopolitan law may simply supersede the potentially conflicting standards of local laws, unifying the human community at a global level beyond the current nation state. However, Kant defends a surprisingly pluralist conception of a global order with many different local identities and political arrangements. The tolerance of ineliminable human diversity is in fact a consequence of cosmopolitan peace, rather than a natural cause of conflict.

Contemporary challenges and defenses of the normative and descriptive aspects of Kant's proposal coalesce around three themes that are necessary for any critical reconstruction of Kant's cosmopolitan ideal. While all the essays in this volume reject Kant's descriptive "guarantees" of peace and his normative principle that states are sovereign "moral persons," they are Kantian to the extent that all agree that the modern ideal of peace must be both positive and cosmopolitan—that is, they all agree that only new institutions and political associations can hope to put "an end to all hostilities."[13] Any contemporary reconstruction of Kant's ideal of peace must respond to three challenges raised by recent historical developments, one concerning the nature of the globalization process on which it is based, a second concerning the status and sovereignty of nation states as political communities within a larger cosmopolitan order, and a third concerning the reconciliation of unity and difference within the cosmopolitan identities of Kant's "citizens of the world." These challenges are taken up to some degree or another in all of the essays.

The first thematic complex reflects the diverse effects of globalization. Most social scientists and philosophers today would argue that the logic of Kant's explanation of progress toward peace is not dialectical enough. While Nussbaum explores the contrast between Kant and the Stoics on natural teleology, criticisms of his faulty dialectical logic and historical teleology can be found in the essays by Jürgen Habermas, Karl-Otto Apel, James Bohman, and David Held, all of whom offer mechanisms for realizing the practical possibility of peace different from that offered by Kant's teleology of human convergence. These revised mechanisms lead to an explanation of the possibility of peace that is consistent with a more dialectical, less progressivist, and less uniform account of the problems and prospects of globalization.

The second thematic complex concerns Kant's insistence on the internal sovereignty of nations as a condition of global order. This assumption is behind many of the conceptual and empirical problems of Kant's conception of peace, particularly his shift away from the world republic of "Theory and Practice" (1793) to his self-described "negative substitute" of a slowly spreading federation of internally peaceful republics in "Toward Perpetual Peace" (1795). Matthias Lutz-Bachmann and Jürgen Habermas challenge this assumption and call for executive, legislative, and judicial components to world organizations that transcend the current nation-state system. Kenneth Baynes and David Held see a need for overlapping institutions and cross-cutting forms of authority and accountability, preferring a cosmopolitan structure that strengthens democratic self-governance at all levels.[14] National sovereignty is therefore a central issue in thinking about cosmopolitanism: it suggests an order that is not simply imposed from a center and yet one that is based on the rule of law.

The third thematic complex concerns the contrast between local and universal identities, between allegiance to particular communities and cosmopolitan citizenship. Martha Nussbaum explores this theme historically, and Baynes discusses it in light of recent communitarian proposals. Both try to show that cosmopolitanism and the moral universalism that underlies it do not have to exclude local attachments and institutional order. A related and difficult issue not discussed by Kant at all—the problem of illiberal societies—is taken up by Axel Honneth and Thomas McCarthy, both of whom defend strong versions of the cosmopolitan ideal of universal human rights. McCarthy insists on Kant's stronger account over John Rawls's weaker "reasonable law of peoples" (which would include illiberal but well-ordered societies).[15] In this regard, the problem of illiberal societies has become pressing: what we think of this problem determines what we think about the political role of human rights in levels of global governance above the nation state. Whereas Kant hesitated to give human rights full legal status as enforceable claims, Habermas explores all the implications of properly distinguishing law and morality in the justification and enforcement of human rights. Such rights of world citizens include the rights of individuals against the nation state. Although Kant neglected these legal rights in "Toward Perpetual Peace," they may be contained in his idea of a "right to hospitality" of each individual who travels and speaks anywhere in the world. Since Kant (following Cicero) insists that hospitality is a "right" and thus a duty rather than an act of benevolence, it is clearly a right that can be asserted against the sovereignty of nation states.

1 The "Dialectics" of Globalization

The process of creating worldwide networks of interaction sets the current parameters for a feasible cosmopolitan order. In general terms, globalization may be defined as the growing interconnectedness of states and societies, creating multiple and rapid networks of interaction and coordination that include the global economic system, global networks of communication and transgovernmental interaction, and forms of multilateral diplomacy and regulation that restrict the policies available to governments and citizens.[16] All these phenomena have existed to some degree since the beginning of the modern period. As Anthony Giddens puts it, "modernity is inherently globalizing."[17] For Giddens, this historical fact also implies that these processes are Western to the extent that it is Western institutions that have made global expansion and interconnection seemingly irresistible. But, for many social theorists, globalization has changed qualitatively in recent years. Not only has economic activity become worldwide in scope; there has been an intensification of the degree of "interaction and interconnectedness among the states and societies that make up international society."[18] These new and rapid interactions bring with them new levels of risk and uncertainty, making the regulatory and political instruments available to states less and less useful, particularly in controlling the effects of the world market. Against Kant, recent sociological analyses of globalization emphasize the two-sidedness of the political phenomena that it produces: globalization presents new opportunities as well as unparalleled risks; it opens up prospects for new forms of governance while threatening existing democracy to the core. Although globalization spreads through the escalation of power in larger and larger social systems and institutions, Honneth points out that it has also (once again dialectically) increased the power of transnational civil society.

Kant's own account of globalization is dialectical in a more specific and typically eighteenth-century sense: it is the unintended consequences of global interconnectedness that propel human beings toward peace, so long as they solve the problems that this form of order poses. Because peace cannot be achieved by some direct revolutionary act, "nature" must provide causal mechanisms that make this possible. The unintended consequences of human activities and the dispositions and inclinations that motivate them produce pacifying effects, particularly with regard to the power of commerce to create communal ties. Kant also counted on a political mechanism to achieve a slow spread of peaceful relations among internally peaceful republics, whose citizens are less likely to go to war as they realize their enlightened self-interests through critical public spheres.

Empirical research has to some extent borne out Kant's hypothesis about peaceable relations among liberal regimes.[19] But while Kant criticizes the grave injustices such regimes perpetrated in pursuit of their colonial ambitions, he does not recognize the ways in which increasing global interconnections under conditions in which resources are distributed unequally may only exacerbate international conflicts and separate the interests of liberal regimes from the rest of world society. As Habermas points out, the very forces unleashed by the world market undermine the effectiveness of Kant's political mechanism for progress toward peace, precisely because states can no longer influence the global processes they have unleashed. As globalization causes states to lose control over the historical process, Kant's teleology has no more social and cultural mechanisms to support it, leaving only the metaphysical appeal to nature's endowment of basic capacities and contradictory dispositions in human beings. In his essay, Apel tries to rethink the metaphysical or invisible-hand basis for such claims, arguing that it must be purified into a moral duty to take advantage of political opportunities to create the conditions of peace. Only in this way can the moral demand for peace be freed from Kant's two-world metaphysics and his teleological philosophy of history.

Habermas argues that the main problem with Kant's proposal is his inadequately dialectical conception of progress. He suggests in its place a more dialectical analysis of globalization—one earned through the bitter disappointments of the last 200 years. By "dialectical" Habermas does not mean simply that the invisible hand has its "backside," in Russell Hardin's apt phrase. Rather, he argues forcefully that historical evidence shows that all the basic trends that Kant identified are two-sided: they have promoted the conditions of peace, but they have also made the task more difficult. This two-sidedness can be seen in the failure of liberal societies to be peaceful in *all* their relations to other states; in the way the networks of global markets have also produced inequalities and powerful transnational actors (such as multinational corporations and banks) that escape the regulatory control of nation states, and in the fact that the global public sphere has emerged at the same time as mass media have undermined the kind of literary public sphere that Kant envisaged. Nonetheless, Habermas argues that globalization produces a constellation of forces that make peace feasible. But this feasibility requires that the promise of Kant's cosmopolitan law be fulfilled—that human rights achieve a *legal* status in the rights of world citizens as individuals, particularly as rights over and against the nation states in which they live. A properly reformed United Nations could be the instrument to implement and enforce this legal status for human rights, and both Habermas and Honneth see trends in this direction in recent events.

Globalization may be even more dialectical and less teleological than Habermas's analysis of new institutional possibilities suggests. It is difficult not to think of globalization in unilinear terms, with new international institutions simply replacing obsolescent local and national ones. Kant himself vacillated on this issue, at first seeing a "world republic" as the only solution to the problem of peace but later replacing this conception with a looser and less institutionally organized federation of republican states.[20] Lutz-Bachmann shows quite convincingly that the logic of Kant's argument, even in "Toward Perpetual Peace," suggests that a world republic with legislative, executive, and judicial powers is a requirement of cosmopolitan law. Although correct with regard to the status of human rights, such arguments may imply that the nation state, like the nation-state system, is historically obsolete, since the global threats of nuclear war and environmental catastrophe can be relieved only by a world government. Nonetheless, Held usefully distinguishes between world government and global governance, arguing that global governance of certain sorts of problems is in no way inconsistent with the continued existence of more local forms of government, including nation states. The problem is that Kant does not provide his federation with the capacities of global governance needed to overcome the current state of violence between states and to implement his innovative idea of a cosmopolitan law.

Furthermore, although globalization may increase interaction among spatially distant actors in different social contexts and geographical regions, the effects of these interactions are not uniform. This may cause "local transformations," shaped by distant events, that may be quite different at different locations. Indeed, such effects may be contradictory. The increased prosperity of the Korean automobile industry may increase poverty and displacement in the American Midwest, and vice versa. Thus, the outcome of globalization is, as Giddens puts it, "not necessarily or even usually a generalized set of changes acting in a uniform direction"; it "consists in mutually opposing tendencies."[21] This means, for example, that even if global social relations diminish nationalist feelings at the nation-state level, they may intensify ethnic or regional identities at a more local level. Thus, the nation state's position in the global order has become more complex: it is now too small for global economic problems and too large to ensure cultural identity. It may well be, in a dialectical twist, that the nation state must be strengthened, at least democratically, in order to make cosmopolitan law and democracy possible. Similarly, it may well be that "the declining grip of the West over the rest of the world is not a result of the diminishing impact of the institutions which first arose there but, on the contrary, a result of their global spread."[22] Thus, a better, less uniform, less unilinear conception of globalization can help us understand not only its effects and the problems that it poses but also the political opportunities for greater democracy that it offers.

Rather than simply the local level and the global level, or national law and cosmopolitan law, we need broader descriptive categories that capture the dialectical quality of the transformative interactions between them. In view of Kant's emphasis on the "guarantees" of peace, the positive ideal of peace requires a more empirically adequate account of globalization. The tendency to see globalization in teleological terms not only overestimates the positive effects of growing interdependence but also misleads practical attempts to approximate the normative ideal of cosmopolitan order.

2   National Sovereignty and Global Order

Another way in which Kant's inadequate descriptive categories skewed his normative approximations of the ideal conditions of peace may be found in his unqualified endorsement of the principle of the internal sovereignty of states, even at the level of cosmopolitan law. At first, Kant clearly rejected this political principle, seeing a strict analogy between exiting the state of nature in the founding of civil society and in the founding of the world republic. The subordination of all states to a world republic would lead to a sort of peace, but it could also produce a "soulless despotism," established on the Hobbesian logic of the need for a supreme coercive power to enforce agreements. Moreover, the unity of reason seems to preclude the possibility of conflicts between republican and cosmopolitan law. But whether he interpreted the nation state as oppressive to human freedom or as the realistic component of his theory that leads him to appeal to the providence of nature, the fact is that Kant accepted the existing states as "legal persons" each having legitimate legal authority.

In the Preliminary Articles to "Toward Perpetual Peace," Kant outlines the necessary conditions for peace among states—particularly the establishment of strict publicity, further ensured by the presence of an enlightened, critical, and educated world public (a role narrowly identified with philosophers in the Second Supplementary Article). World citizens maintain the cosmopolitan public sphere in their societies and expose violations of human rights to the verdict of world public opinion. Bohman argues that there are indeed many different and overlapping and transnational public spheres for world citizens, and that public opinion rather than coercive law seems to be the sole mechanism for the enforcement of human rights. All other political mechanisms and institutions seem ruled out by the principle of sovereignty that grants each state "supreme power" over its territory. But a truly transnational public sphere requires at the very least a shift in power from the state to civil society. Kant's "right to hospitality" and his requirement that states have the consent of the people to wage war already set out normative conditions for a transformation of power in favor of transnational civil society.[23]

All the philosophers in this volume reject the unqualified principle of internal sovereignty, especially as it is incorporated in the international law of the existing nation-state system. Most seek something stronger than Kant's "federation of free states" but weaker than a single world republic. For many the globalization of economic processes and environmental risks requires the creation of more effective political and regulatory instruments at the supranational level. Moreover, most argue that the rule of law at the international level must in some way institutionalize basic human rights. All acknowledge, however, that constitutions that would make the rule of law possible at the global level have not yet been formulated.

Despite this general agreement about the need for global governance, fundamental differences remain in how to get there from here. These turn on whether or not the institutionalization of cosmopolitan law requires a strengthening or a weakening of sovereignty at more local levels, including that of the nation state. Of course, the introduction of any effective supranational rule of law would require some limits on the powers and policies of existing states, particularly nation states that violate human rights in pursuit of their national goals. However, it is hard to see how such supranational protections could be implemented except via a legitimate legal system operating at the local level.

If we reject the view that globalization simply means the obsolescence of the nation state and the irrelevance of local communities, then it is plausible to argue that local sovereignty must be strengthened for the sake of effective global governance. Such sovereignty might now be concerned with regulatory control, such as giving local communities influence over environmental policies. This interactive view, particularly well developed by Held, argues against simply transferring sovereignty to the supranational level, instead seeing it as dispersed and overlapping into many different levels, from local to national to global. Baynes also defends a conception of "differentiated sovereignty" and, along with Held and Bohman, sees it as part of introducing the concept of democracy into Kant's cosmopolitanism. Global governance requires local forms of sovereignty in order to allow for citizen accountability. At the same time, the publics that are affected by a problem or a policy may extend beyond any particular political unit, requiring that the sovereignty of world citizens be built up out of cosmopolitan and transnational interconnections between publics to allow for real accountability on the global scale.

Kant's unease about world government is reflected by the many contemporary critics for whom cosmopolitanism has become a derogatory term. In *Cosmopolis*, Stephen Toulmin identifies cosmopolitanism as a hidden and essentially oppressive political agenda of modernity "dominated by the Newtonian image of massive power, exerted by sovereign agency through the operation of central force."[24] This central force or apex of power is primarily the modern nation state. In light of such objections, it is one of the strengths of "Toward Perpetual Peace" that Kant insists upon the disanalogies between the state and global governance. As opposed to such centralized vision, the Kantian proposal can be reinterpreted as a defense of a democratic sovereignty of citizens that is differentiated and polycentric. Held sees this as leading to a variety of interactions involving transnational, subnational, national, and multinational institutions. For these connections, Kant relied on mechanisms of influence rather than force. Habermas, on the contrary, argues that human rights that genuinely protect individuals' rights must be backed by the coercive and constitutional power of an international court that understands violations of human rights as crimes against an enforceable cosmopolitan law.

Other critics of cosmopolitanism see it as overly unifying and contrast it sharply with pluralism. Amy Guttman opposes multiculturalism to "the cosmopolitan view of most people sharing a similar mixture of cultures that assimilates everyone into one cosmopolitan culture."[25] Similarly, Michael Walzer explicitly contrasts pluralism and cosmopolitanism, criticizing the latter for its abstract universalism.[26] As Habermas notes, existing international institutions perform a "real abstraction," employing an implicit model of the state that only a few of its members live up to internally. But cosmopolitan law does not require such abstraction. Baynes argues that linking cosmopolitanism to more differentiated and dispersed democratic sovereignty goes a long way toward meeting communitarian objections. Nussbaum notes that even among the Stoics the moral attitude of cosmopolitanism did not preclude local attachments and particular loyalties. Rather, it permits a tolerant and encompassing moral pluralism that allows people to "think from the standpoint of everyone else." Cosmopolitanism needs to balance both sorts of claims by recognizing the unity that each of us has with all others as world citizens, as well as the diversity of societies and their values. It is this type of universalist politics that promotes peace and allows diversity to flourish.

Even if the term 'cosmopolitanism' can be reclaimed for this type of pluralist politics, difficult practical issues of multiculturalism and social complexity remain.[27] First, cosmopolitan politics must face the possibility of deep conflicts among these groups and societies that would make it difficult for all to agree on methods and procedures of adjudication. As the largest political community, the community of world citizens would be characterized by many cross-cutting and potentially conflicting allegiances and obligations. The forms of agreement that hold it together would have to be suitably pluralistic without surrendering the basis for cooperative and peaceful relations.[28] Moreover, such a society faces problems of unprecedented size and complexity, both of which challenge the very idea of democratic control over social processes. In moral theory, many accept that universality need not be embodied in a single perspective. The key here is to create structures that do not demand that a single set of institutions or actors solve these problems.

3 Pluralism, Cosmopolitanism, and the Problem of Illiberal Societies

If properly organized, cosmopolitan institutions need not be inimical to pluralism. With "differentiated sovereignty" there is room for cross-cutting and overlapping levels of regulation and control, and there is space for the formation of particular cultural identities and communal ties. Kant allowed for such pluralism in his idea of a world federation, although he believed that only republics, with the rule of law and with self-rule by citizens, could be peaceful enough to respect the integrity of one another's communal ties and boundaries. But the greater the pluralism, the greater the potential for conflicts at the cosmopolitan level. This raises the deep problem of the limits of toleration and the status of illiberal societies and antidemocratic regimes. Kant avoids this problem, since he argues that the mutual recognition of law-abiding republican states is the only way that peace will be spread by influence rather than by force. The reformulation of the idea of sovereignty and of cosmopolitan institutions suggested above also seems to support a similar idea, in that differentiated sovereignty seeks to promote democratization at different levels of political integration. It is hard to imagine democratization of the nation state without a robust and democratic civil society and public sphere. Similarly, it is hard to imagine democratic and accountable institutions at the local and cosmopolitan levels without democratic and accountable institutions at the regional and national levels and without a robust transnational civil society. Where do nondemocratic regimes stand in such a polycentric cosmopolitan order?

In his essay "The Law of Peoples," John Rawls has provided perhaps the best Kantian response to this problem—one that retains the Kantian pluralism of societies and states along with a conception of international justice. As did Kant, Rawls thinks of the political problem here as that of any political association: to create a social world in which reasonable persons, as free and equal, "can cooperate freely with others on terms all can accept."[29] It is particularly important that each society decide on its own acceptable constitutional regime that directs the legitimate exercise of public power. In view of the "fact of oppression" in pluralistic societies and the fact that international society will have the highest degree of pluralism, the law of peoples requires Rawls to go beyond the liberal conception in order "to yield a more general law of peoples without prejudging the case against nonliberal societies."[30] Rawls argues on the basis of a principle of toleration that we must accept that there are other "reasonable ways of ordering society." He specifies the general criteria for the admission of nonliberal societies into the community of peoples: that they be "well-ordered hierarchical societies," that they not be expansionist, that they be informed by a conception of the common good, that they have a consultation hierarchy (instead of a public sphere), and that they respect the basic rights of their members (although this does not include some civil rights endorsed by the United Nations Charter, such as rights of free expression). In his essay, McCarthy questions whether *liberal* societies ought to surrender such basic political principles as the free use of public reason for the sake of making an agreement on the law of peoples with societies that do not share those principles.

As in his previous criticisms of Rawls's method of avoidance, McCarthy (like Habermas) rejects Rawls's expansion of the notion of the reasonable to the point that it seems only to countenance the de facto pluralism of the status quo.[31] Rawls seems to undermine any basis for the goal of his own nonideal theory: that liberal societies have the duty to assist others now burdened with "unfavorable conditions" in achieving a well-ordered society. This assistance is directed not only to resource inequalities but also to problems related to public political culture. To this extent, any account of the spread of processes of enlightenment of public opinion—Kant's "negative substitute" for a world state and main mechanism for achieving conditions of peace—must consider creating favorable social, economic, and political conditions for peace, including overcoming the profound asymmetries of wealth and power typical of current transnational interactions. Although (as Habermas too points out) Kant does not consider such conditions in his definition of peace, Rawls neglects the necessary conditions for a process of enlightenment within societies. Honneth defends "the politics of human rights," which seeks to protect transnational civil society from illiberal states, against the objections of a Hobbesian and consequentialist version that has been made popular by Hans Magnus Enzensberger in Germany.[32] With the escalation of power typical of modern societies and states, Honneth argues, it is an illusion to think that coercive international law can substitute for creating the democratic and economic basis for human rights in each society.

If this is the process of enlightenment that promotes peace, what would a global order that achieved the free exchange of public opinion look like? What is the outline of a more robust "ideal theory" of the law of peoples? This issue is explored most fully in the second half of Habermas's essay. After rejecting Carl Schmitt's arguments against any politics of human rights as an ethnocentric imposition, he argues that human rights ought to be understood not as merely moral rights but as legal rights in the first instance. It is here that we might see a very specific rejection of the unlimited role of internal sovereignty in current international law. Consistent with the theme of democratization at various levels developed above, it is important that human rights be enshrined at all levels of local and global governance. But if Habermas is right, then human rights must be the domain of cosmopolitan law, which institutionalizes basic rights of individuals and the rule of law at the supranational level. As Hannah Arendt argued in light of the rightless condition of "stateless peoples," human rights cannot any longer be enforceable only by nation states. If there is any room for coercion in cosmopolitan law, it is in the enforcement of human rights precisely against states that use their sovereignty to abuse human rights for particular political, religious, or nationalist goals. If the regulation of global processes such as market effects is the legislative side of global governance, then enforcing claims of citizens against states is its judicial side.

Pluralism requires a broader and more inclusive conception of peace, with a broader and more inclusive set of rights, including rights of cultural membership.[33] Such a revision, however, means rewriting the necessary conditions for the spread of peace contained in Kant's Preliminary Articles to include just those basic rights necessary for free processes of enlightenment, which would take different forms in different political cultures. In this particular sense of inhibiting enlightenment, the sovereignty of nation states stands in the way of cosmopolitan law. Some mechanism of world public opinion and input must be developed to limit the use of such force by institutions of global governance to creating these social conditions and only these social conditions, lest cosmopolitan order begin to take on the features that Toulmin and Walzer find so objectionable and that Kant found "despotic." Escaping the dilemmas of despotism and fragmentation remains the most difficult institutional challenge of a cosmopolitan order; showing how the public use of reason permits both unity and difference is a task that the Kantian conception of reason has yet to solve.

4 Cosmopolitanism and Its Critics

Three misconceptions about cosmopolitanism are especially inappropriate to reconstructed versions of Kant's ideal. First, it is important to see that globalization is not a unilinear or uniform process.

Rather, it is dialectical in the fullest sense, in that global interactions may have opposing effects at different sites and may also reinforce certain local forms of power or identity. Second, cosmopolitanism requires not a unified center of political power but a differentiated institutional structure with various levels of democratic sovereignty. Third, cosmopolitanism and universal human rights are not inimical to pluralism but are consistent with a variety of local attachments and identities. A politics that promotes more than de facto pluralism would have to ensure that all societies have access to the social and economic conditions of enlightenment—that is, the necessary conditions for the public use of reason by their members. Since asymmetries with regard to such things as access to resources and power have not been overcome even at the nation-state level, we are still a long way from fair and democratic global governance. A better-developed transnational civil society consisting of self-organized groups below the nation-state level is a condition for building global governance and making it work democratically.

Many critics rightly fear that cosmopolitan law backed by centralized coercive power might only heighten the asymmetries of power already present in the nation-state and global-market systems. This might be true if cosmopolitan law were conceived on a different model of politics, with less differentiated, less pluralistic, and less polycentric institutional forms. It would also be true for a conception of enlightenment that did not promote the emergence of indigenous public spheres, each of which is potentially cosmopolitan. However, it is clear from the existing large inequalities of resources and asymmetries of power that vibrant cultural pluralism in transnational civil society is a necessary condition for introducing the powerful instrument of law into transnational institutions and practices. The pluralism that exists at present promotes neither justice nor peace.

A proper understanding of the dialectics of globalization, of the limits and scope of national sovereignty, and of a fully multicultural cosmopolitanism is now needed in order to restore the political attractiveness of the cosmopolitan ideal for an age disillusioned with progress. Cosmopolitan law and institutions are, if anything, solutions to contemporary problems more urgent and threatening than the threat of war was for Kant. Aside from the inescapable connections between the fate of Western democracies and the fates of all other political communities resulting from such dangers as global warming and new forms of violence, it is clear that living up to democratic ideals of political and economic justice (democratic self-determination and freedom from destitution, abject suffering, hunger, and environmental catastrophe) is now truly and unavoidably a cosmopolitan project.

Notes to Introduction

1. Kant, "Toward Perpetual Peace: A Philosophical Sketch," in *Kant's Political Writings*, ed. H. Reiss (Cambridge University Press, 1970), p. 105.

2. Kant, "Toward Perpetual Peace," p. 104. Kant makes a similar claim in *The Metaphysics of Morals*: "The moral practical reason within us pronounces its irresistible veto: There shall be no war, either between individuals in the state of nature or between separate states. . . ." (*Political Writings*, p. 194) The essays in this volume will employ the Cambridge translation for the sake of consistency, despite its inadequacies. It is particularly problematic in its translations of *Recht*; when translated as "right," the term does not convey the real innovation of Kant's "Toward Perpetual Peace," the development of a distinctly cosmopolitan *law* of peoples. Such cosmopolitan law goes beyond international law even as it is understood today, either by modern natural-right theory or contemporary neo-Hobbesian realism. Furthermore, the term *Völker* is ambiguous; it means "peoples," even though *Völkerrecht* is the standard German term for international law. Whenever Kant does not mean traditional international law, we have translated it as "peoples." It does not mean "nations," a term more associated with nationalism and a term that did not yet exist in Kant's time; Kant also clearly discusses peoples as a cultural category different from states, the form of political organization (to paraphrase Weber) requiring coercive law and the monopoly of the means of violence in a territory. All these translation problems increase the difficulties of interpreting Kant's already ambiguous text.

3. For a collection of the entire discussion about world peace around 1800 in Germany, see *Ewiger Frieden? Dokumente einer deutschen Diskussion um 1800*, ed. A. and W. Dietzen (Kiepenheuer, 1989).

4. Kant, "Toward Perpetual Peace," p. 115.

5. The complete set of conference papers has been published in German as *Frieden durch Recht*, ed. J. Bohman and M. Lutz-Bachmann (Suhrkamp, 1996). The present volume presents a selection of these essays for an English-language audience, with a new introduction and a contribution by Karl-Otto Apel added.

6. As noted above, the extant translations do not do justice to the myriad ambiguities of the term *Recht* in "Toward Perpetual Peace." It is clear that the pacifying effect of law is fundamental to Kant's proposal for an "eternal" peace and to his entire political philosophy; in this essay he is concerned with cosmopolitan law (*ius cosmopolitikon*), which he was to distinguish from classical international law. Kant calls Pufendorff, Grotius, and Vattel "sorry panderers" who are "dutifully quoted in justification of military aggression" (p. 103). The invented word "right" tries to retain this

Introduction

basic ambiguity and reflects how Kant clearly thinks that this new form of *law* establishes the *rights* of the world citizen qua person or human being. But, as a neologism, "right" conveys very little, so we have attempted to avoid its use where possible. The translated essays in this volume try to preserve these ambiguities as well as Kant's basic innovation: the idea of a cosmopolitan *law*.

7. This is often referred to as "Theory and Practice."

8. See, for example, Robert Keohane and Joseph Nye, *Power and Interdependence: World Politics in Transition* (Little, Brown, 1977).

9. On the contrast between the Westphalian and cosmopolitan models of global order, see David Held, *Democracy and Global Order* (Polity, 1995), pp. 74–98.

10. On the contrast between these two basic approaches in study of international relations, see of Janna Thompson, *Justice and World Order* (Routledge, 1992), part I. Thompson defends a modified version of the Kantian program.

11. Kant, "Idea for a Universal History with a Cosmopolitan Purpose," *Political Writings*, p. 49. Enlightenment is crucial to the process by which "a pathologically enforced social union is transformed into a moral whole" (p. 45).

12. Kant, "Toward Perpetual Peace," pp. 112–113.

13. Ibid., p. 93.

14. For the most developed account of this approach, see Held, *Democracy and Global Order*, chapter 9.

15. See John Rawls, "The Law of Peoples," in *On Human Rights: The Oxford Amnesty Lectures 1993* (Basic Books, 1993), p. 50ff.

16. This discussion of globalization owes much to Anthony Giddens, *The Consequences of Modernity* (Stanford University Press, 1990); see p. 63ff. For a more directly political analysis of the consequences of globalization for democracy in the nation state, see David Held, "Democracy, the Nation State and the Global System," in *Political Theory Today*, ed. D. Held (Stanford University Press, 1991).

17. Giddens, *Consequences of Modernity*, p. 63.

18. Held, "Democracy, the Nation State and the Global System," p. 206.

19. This empirical regularity has in fact been called "Doyle's Law." For its initial formulation see Michael Doyle, "Kant, Liberal Legacies and Foreign Affairs (Part I)," *Philosophy and Public Affairs* 12, no. 3 (1983): 205–235 and "Part II," 12, no. 4: 323–353.

20. Kant, "Theory and Practice," in *Political Writings*, p. 92.

21. Giddens, *Consequences of Modernity*, p. 64.

22. Ibid., p. 52.

23. Pauline Kleingeld has pointed out to us that these two normative demands on the state show that the principle of sovereignty is not inviolable for Kant. Above all, the

"Third Definitive Article" on the right of universal hospitality could be used to respond to some of the criticisms of Kant's conception of state sovereignty. See "Toward Perpetual Peace," pp. 105–108. Dvid Held discusses this right in his essay below.

24. Stephen Toulmin, *Cosmopolis: The Hidden Agenda of Modernity* (University of Chicago Press, 1990), p. 209.

25. Amy Guttman, "The Challenge of Multiculturalism in Political Ethics," *Philosophy and Public Affairs* 22, no. 3 (1993), p. 184. Cosmopolitanism is rejected because it is "comprehensive universalism," which "overlooks cases of moral conflict where no substantive standard can legitimately claim a monopoly on reasonableness or justification" (ibid., p. 194). Guttman weakens universalism in a way similar to Rawls's relaxation of the criterion of reasonableness for the Law of Peoples. We need not, however, reserve the term cosmopolitan for such assumptions about the singularity of public reason or the standards of moral agreement. Instead, we may think of the cosmopolitan ideal in more Kantian terms: the maximum amount of pluralism consistent with social and global peace. On pluralism, moral conflict, and the political use of public reason, see James Bohman, "Cultural Pluralism and Public Reason: The Problem of Moral Conflict in Political Liberalism," *Political Theory* 23, no. 2 (1995): 253–279.

26. Compare Michael Walzer's discussion of abstract universalism as a "moral Esperanto" in *Interpretation and Social Criticism* (Harvard University Press, 1987), p. 14; see also his "Pluralism: A Political Perspective," in *The Rights of Minority Cultures*, ed. W. Kymlicka (Oxford University Press, 1995).

27. On these problems for democratic self-rule in large-scale, complex, pluralistic societies, see chapters 2 and 4 of James Bohman, *Public Deliberation* (MIT Press, 1996).

28. On the emphasis on pluralism in Hannah Arendt's conception of human rights and her analysis of the potential conflicts of pluralism and equality in cosmopolitan societies, see James Bohman, "The Moral Costs of Political Pluralism: The Dilemmas of Equality and Difference in Arendt's 'Reflections on Little Rock,'" in *Hannah Arendt: Twenty Years Later*, ed. L. May and J. Kohn (MIT Press, 1996).

29. John Rawls, *Political Liberalism* (Columbia University Press, 1993), p. 50.

30. Rawls, "The Law of Peoples," p. 65.

31. See Thomas McCarthy, "Kantian Constructivism and Reconstructivism: Rawls and Habermas in Dialogue," *Ethics* 105, no. 1 (1994): 44–63. For an even stronger defense of Kantian practical reason against Rawls "political" turn, see Habermas, "Reconciliation through the Public Use of Reason: Remarks on John Rawls' Political Liberalism," *Journal of Philosophy* 52 (1995): 109–131.

32. For a particularly pessimistic version of German neo-Hobbesianism, see Hans Magnus Enzensberger, *Aussichten auf den Bürgerkrieg* (Suhrkamp, 1993); Honneth criticizes Enzensberger's historical, descriptive and anthropological assumptions in his essay in this volume. These criticisms can be generalized to other neo-Hobbesian, consequentialist arguments against the political significance of human rights.

33. On these cultural rights, see Will Kymlicka, *Multicultural Citizenship* (Oxford University Press, 1995).

I

Kant's Cosmopolitan Ideal in "Toward Perpetual Peace": Historical Reconstructions

1

Kant and Cosmopolitanism

Martha C. Nussbaum

The peoples of the earth have . . . entered in varying degrees into a universal community, and it has developed to the point where a violation of laws in *one* part of the world is felt *everywhere*. The idea of a cosmopolitan law is therefore not fantastic and overstrained; it is a necessary complement to the unwritten code of political and international law, transforming it into a universal law of humanity.
—*Kant, "Toward Perpetual Peace"*[1]

Let us take hold of the fact that there are two communities—the one, which is truly great and truly common, embracing gods and men, in which we look neither to this corner nor to that, but measure the boundaries of our state by the sun; the other, the one to which we have been assigned by our birth.
—*Seneca, De Otio*

1

In recent years it has become fashionable for philosophers to look to the ancient Greeks for alternatives to the Enlightenment and its idea of a political life based on reason. Under the influence of Nietzsche, eminent thinkers of quite different sorts have felt dissatisfaction with a politics based on reason and principle, and have believed that in the ancient Greek *polis* we could find an alternative paradigm for our own political lives, one based less on reason and more on communal solidarity, less on principle and more on affiliation, less on optimism for progress than on a sober acknowledgment of human finitude and mortality. Thinkers in this Nietzschean tradition have differed about which Greeks they take to be the good Greeks—since usually it will be granted that reason took over and killed off the good developments at some point. For Nietzsche, famously, the bad times begin with Euripides. For Heidegger, they seem to have begun even sooner, with the death of Parmenides or Heraclitus, whichever came first. For Bernard Williams,[2] things do not get really bad until Plato, but then they get very bad quite rapidly. And for Alasdair MacIntyre,[3] it would seem that the good times persist at least through the lifetime of Aristotle and his medieval successors, and do not get really awful until Hume and Kant.

Nor do thinkers in this tradition agree precisely about what they take to be good in the Greeks and bad in their Enlightenment successors. For Nietzsche and for Bernard Williams, who is the closest of this group to Nietzsche's original idea, the good thing was to base politics on the recognition that the world is horrible and fundamentally unintelligible; the bad thing was to pretend that it has an intelligible rational structure *or* anything to make us optimistic about political progress. In a paper written after his book,[4] Williams has criticized more or less all of Western political philosophy, and in particular the philosophies of Hegel and Kant,[5] for bringing us "good news," and has praised Sophoclean tragedy for directing us simply to contemplate "the horrors." For MacIntyre and for Heidegger—and there are certainly elements of this position in Williams also—the good thing is to suppose that in a well-ordered community we execute our tasks without reflection; the bad thing is to suppose that each political act needs, and can have, a rational justification.[6] For Heidegger, again, the good thing is to wait somewhat passively for the revelation of Being, the way a poet waits for the voice of inspiration or the believer for the voice of God. The bad thing is to take matters into our own hands, crafting our politics to suit our own perceived human purposes. All agree, at any rate, in their opposition to a hopeful, active, and reason-based politics grounded in an idea of reverence for rational humanity wherever we find it.

It is not my purpose to quarrel with these thinkers' interpretation of the Greek *polis*—though in fact I believe that they vastly underrate the importance of rational justification and rational argument to the fifth-century *polis* and fifth-century tragedy, and hence underrate the continuity between the *polis* and its philosophers.[7] I have more sympathy, in this regard, with the view of G. E. R. Lloyd, who throughout his career has perceptively stressed the difference that a rational style of political life made to the unfolding of science and philosophy in the ancient Greek world.[8] Nor is it my purpose to quarrel directly with the lessons these thinkers take from the Greeks and apply to modern political thought—although in some respects it will become clear what my attitude to those lessons is.

My purpose in this paper, instead, is to begin writing a different chapter in the history of our classical heritage, one from which I think we can derive lessons of direct political worth. For all the Nietzschean thinkers I have named, perhaps the arch-foe is Immanuel Kant.[9] Kant, more influentially than any other Enlightenment thinker, defended a politics based upon reason rather than patriotism or group sentiment, a politics that was truly universal rather than communitarian, a politics that was active, reformist, and optimistic, rather than given to contemplating the horrors, or waiting for the call of Being. The struggle between Kantians and Nietzscheans is vigorous in the Germany of today, as Habermas's Kantian program for politics does battle with the legacy of Heidegger. The same struggle is joined in the Anglo-American world, as the Kantian politics of John Rawls is increasingly at odds with forms of communitarian political thought favored by Williams, MacIntyre, and others. In 1995 we had a special reason to reassess Kant's political legacy, since we celebrated the two-hundredth anniversary of the publication of "Toward Perpetual Peace," in which he mapped out an ambitious program for the containment of global aggression and the promotion of universal respect for human dignity. My aim in this paper will be to trace the debt Kant owed to ancient Stoic cosmopolitanism. It will be my contention that Kant—and, through him, Seneca, Marcus Aurelius, and above all Cicero—present us with a challenge that is at once noble and practical; that trying to meet this challenge will give us something far better to do with our time than to wait for the call of Being, or even to contemplate the horrors, many though there surely are to contemplate—that, in short, if we want to give the world a paradigm from the ancient Greco-Roman world to inform its engagement with the political life, in a time of ethnic violence, genocidal war, and widespread disregard for human dignity, it is this one that we should select.

2

Kant's "Toward Perpetual Peace" is a profound defense of cosmopolitan values. The term "cosmopolitan" occurs frequently throughout Kant's political writings, often in close proximity to classical citations and references.[10] Although his own version of cosmopolitanism grows out of a distinctive eighteenth-century tradition, both the tradition itself and Kant's own approach to it are saturated with the ideas of ancient Greek and especially Roman Stoicism, where the idea of the *kosmou politês* (world citizen) received its first philosophical development.[11] Although Kant characteristically discusses Stoic ideas only in a brief and general way, without precise textual detail, he seems nonetheless to have been profoundly shaped by them, or at least to have found in them a deep affinity with his own unfolding ideas about cosmopolitan humanity. Some of the Stoic influence on him derives, certainly, from his reading of modern writings on natural law that are themselves heavily indebted to Cicero and other ancient thinkers. But Kant's deep familiarity with the major Roman authors shapes his engagement with their ideas in a very close and detailed manner. We know, for example, that Cicero's *De Officiis*, a pivotal text in the moral philosophy of the period, was especially important to Kant at the time when he was writing the *Groundwork* and the later ethical/political works. Klaus Reich has shown in detail that the argument of the *Groundwork* follows Cicero closely, especially in its way of connecting the idea of a universal law of nature with the idea of respect for humanity.[12] Seneca seems to have been important throughout this period also. The influence of Marcus Aurelius appears to have been less direct, but one may still discern its presence, especially in Kant's fondness for the term "citizen of the world."[13]

The attempt proves of interest in part because of similarities it discloses; even more fascinating, however, are some profound differences of aim and philosophical substance that come to light. Seeing where Kant diverges from thinkers with whom he is so solidly allied, with respect to the twin goals of containing aggression and fostering respect for humanity, assists us in no small measure in understanding his political project. I shall therefore first set out in a schematic way the general outlines of Stoic cosmopolitanism as Kant was aware of it, combining, as he does, the contributions of various thinkers, including Cicero, Seneca, and Marcus; then I shall show the extent of Kant's affinity with those ideas. Finally, I shall explore two important differences between the Kantian and the Stoic projects concerning aggression, war, and peace in the areas of *teleology* and *theory of passions.*

3

Asked where he came from, Diogenes the Cynic replied "I am a citizen of the world."[14] He meant by this, it appears, that he refused to be defined by his local origins and local group memberships, so central to the self-image of a conventional Greek male. He insisted on defining himself, primarily, in terms of more universal aspirations and concerns. It would appear that these concerns focused on the worth of reason and moral purpose in defining one's humanity. Class, rank, status, national origin and location, and even gender are treated by the Cynics as secondary and morally irrelevant attributes. The first form of moral affiliation for the citizen should be her affiliation with rational humanity; and this, above all, should define the purposes of her conduct.[15]

We know relatively little about what more the Cynics made of these ideas, although it is obvious that they had a major influence on later Greco-Roman cosmopolitan thought. The Stoics, who followed the Cynics' lead, developed the image of the *kosmopolitês* (world citizen) more fully, arguing that each of us dwells, in effect, in two communities: the local community of our birth and the community of human argument and aspiration. The latter is, in Seneca's words, "truly great and truly common, in which we look neither to this corner nor to that, but measure the boundaries of our nation by the sun."[16] The Stoics held that this community is the source of our most fundamental moral and social obligations. Plutarch summarizes:

The much admired *Republic* of Zeno is aimed at this one main point, that we should not organize our daily lives around the city or the deme, divided from

one another by local schemes of justice, but we should regard all human beings as our fellow demesmen and fellow citizens, and there should be one way
of life and one order, just as a herd that feeds together shares a common nur-
turance and a common law. Zeno wrote this as a dream or image of a well-
ordered and philosophical community.[17]

It is not clear whether the Greek Stoics really wished to establish a
single world state. Zeno did propose an ideal city, but we know very little about its institutional structure.[18] More important by far is the
Stoics' insistence on a certain way of perceiving our standing in the
moral and social world. We should view ourselves as fundamentally
and deeply linked to humankind as a whole, and take thought in our
deliberations, both personal and political, for the good of the whole
species. This idea is compatible with the maintenance of local forms
of political organization, but it does direct political as well as moral
thought. In the Roman world the directly political side of cosmopolitanism could come into its own in a very practical way, as Roman Stoic
philosophers had a major influence on the conduct of political life.
Cicero, following the Middle Stoic Panaetius, applies Stoic precepts to
the conduct of affairs in the Roman Republic. Seneca was regent of
the emperor under Nero; Marcus Aurelius was, of course, emperor at
the height of Roman influence. Both closely connected their philosophical with their political endeavors.[19] Also during the Roman period, Stoicism provided the impetus for some republican anti-imperial
movements, such as the conspiracies of Thrasea Paetus and Piso during the reign of Nero. (Seneca lost his life on account of his involvement in the latter.[20])

According to the Stoics, the basis for human community is the
worth of reason in each and every human being.[21] Reason, in the
Stoic view, is a portion of the divine in each of us. And each and every
human being, just in virtue of being rational and moral (for Stoics,
reason is above all a faculty of moral choice) has boundless worth.
Male or female, slave or free, king or peasant, all are of boundless
moral value, and the dignity of reason is worthy of respect wherever it
is found. This reason, the Stoics held, makes us fellow citizens. Zeno,
it would appear, already spoke of rational humanity as grounding a
common idea of law.[22] Similarly, Cicero in the *De Officiis* (III, 27–28)
holds that nature ordains that every human being should promote the

good of every other human being just because he is human: "And if this is so, we are all subject to a single law of nature, and if this is so we are bound not to harm anyone."[23] Marcus develops this idea further (IV, 4): "If reason is common, so too is law; and if this is common, then we are fellow citizens. If this is so, we share in a kind of organized polity. And if that is so, the world is as it were a city state."[24]

This being so, Stoic cosmopolitans hold, we should regard our deliberations as, first and foremost, deliberations about the problems common to all human beings emerging in particular concrete situations, not problems growing out of a local or national identity that confines and limits our moral aspirations. The accident of where one is born is just that, an accident; any human being might have been born in any nation. As Marcus puts it (X, 15), "It makes no difference whether a person lives here or there, provided that, wherever he lives, he lives as a citizen of the world."[25] Recognizing this, we should not allow differences of nationality or class or ethnic membership or even gender[26] to erect barriers between us and our fellow human beings. We should recognize humanity wherever it occurs, and give its fundamental ingredients, reason and moral capacity, our first allegiance and respect.[27]

Even in its Roman incarnations, this proposal is not, fundamentally, a proposal for a world state. The point is more radical still: that we should give our first moral allegiance to *no* mere form of government, no temporal power. We should give it, instead, to the moral community made up by the humanity of all human beings. One should always behave so as to treat with equal respect the dignity of reason and moral choice in each and every human being. And, as Marcus holds, this will generate both moral and legal obligations.

The attitude of the world citizen is held to be strategically valuable in social life. We will be better able to solve our problems if we face them in this way, as fellow human beings respecting one another. No theme is deeper in Stoicism than the damage done to our political lives by faction and intense local loyalties. Marcus Aurelius writes about this topic with especial eloquence, noting that Roman political life tends to be dominated by divisions and parties of many sorts, from the divisions of class and rank and ethnic origin to the division of parties at public games and gladiatorial shows. Part of his own Stoic education, he writes (I, 5), is "not to be a Green or Blue partisan at the races, or a supporter of the lightly armed or heavily armed gladiators at the Circus." The Stoic claim is that a style of political life that recognizes the moral and rational community as fundamental promises a more reasonable style of political deliberation and problem solving, even when institutions are still based on national divisions.

Furthermore, the political stance of the cosmopolitan is intrinsically valuable, for it recognizes in persons what is especially fundamental about them, most worthy of reverence and acknowledgment. This aspect may be less colorful than some of the more eye-catching morally irrelevant attributes of tradition, identity, and group membership. It is, however, the Stoics argue, both deeper and ultimately more beautiful.[28] Seneca is especially eloquent in his description of the beauty of the moral substance of humanity in each person, and in the attitude of quasi-religious awe with which he is inspired by his contemplation of a human being's rational and moral purpose. In a passage that seems to have profoundly influenced Kant, he writes:

God is near you, is with you, is inside you. . . . If you have ever come on a dense wood of ancient trees that have risen to an exceptional height, shutting out all sight of the sky with one thick screen of branches upon another, the loftiness of the forest, the seclusion of the spot, your sense of wonder at finding so deep and unbroken a gloom out of doors, will persuade you of the presence of a deity. . . . And if you come across a man who is not alarmed by dangers, not touched by passionate longing, happy in adversity, calm in the midst of storm . . . is it not likely that a feeling of awe for him will find its way into your heart? . . . Praise in him what can neither be given nor snatched away, what is peculiarly human. You ask what that is? It is his soul, and reason perfected in the soul. For the human being is a rational animal. *(Ep. Mor.*, 41)

The Stoics stress that to be a world citizen one does not need to give up local identifications and affiliations, which can be a great source of richness in life. Hierocles, a Stoic of the first and second centuries A.D., using an older metaphor found also in Cicero's *De Officiis*, argued that we should regard ourselves not as devoid of local affiliations but as surrounded by a series of concentric circles. The first circle is drawn around the self; the next takes in one's immediate family; then follows the extended family; then, in order, one's neighbors or local group, one's fellow city dwellers, and one's fellow countrymen. Outside all these circles is the largest one, that of humanity as a whole. Our task as citizens of the world will be to "draw the circles somehow toward the center," making all human beings more like our fellow city dwellers, and so forth.[29] In general, we should think of nobody as a stranger, as outside our sphere of concern and obligation. Cicero here borrows Terence's famous line "Homo sum: humani nihil a me alienum puto." ("I am a human being; I think nothing human alien to me.")[30] In other words, we may give what is near to us a special degree of attention and concern. But, first, we should always remember that these features of placement are incidental and that our most fundamental allegiance is to what is human. Second, we should consider that even the special measure of concern we give to our own is justified not by any intrinsic superiority in the local but by the overall requirements of humanity. To see this, consider the rearing of children. Roman Stoics tend to disagree strongly with Plato and with their Greek Stoic forebears, who seem to have followed Plato in abolishing the nuclear family.[31] The Roman Stoics held, it seems, that we will not get good rearing of children by leaving all children equally to the care of all parents. Each parent should care intensely for his or her own children, and not try to spread parental concern all around the world. On the other hand, this should be done not from a sense that my children are really more worthwhile than other people's children, but from a sense that it makes most sense for me to do my duties where I am placed, that the human community is best arranged in this way. That, to a Stoic, is what local and national identities should be like, and that is how they can be fortified and encouraged without subverting the primary claim of humanity.

Stoic cosmopolitans are aware that politics divides people and that it encourages them to think of other groups as alien and hostile. They therefore insist strongly on a process of empathetic understanding whereby we come to respect the humanity even of our political enemies, thinking of ourselves as born to work together and inspired by a common purpose. In the words of Marcus, who develops this idea especially fully, we should "enter into the mind" of the other, as far as is possible, and interpret the other's action with understanding (VI, 53; VIII, 51; XI, 18).

A favored exercise, in this process of world thinking, is to conceive of the entire world of human beings as a single body, and its many people as so many limbs. Referring to the fact that it takes only the change of a single letter in Greek to convert the word *melos* ("limb") to *meros* ("[detached] part"), Marcus concludes (VII, 13): "If, changing the word, you call yourself merely a [detached] part rather than a limb, you do not yet love your fellow men from the heart, nor derive complete joy from doing good; you will do it merely as a duty, not as doing good to yourself." Adoption of this organic model need not entail the disregard of the separateness of persons and the importance of political liberty: Stoics were intensely concerned about both of these things, in their own way,[32] and never conceived of the satisfactions of different persons as fusable into a single system. But it does entail that we should think at all times of the way in which our good is intertwined with that of our fellows, and indeed conceive of ourselves as having common goals and projects with our fellows.

It is in this thought of common goals and projects that the Stoics find one of the strongest incentives toward the containment of enmity and aggression. As I shall discuss at length below, the Stoics believed that a central goal of the world citizen was the complete extirpation of anger, both in oneself and in the surrounding society.[33] But it is difficult to teach oneself not to mind slights and insults, especially when one is aware that the political world contains much that is malicious and morally unpleasant. Marcus Aurelius speaks to himself as a person very prone to indignation and resentment. He gives himself the following cosmopolitan advice:

Say to yourself in the morning: I shall meet people who are interfering, ungracious, insolent, full of guile, deceitful and antisocial. . . . But I, . . . who know that the nature of the wrongdoer is of one kin with mine—not indeed of the same blood or seed but sharing the same kind, the same portion of the divine—I cannot be harmed by any one of them, and no one can involve me in shame. I cannot feel anger against him who is of my kin, nor hate him. We were born to labor together, like the feet, the hands, the eyes, and the rows of upper and lower teeth. To work against one another is therefore contrary to nature, and to be angry against a man or turn one's back on him is to work against him.[34]

Here the cosmopolitan thought of connectedness and common purposes steps in to give Marcus a new view of his political enemies. This humane view, in turn, permits him to cultivate his own humanity toward them, and to persist in the goals of cosmopolitanism, rather than relapse into the faction-ridden style of politics he has sought to avoid. Because he sees them as fellow humans, sharing purposes and ends with him, he can treat them as ends rather than merely as obstacles in the way of his policies.

The Stoics are aware that the life of the cosmopolitan, and the cosmopolitan's concern with goals of world cooperation and respect for personhood, may be difficult to sell to citizens who are hooked on local group loyalties, with their colorful slogans and the psychological security they can inspire. The life of the world citizen is, in effect, as Diogenes the Cynic said, a kind of exile[35]—from the comfort of local truths, from the warm nestling feeling of local loyalties, from the absorbing drama of pride in oneself and one's own. In the writings of Marcus especially, one sometimes feels a boundless loneliness, as if the removal of props of habit and local boundaries had left life bereft of a certain sort of warmth and security. A person who as a child loved and trusted his parents is tempted to want to reconstruct citizenship along the same lines, finding in an idealized image of a group or a nation a surrogate parent who will do his thinking for him.[36] Cosmopolitanism, in contrast, requires a nation of adults who do not need a childlike dependence upon omnipotent parental figures.[37]

Whatever form political institutions take, they should be structured around a mature recognition of equal personhood and humanity. Cicero, following Panaetius, took this to entail certain duties of hospitality to the foreigner and the other (*De Officiis* I, 51ff.). Marcus insisted on the duty to educate oneself about the political affairs of the world as a whole, and to engage actively in those affairs in a way that shows concern for all world citizens. All Stoics took cosmopolitanism to require certain international limitations upon the conduct of warfare—in general, the renunciation of aggression and the resort to force only in self-defense, when all discussion has proven futile (ibid., 34), and also the humane treatment of the vanquished, including, if possible, the admission of the defeated people to equal citizenship in one's own nation (ibid., 35). In general, all punishments meted out to wrongdoers, whether as individuals or collectively, must preserve respect for human dignity in them (ibid., 89). Wars motivated by group hatred and wars of extermination come in for especially harsh condemnation.

4

Kant's debt to Stoic cosmopolitanism cannot be well understood if the discussion is confined to the political sphere and the political writings. That is why, in my own characterization of Stoicism, I have started from the moral core of the Stoics' ideas about reason and personhood, rather than from a more superficial description of their institutional and practical goals. It is this deep core that Kant appropriates—the idea of a kingdom of free rational beings, equal in humanity, each of them to be treated as an end no matter where in the world he or she dwells. In Kant as in Stoicism, this idea is less a specific political proposal than a regulative ideal that should be at the heart of both moral and political reflection and that supplies constraints upon what we may politically will. It also supplies moral motives of respect and awe that provide powerful incentives to fulfill the moral law. One can easily recognize these ideas as formative in the *Groundwork*, where, as Reich has argued, Kant's way of connecting the Formula of Universal Law to the Formula of Humanity is his own nonteleological recasting of the argument of *De Officiis*, where Cicero interprets the Stoic idea of life in accordance with nature as entailing a universal respect for humanity (III, 26–27). (As Reich shows, there are so many other points of contact between the two works that it appears likely that Kant followed the lines of Cicero's argument closely.) Stoic ideas also appear formative in the Second Critique, whose famous conclusion concerning the mind's awe before the starry sky above and the moral law within closely echoes the imagery of Seneca's Letter 41, expressing awe before the divinity of reason within us. A particularly important reference to Stoic ideas of world citizenship occurs in the *Anthropology*, where Kant, apparently following Marcus or at least writing in his spirit,[38] insists that we owe it to other human beings to try to understand their ways of thinking, since only that attitude is consistent with seeing oneself as a "citizen of the world"

(*Anthropologie*, 2). And one can see these core notions of humanity and world citizenship as formative in the political writings too, especially in "Toward Perpetual Peace."

As do Marcus and Cicero, Kant stresses that the community of all human beings in reason entails a common participation in law (*ius*), and, by our very rational existence, a common participation in a virtual polity, a cosmopolis that has an implicit structure of claims and obligations regardless of whether or not there is an actual political organization in place to promote and vindicate them. When Kant refers to "the idea of a cosmopolitan law" and asserts that this law is "a necessary complement to the unwritten code of political and international law" (*PP*, 108), he is following very closely the lines of analysis traced by Cicero and Marcus. So too when he insists on the organic interconnectedness of all our actions: "The peoples of the earth have thus entered in varying degrees into a universal community, and it has developed to the point where a violation of laws in *one* part of the world is felt *everywhere*." (*PP*, 107–108)

In the details of his political proposals, Kant's debt to Cicero's *De Officiis* is, as in the *Groundwork*, intimate and striking. Kant's discussion of the relationship between morality and politics in the first appendix follows closely Cicero's discussions of the relation between morality and expediency (see II, 83 and III, 16ff.). Both thinkers insist on the supreme importance of justice in the conduct of political life, giving similar reasons for their denial that morality should ever be weighed against expediency. There are close parallels between the two thinkers' discussions of the hospitality right (II, 64; cf. *PP*, 105),[39] and between their extremely stringent accounts of proper moral conduct during wartime and especially of justice to the enemy (Cicero I, 38ff.; cf. *PP*, 96ff.). Both insist on the great importance of truthfulness and promise keeping even in war, both denounce cruelty and wars of extermination, and both insistently oppose all treacherous conduct even toward the foe. Kant is again close to the Stoic analysis when he speaks of the right of all human beings to "communal possession of the earth's surface" (106), and of the possibility of "peaceful mutual relations which may eventually be regulated by public laws, thus bringing the human race nearer and nearer to a cosmopolitan constitution" (ibid.).

Especially fascinating is the way in which Kant appropriates Cicero's ideas about the duty of the philosopher to speak freely for the public good. In an Appendix entitled "Secret Article of a Perpetual Peace" he tells the reader that the containment of aggression has one condition that governing bodies will not want to admit publicly, and therefore will not write into their public documents. The "secret article" is that governing bodies working on this issue need help from philosophers:

> Although it may seem humiliating for the legislative authority of a state, to which we must naturally attribute the highest degree of wisdom, to seek instruction from *subjects* (the philosophers) regarding the principles on which it should act in its relations with other states, it is nevertheless extremely advisable that it should do so. The state will therefore invite their help *silently*, making a secret of it. In other words, it will *allow them to speak* freely and publicly on the universal maxims of warfare and peace-making, and they will indeed do so of their own accord if no-one forbids their discussions.

There remain some important differences between the Roman Stoics and Kant. For example, the Stoics did not and could not conclude, as Kant does (*PP*, 106–107), that colonial conquest is morally unacceptable. Seneca certainly could not have uttered such sentiments had he had them, and Marcus focuses on the task of managing the existing empire as justly and wisely as he can rather than on the question whether he ought not instead to dismantle it. But we should observe that what Kant objects to in colonialism is the oppressive and brutal treatment of the inhabitants (106) more than the fact of rule itself; and, on the other hand, Marcus, in his dying words, insists, not altogether implausibly, that he has ruled his empire by persuasion and love rather than fear: ". . . neither can any wealth, however abundant, suffice for the incontinence of a tyranny, nor a bodyguard be strong enough to protect the ruler, unless he has first of all the good-will of the governed."[40] If we make allowances for the differences of station in which life located these two philosophers, we may perhaps say that they pursued the goals of cosmopolitanism in parallel ways, each executing as well as possible the task of world citizenship in the sphere of life and work to which luck and talent assigned him.

Again, both the Stoics and Kant have blind spots, and not always in the same place. Kant's cosmopolitanism allows him to fall short of the

Greek and even the Roman Stoics with regard to the equal personhood and dignity of women,[41] and the Stoics' general tendency to
accept the institution of slavery, if not all the practices associated with
it, is especially shocking.[42] For both Kant and the Stoics, there is sometimes and in some ways a tendency to treat the moral imperative as
displacing the political imperative, respect for dignity at times taking
the place of rather than motivating changes in the external circumstances of human lives, given that for both the good will is invulnera-
ble to disadvantages imposed by these circumstances. But one should
not exaggerate the indifference of either the Stoics or Kant to political
change. Both hold that we have a duty to promote the happiness of
others, and both hold that this entails constructive engagement with
the political life. Cicero is especially vehement on this point, and it is
the example of Cicero that Kant follows most closely.

In general, we may say that Kant's conception of a world politics in
which moral norms of respect for humanity work to contain aggression and to promote mutual solidarity is a close adaptation of Cicero's
Stoic ideas to the practical problems of his own era.

5

But there are two deep philosophical differences between Kant and
his Stoic forebears that have important implications for the argument
of "Toward Perpetual Peace." These differences concern *teleology* and
the view of the passions.

It is, of course, fundamental to Kant's moral philosophy, and a central point in his criticism of ancient Greek moral theories throughout
his work, that practical reason may not rely on any metaphysical picture of the world of nature, and therefore *a fortiori* may not rely on a
picture of nature as teleologically designed by a beneficent and wise
deity for the sake of the overall good. It is precisely on such a picture
of nature that Stoic ethics rests—although the importance of this idea
to the moral arguments of the Stoic thinkers has been disputed, and
although it may have different degrees of importance for different
Stoic thinkers.[43]

In Kant's political writings, however, things are more complex. The
idea of Providence appears, in something like a Stoic form, but Kant is

careful to qualify his allegiance to it. In "On the Common Saying, 'This May be True in Theory, but it does not Apply in Practice,'" Kant, discussing the envisaged progress in international justice as seen "from a universal, i.e. cosmopolitan point of view,"[44] makes use of a very Stoic notion of nature's providential design:

If we now ask what means there are of maintaining and indeed accelerating this constant progress toward a better state, we soon realize that . . . [we] must look to nature alone, or rather to *providence* (since it requires the highest wisdom to fulfill this purpose), for a successful outcome which will first affect the whole and then the individual parts.

This appeal to providence returns in "Toward Perpetual Peace," with especially fascinating ambiguity, in the section entitled First Supplement: On the Guarantee of a Perpetual Peace:

Perpetual peace is *guaranteed* by no less an authority than the great artist Nature herself (*natura daedala rerum*). The mechanical process of nature visibly exhibits the purposive plan of producing concord among men, even against their will and indeed by means of their very discord. This design, if we regard it as a compelling cause whose laws of operation are unknown to us, is called *fate*. But if we consider its purposive function within the world's development, whereby it appears as the underlying wisdom of a higher cause, showing the way towards the objective goal of the human race and predetermining the world's evolution, we call it *Providence*. We cannot actually observe such an agency in the artifices of nature, nor can we even *infer* its existence from them. But as with all relations between the form of things and their ultimate purposes, we can and must *supply it mentally* in order to conceive of its possibility by analogy with human artifices. . . . But in contexts such as this, where we are concerned purely with theory and not with religion, we should also note that it is more in keeping with the limitations of human reason to speak of *nature* and not of *Providence*, for reason, in dealing with cause and effect relationships, must keep within the bounds of possible experience. *Modesty* forbids us to speak of providence as something we can recognize, for this would mean donning the wings of Icarus and presuming to approach the mystery of its inscrutable intentions.

In this complex paragraph (which is accompanied by an even more complex and very obscure footnote on the different varieties of Providence), Kant first states confidently that perpetual peace is guaranteed by nature's design; following the Stoics, he gives this design the dual names "fate" and "Providence." Already here, however, there is complexity: the Latin phrase that characterizes nature is taken from Lucretius's *De Rerum Natura*, a work much loved by Kant but one that resolutely denies that any teleological design is to be discerned in the workings of nature.[45] Kant now goes on to make this uncertainty official, reminding his readers that we must not speak of providence with any confidence, since that would be to attempt to transcend the limits of human nature. In other words, he repudiates the Stoic approach that insists on grounding cosmopolitanism in a securely asserted teleology.

In the next paragraph, however, Kant goes straight back to the Stoic picture as if no qualification had intervened: "We may next enquire in what manner the guarantee is provided. Nature's provisional arrangement is as follows." What is especially fascinating to a classicist is that the material that ensues seems to be evidence that the strange reference to Lucretius is no accident. Kant follows closely the course of Lucretius's actual argument denying providential design in nature, but simply asserts the contradictory at every point. Lucretius says that more than half of the earth is simply uninhabitable because of climate, and that the rest is extremely inhospitable to humans on account of the presence of wild beasts. Kant asserts, without argument, that nature "has taken care that human beings are able to live in all the areas where they are settled" and has "see[n] to it that men *could* live everywhere on earth." Again, Lucretius cites war as an example of the disordered and nonprovidential nature of things; Kant immediately cites war as part of nature's providential design, in order to cause humans to scatter, inhabiting "even the most inhospitable regions." For Lucretius, legal arrangements originated because human beings, finding themselves in an intrinsically disordered universe, decided to agree to their own order; for Kant, in the next sentence, legal arrangements result from strife that is caused, in turn, by nature's providential design.

In short, I think there can be little doubt that Kant is struggling against Lucretius's anti-teleological view of nature and allying himself with Stoic providential religion. His argument gives many signs of this internal debate: for example, in a strange footnote he ponders a hypothetical objection that settlers in remote Arctic lands might someday run out of driftwood, and responds that the settlers will be able to barter for wood by using "the animal products in which the Arctic coasts are so plentiful." This is of course not an objection to teleology to be found in Lucretius; but it is just the *sort* of point Lucretius does raise, and just what we would expect an eighteenth-century Epicurean to assert.[46] Kant, then, appears to enroll himself as an enthusiastic partisan of Stoic views, despite the modesty that his official view enjoins.[47]

There remains, however, a large difference between Kant and the Stoics—or at least between Kant's claim about all human beings and what Stoics claim about the sage. (With respect to non-sages the Stoics' view is difficult to distinguish from Kant's.) The Stoic sage knows with certainty the design of the universe in all its workings, and knows that it is providential. He is like Zeus in his knowledge, with the one exception that he lacks knowledge of future contingent particular events. Kant's human being, by contrast, hopes for providence, and makes up arguments about it, but thinks it inappropriate to claim actually to recognize it or to approach the mystery of its intentions—however much Kant himself appears at times to do all this. Providence is, at best, a "practical postulate," a confidently held practical hope.

How important is this hope to Kant's cosmopolitanism? This is obviously of great concern to us, since what appears attractive in Kant's version of Stoic cosmopolitanism is its attempt to preserve the moral core of the view without pinning it to a teleology that most of us can no longer believe. Here I am in agreement with Bernard Williams[48]: if the good news that Kant's Stoicism brings us is inseparable from a view that rational purpose is inherent in the universe, we are much less likely to accept it.

The hope of Providence was clearly of importance to Kant personally, and he seems to think it important that cosmopolitans should be able to share it. That is why, in "Toward Perpetual Peace" more than elsewhere, his rhetoric is full of appeals to that hope. But I believe it is clear that the moral core of Kant's argument is altogether separable from this sort of wishful thinking—and I believe that he is correct to think that one may appropriate this moral core of Stoicism without its teleology of design. We are told that our moral acts must take their bearings from the equal worth of humanity in all persons, near or far, and that this moral stance leads politics in a cosmopolitan direction; we are told that morality should be supreme over politics, giving political thought both constraints and goals. Following Cicero, Kant focuses on that moral imperative and its basis in reverence for humanity, and adds the appeals to providence only as a kind of reassurance to the faint-hearted.

Do we need to follow Kant in alluding to providence as at least a practical postulate, a reasonable hope, if we wish either to be cosmopolitans or to persuade others that they should define themselves in accordance with cosmopolitan aims and aspirations? I believe we do not. Humanity can claim our respect just as powerfully whether we think the universe is intrinsically well ordered or whether, with Lucretius, we think that things look pretty random and unprovidential. However humanity emerged, whether by design or by chance, it is what it is and it compels respect.[49] In a sense there is a special dignity and freedom in the choice to constitute our community as universal and moral in the face of a disorderly and unfriendly universe, for then we are not following anyone else's imperatives but our very own.

6

We now arrive at what is perhaps the central difference between Kant and the Stoics. For Kant, the search for peace requires a persistent vigilance toward human aggression, which Kant views as innate, ineliminable from human nature, and more or less brutish and ineducable. "War," he writes (*PP*, 111), "does not require any particular kind of motivation, for it seems to be ingrained in human nature." If we were looking only at a single nation, he says, we could deny that bad things result from "any inherent wickedness rooted in human nature" (120), and blame them instead on "the deficiencies of their as yet underdeveloped culture (i.e. their barbarism)." But Kant concludes that the fact that all states, however developed, behave badly in their external relations gives "irrefutable" evidence of inherent wickedness. Similarly, in "Idea for a Universal History" he says that when one contemplates human actions one sees that "everything as a whole is made up of folly and childish vanity, and often of childish malice and destructiveness" (42). Influenced, it would appear, both by Augustinian

Christianity and by Romanticism's strong distinction between passion and culture, Kant appears throughout his career to conceive of the passions, including aggression, as natural, precultural, and not removable from human nature.

For the Stoics, however, none of the passions is seated in human nature. Bodily appetites do, of course, have an innate bodily basis. But the passions themselves (grief, fear, love, hatred, envy, jealousy, anger) not only require learning and belief; they are actually identified by the Stoics with a certain type of evaluative judgment—that is, with an assent to a certain sort of value-laden view of the way things are. The common characteristic of all these value-laden views is that they ascribe considerable importance, with respect to the person's own flourishing, to things and persons outside the self that the person does not control.[50] They all involve, therefore, a kind of passivity toward the world of nature, a form of life in which one puts oneself at the mercy of the world by allowing one's good to reside outside the boundaries of that which one can control. To a Stoic, such a form of life is profoundly irrational, because it is always bound to lead to instability and pain, and indeed very likely to lead, through retaliatory aggression, to the infliction of harm on others. It is always in our power to withhold assent to these ways of seeing the importance of external things, no matter how pervasive they are in our society, and to judge that one's own virtue is sufficient for one's flourishing.

It is, then, a consequence of this view that there will be no passions of anger and hatred, and no desire for retaliation, if there are no unwise attachments to external things and persons. The Stoics' diagnosis—like and the basis for Spinoza's—is that anger does not derive from any innate aggressive instinct in human nature. They see no reason to posit such an instinct, and much reason in the early behavior of children, to doubt it.[51] On the other hand, when we become attached to things outside our will—our possessions, our reputation, our honor, our bodily good looks and health—we put our dignity at the world's mercy, setting ourselves up to be slighted and damaged. To those slights and damages, anger will be the natural response—natural in the sense that a judgment that an important element of my good has been damaged or slighted is a sufficient condition for it, but not in the sense that the response itself is instinctual or (apart from the questionable value judgments) inevitable.

Nor will the Stoics accept the claim (made by Aristotelians in their philosophical culture,[52] and by many ordinary people consulting their intuitions) that anger is an essential part of public life in the sense of being a necessary motivation for valuable actions defending oneself, one's family, or one's country. They like to point out that an angry army is very likely to be an inept, aggressive army, and that actions in defense of one's own can appropriately be taken by consulting duty alone. If one acts because the action is right, not because one is oneself aggrieved, one's action will be more likely to be a balanced and measured one. The Stoics certainly do not envisage that putting an end to anger will put an end to war, for, like Kant, they conceive of some wars as appropriate responses to the aggression of others. But they do believe, as I have said, that human beings are born for mutual aid and mutual concord, and that the removal of anger will remove the vindictive and destructive elements in war and cut down greatly on the world's total of conflict.

To what extent do Stoics think that the passions—and in particular anger and hatred—can really be removed from human life? In any actual society (say, Seneca's Rome), the roots of the passions are taught so early in a child's moral education that the adult who undertakes a Stoic education will have to labor all his life against his own habits and habit-based inclinations. Seneca examines himself at the end of every day,[53] noting that he has become inappropriately angered at this or that slight to his honor—being seated too low at a dinner table and so forth. This sort of patient self-examination and self-criticism is necessary for passional enlightenment. But as it is carried on with increasing success, the personality becomes enlightened all the way down, so to speak. Reason and respect for humanity will gradually infuse the whole of Seneca's personality, shaping not only his philosophical and juridical ruminations but also his very propensities for fear, for grief, for anger and hatred. Because these passions are not a part of the soul apart from thought but rather a certain sort of (misguided) thought, they can themselves be enlightened. And therefore the Stoics hold out the hope that the society they live in, through the patient labors of individual souls, can itself become an enlightened one.

It is especially important to see how the Stoics link the goal of world citizenship to the goal of passional enlightenment. Briefly put, their recipe is that love of humanity as such should be our basic affective attitude.[54] This will not be a passion in the technical sense in which passion is linked with upheaval and instability, but it will be a reliable motivation that will steer us in the world and give us joy. At the same time, their instructions about the proper way to view the alien, the other, or the enemy—not as objects of fear and hate, but as members of one common body with one set of purposes—provide powerful devices for the undoing of the negative attitudes that often inform situations of national or ethnic conflict. Their claim is that these attitudes are constructed by social evaluations and can be undone by the patient work of philosophy.

To enlighten the passions need not mean to remove them, although it is this goal that the Stoics actually adopt. Another sort of cognitive passion-theorist, say an Aristotelian, can hold that the passions can be enlightened in such a way that they still are on the scene in some cases but they always select appropriate objects—so that anger, for example, manifests itself only toward the appropriate targets at the appropriate time. (For the Stoics no such targets are appropriate; for Aristotle it is right to be angry about certain damages to one's body, one's loved ones, or one's country.) Such an Aristotelian view of the passions has wide currency throughout history. (It is, for example, the dominant view of emotion in the Anglo-American common-law tradition of criminal law, and is responsible for standard definitions of notions such as "reasonable provocation" and duress.[55]) So it is important to state that we can adopt the Stoics' goal of passional enlightenment without adopting the specific content they give to that notion, which requires a radical detachment from some attachments that we might judge it reasonable to foster, even in a cosmopolitan society.

Kant cannot set such a high goal for human personal enlightenment; his related conception of social enlightenment must therefore be defined in terms of the suppression of the evil forces in human beings rather than in terms of their education. It is more than a little odd, it seems to me, that Kant, familiar as he clearly was with Stoic ideas, including ideas about the passions,[56] did not seriously consider their view as a candidate for truth in this area. This fact is all the odder given that Spinoza adopted the Stoic picture more or less unchanged and made the adoption of that picture and its associated conception of enlightenment a linchpin of his own project of cosmopolitan reform. Rousseau, moreover, though he did not analyze the passions in detail, seems to have been convinced of the natural goodness of humanity, and he discussed the formation of passion against the background of that commitment.[57] It seems clear to me that Kant could have taken over the Stoic/Spinozistic analysis of passion with very few other changes in his overall moral and political view,[58] and that the Stoic conception would in many ways have served his view better than the one he in fact adopted. The pessimistic view of human evil implied by his acceptance of innate aggression is always a difficulty for him, and he must struggle against it to find a place for his own characteristic political optimism, an optimism he clearly shares with Spinoza and Rousseau. In "Theory and Practice," for example, he begins the section on international justice with the question "Is the human race as a whole likable, or is it an object to be regarded with distaste?" And he shortly declares that a belief in immutable natural evil can cause us to turn our backs on our fellow human beings, and on ourselves:

. . . however hard we may try to awaken feelings of love in ourselves, we cannot avoid hating that which is and always will be evil, especially if it involves deliberate and general violation of the most sacred laws of humanity. Perhaps we may not wish to harm men, but shall not want to have any more to do with them than we can help. (87)

Seneca's arguments against the idea of innate aggression would have provided Kant with a strong counterweight to these pessimistic thoughts, and would have opened up prospects of enlightenment that would give new substance to the hope for cosmopolitanism.

Suppose, now, we substitute the Stoic view of passions for the view Kant actually holds, and consider the prospects of human enlightenment in the perspective of that view. How much hope does the Stoic picture give us, with respect to the containment of anger and aggression in our own world? Not much, without some fairly radical changes in moral education on a large scale, so that people will increasingly define themselves in terms of their reason and character rather than in terms of honor, status, wealth, power, and the other things that are the common occasions of slights and damages and thus of retaliatory anger.

Furthermore, seeing the Stoic analysis of passions as based on a certain type of evaluative belief does not, as I have said, commit us to the normative Stoic view. We will have to ask, on Kant's behalf and on our own, to exactly what extent the goal of a complete eradication of anger is an appropriate moral goal. I myself would not have us follow the Stoics in refusing anger at social injustice, or at damages to loved ones, or to our own bodily integrity. I would support a more Aristotelian course. But this qualification means that some appropriate causes of anger will still remain in human life, and peace will still require Kant's careful institutional guarantees.

However, certain especially pernicious forms of anger and hatred can indeed be eradicated by patient reform following Stoic conceptions. The hatred of members of other races and religions can be effectively addressed by forms of early education that address the cognitive roots of those passions by getting children to view these people in the Stoic cosmopolitan way, as similarly human, as bearers of an equal moral dignity, as members of a single body and a single set of purposes, and as no longer impossibly alien or threatening. If one looks at the way in which racial hatred and aggression can be and occasionally has been eradicated in a person or a community (if, for example, one looks at successes in the rearing of nonracist children), one sees that the success, insofar as there is success, is a Stoic success, achieved through enlightenment of the images we bring to our encounters with the other, through gradual changes in *evaluation*, rather than through suppression of a brute and undiscriminating urge to harm. Consider how the equal respect for women is fostered (when it is) in an individual or a group. Once again, I believe that it is achieved in the Stoic way, well described by Musonius Rufus: it is through enlightenment of the images of rational and moral humanity that we bring to our mutual encounters, rather than through suppression of an allegedly innate and unreasoning misogyny. The powerful Stoic idea that our destructive passions are socially constructed and fostered in the images of self and other we use suggests a program of reform that, while unlikely to achieve full success, can quite realistically be expected to shape the ways our children regard one another and the ways in which marriages and partnerships of all sorts take shape. Again, where we see suspicion and hatred of the foreigner, we can always try to address it through programs of education that will make the Stoics' and Kant's idea of world citizenship real in our schools and universities, teaching young people to regard the alien, with Marcus, as one from whom they might actually learn something, and, indeed, someone who, given a change of situation, they might themselves be. We may make the same point about contempt distributed along lines of wealth and social class. Recognizing the cogency of the Stoic view of passions gives us a duty: it tells us that we have great power over racism, sexism, and other divisive passions that militate against cosmopolitan humanism, if we will only devote enough attention to the cognitive moral development of the young. It is this noble Stoic idea that I believe to be at the heart of the much-maligned American interest in "political correctness," by which is meant the careful scrutiny of the imagery and the speech we use when we talk about those we are in the habit of regarding as unequally human. In its best form[59] this is not in the least a totalitarian idea, but one connected with the Stoic and the Kantian ideas of a truly free person. This ideal gives us a lifetime full of work to do if only we will do it.

Moreover, where such enlightenment of divisive passions cannot be achieved in the lives of individuals, we may view it as a regulative ideal and design institutions in ways that appropriately reflect the respect for humanity involved in it. Where we cannot altogether eradicate racial hatred, we can ensure that heavy penalties for ethnic and racial hate crimes are institutionalized in our codes of criminal law—and this is now being done. Where we cannot altogether ensure that foreigners be treated with Ciceronian hospitality, we can always seek to enact constitutional protections for the alien on our soil, and for that alien's children. Where we see the rights of women, or racial or ethnic minorities, being grossly violated anywhere in the world, we can support approaches to these problems through the international human rights movement, through nongovernmental organizations of many types, and through, let us hope, our own governments, if they will show themselves capable of minimal courage. We do not need to have exaggerated optimism about the triumph of enlightenment in order to view these as goals toward which we may sensibly strive, and in order to believe that this striving may achieve many local victories.

One must acknowledge that we do not see a triumph for cosmopolitanism right now in the United States, which seems increasingly indifferent to cosmopolitan goals and increasingly given over to a style of politics that does not focus on recognizing the equal humanity of the alien and the other; which seems increasingly hostile, too, to the intellectuals whom Kant saw as crucial to the production of such an enlightenment. We may well conjecture that were either Kant or Cicero and Marcus Aurelius to look at America they would see much that would distress them: not just the dominance of anger and aggression, but also an indifference to the well-being of the whole world that would make them think of America as one of the cut-off limbs of the world body that Marcus was so fond of describing in scathing and mordant language.[60]

Nor is it only in America that cosmopolitanism seems to be in grave jeopardy. The state of things in very many parts of the world gives reason for pessimism: when, 200 years after the publication of Kant's hopeful treatise, we see so many regions falling prey to ethnic and religious and racial conflict; when we find that the very values of equality, personhood, and human rights that Kant defended, and indeed the Enlightenment itself, are derided in some quarters as mere ethnocentric vestiges of Western imperialism; when, in a general way, we see so much more hatred and aggression around us than respect and love.

And yet we may agree with Kant here as well: certain postulates of practical reason, and therefore certain hopes for at least a local and piecemeal sort of progress—even though they are not clearly supported by what we can observe—should be adopted because they appear necessary for our continued cultivation of our humanity, our constructive engagement in political life. Concerning this hope, Kant writes:

. . . however uncertain I may be and may remain as to whether we can hope for anything better for mankind, this uncertainty cannot detract from the maxim I have adopted, or from the necessity of assuming for practical purposes that human progress is possible.

This hope for better times to come, without which an earnest desire to do something useful for the common good would never have inspired the human heart, has always influenced the activities of right-thinking people.[61]

This hope is, of course, a hope in and for reason. When, as scholars, we turn to classical antiquity in order to bring its resources to our own political world, we would do better, I believe, to appropriate and follow this Stoic/Kantian tradition of cautious rational optimism than to look to ancient Athens for a paradigm of a politics that simply directs us, as Bernard Williams puts it, to contemplate the horrors. There are always too many horrors, and it is all too easy to contemplate them. But, as Kant and his Stoic mentors knew, it is also possible to stop contemplating and to act, doing something useful for the common good.

Acknowledgments

I wish to thank Matthias Lutz-Bachmann and Angelika Krebs for valuable comments, and also to thank Richard Posner and Cass Sunstein for written comments on an earlier version of this paper. The paper was also presented as a plenary address at the Triennial Conference of the British Classical Association in Oxford; I am grateful to Fergus Millar, Miriam Griffin, and Richard Seaford for comments on that occasion. Finally, I am grateful to O'Nora O'Neill and to an anonymous reader for suggestions that improved the paper in the final stages of revision, and to Nancy Sherman for helpful discussions of Kant's view of the passions.

Notes to Chapter 1

1. All citations from Kant's political writings are taken from the second enlarged edition of *Kant: Political Writings*, ed. H. Reiss (Cambridge University Press, 1991). I have, however, in some cases differed with Nisbet about the translation of some terms, and have in those cases altered the translation. In particular, I have translated *Recht* in this passage as "law" rather than "right." *Recht*, as many texts make clear, is Kant's German rendering of Latin *ius*; he often puts the Latin in parentheses after the German term. *Ius*, of course, does not import any distinctively eighteenth-century notion of rights; it is best translated as "law" in many contexts, especially those concerning a notion of unwritten law. (In the introduction to the *Rechtslehre* of the *Metaphysik der Sitten*, Kant alludes to the classical concept of *ius naturae*: "Die letztere Benennung kommt der

systematischen Kenntniss der natürlichen Rechtslehre (*ius naturae*) zu. . . .") We can best appreciate Kant's continuity with Cicero if we bear these facts in mind.

2. Bernard Williams, *Shame and Necessity* (University of California Press, 1993).

3. Alasdair MacIntyre, *After Virtue* (Notre Dame University Press, 1981); MacIntyre, *Whose Justice? Which Rationality?* (Notre Dame University Press, 1987).

4. "The Women of Trachis: Fictions, Pessimism, Ethics," in *The Greeks and Us: Essays in Honor of Arthur W. H. Adkins*, ed. R. Louden (University of Chicago Press, 1996). This paper is continuous with and further develops the picture of the development of Greek ethics presented in Williams's important book *Shame and Necessity* (University of California Press, 1993).

5. Hegel's views are criticized for the universal teleology they posit, Kant's for informing us that the good will is still admirable even when nature has done its worst. It is not clear to me why Sophoclean tragedy should be thought to be opposed to that latter idea. The Sophoclean hero has different traits than the Kantian "hero," but both show an undiminished integrity in the face of "stepmotherly nature." For a related criticism of Williams, see Robert Louden, "Bad News about Good News: Response to Bernard Williams," in *The Greeks and Us.* Louden effectively compares Kant's demand that we pursue justice "even though the heavens may fall" with Deianeira's demand not to be cheated of the truth, even though calamity will ensue.

6. See especially *Whose Justice*, pp. 140–141, where MacIntyre illustrates the allegedly unreflective attitude to practice in the Greek *polis* and in Aristotle's *Ethics* through the picture of a hockey player who has an opportunity to pass in the closing minutes of a game and perceives the need to do so if the team is to have a chance to score. This is supposed to illustrate a form of life in which roles structure action, goods are "unambiguously ordered," and reflection is not required. MacIntyre gives hockey players much too little credit for creativity, flexibility, and initiative—the fact that they do not sit down to think does not mean that they are not thinking. But even if he were fair to hockey, MacIntyre is quite unfair to the Greek *polis*, where nothing seems to have happened without an argument. (The speeches in Thucydides—an author much admired by both Williams and MacIntyre—show, whether historical or not, the sort of extended and often very abstract reflection that was taken to be the sort of thing political actors would say.) For a more detailed criticism of MacIntyre, see my "Recoiling from Reason" (a review of *Whose Justice?*), *New York Review of Books*, November 1989.

7. See my "Aristotle on Human Nature and the Foundations of Ethics," in *World, Mind, and Ethics: Essays on the Ethical Philosophy of Bernard Williams*, ed. J. Altham and R. Harrison (Cambridge University Press, 1995).

8. G. E. R. Lloyd, especially *Magic, Reason, and Experience* (Cambridge University Press, 1981).

9. Williams's attack on "good news," as I have said, divides its energies between Hegel and Kant; even Schopenhauer comes in for criticism, for bringing us the "good news" that we can find consolation in art. In a different way, Hegel and Kant are also Heidegger's arch-enemies. MacIntyre focuses on British liberalism and strangely neglects Kant, but his attack is directed in a general way against the whole of the liberal Enlightenment.

10. The ancient authors referred to in the political works include Epicurus, Lucretius, Virgil, Horace, Cicero, Seneca, Marcus Aurelius, and Persius. All of these but Epicurus and Marcus are Latin authors, and Kant clearly read them in the original. (His education was rich and deep on the Latin side, beginning with his school days at the Fridericianum, and he wrote Latin fluently; on the other hand, as Ernst Cassirer puts it, he "seems to have been affected hardly at all by the spirit of Greek, which was taught exclusively by use of the New Testament" (*Kant's Life and Thought* (Yale University Press, 1981), pp. 14–15)). Kant did become acquainted with some Greek authors in German or Latin translations, but it was the Romans who remained close to his heart. He appears to have known Epicurus primarily through Lucretius, who, with Virgil, appears to have been among his best-loved poets; he mentions Marcus without showing clear evidence of knowing the text. Most of Kant's knowledge of Stoicism would have derived from Seneca, Cicero, and possibly translations of Epictetus and Marcus. In the case of cosmopolitanism, the most important sources would be Cicero's *De Officiis*, Seneca's *Epistulae Morales*, and, if Kant read him, Marcus. Kant's earliest published paper, "Thoughts on the True Estimation of Living Forces," bears an epigraph from Seneca that evidently expresses his sense of his own career: "Nihil magis praestandum est quam ne pecorum ritu sequam." ("There is nothing more important than that we should not, like sheep, follow the flock that has preceded us, going not where we should go, but where people have gone.")

11. The term *kosmou politês* is apparently Cynic in origin: Diogenes the Cynic, asked where he came from, replied "I am a *kosmopolitês*." (Diogenes Laertius VI, 3) Marcus generally prefers not the single coined term but the phrase *politês tou kosmou*. Diogenes did apparently mean to assert that local affiliations were of lesser importance than a primary affiliation with humanity; but he seems to have had little in the way of developed philosophical thought, certainly not political thought. His life was strikingly apolitical and defiant of all earthly authority. The Cynic background is very important historically for the Stoics, both Greek and Roman. For the Roman influence see Miriam Griffin, "Le mouvement cynique et les romains: attraction et répulsion," in *Le Cynisme ancien et ses prolongements* (Presses Universitaires Français, 1994); see also M.-O. Goulet-Cazé, "Le cynisme à l'époque impériale," *Aufstieg und Niedergang der römischen Welt* II.36, no. 4 (1990): 2720–2833. But we may disregard it here, since there is no evidence that Kant thought seriously about the Cynics, and since it was the Stoics' arguments and developed ideas that shaped his thought.

12. Klaus Reich, "Kant and Greek Ethics," *Mind* 48 (1939): 338–354, 446–463.

13. See the reference to Kant's *Anthropology* below.

14. Diogenes the Cynic, in Diogenes Laertius, *Lives of the Philosophers*, VI, 63. For an English version see the Loeb translation by R. D. Hicks (Harvard University Press, 1970). All translations from Greek and Latin are my own unless noted otherwise.

15. See, among other sources, Griffin, "Le mouvement cynique"; *The Cynics*, ed. B. Branham (University of California Press, 1996); D. R. Dudley, *A History of Cynicism* (Ares, 1980); J. Moles, "'Honestius quam ambitiosius'? An Exploration of the Cynic's Attitude to Moral Corruption in His Fellow Men," *Journal of Hellenic Studies* 103 (1983): 103–123.

16. Seneca, *De Otio*, 4.1, translated as in *The Hellenistic Philosophers*, ed. A. Long and D. Sedley (Cambridge University Press, 1987), p. 431.

17. Plutarch, *On the Fortunes of Alexander*, 329A–B, my translation; see Long and Sedley, p. 429. For other relevant texts see Long and Sedley, pp. 429–437.

18. See Malcolm Schofield, *The Stoic Idea of the City* (Cambridge University Press, 1991).

19. See M. Griffin, *Seneca: A Philosopher in Politics* (Clarendon, 1976); see also her "Philosophy, Politics, and Politicians at Rome," in *Philosophia Togata*, ed. M. Griffin and J. Barnes (Clarendon, 1989). On Marcus see R. B. Rutherford, *The Meditations of Marcus Aurelius: A Study* (Clarendon, 1989).

20. See Griffin, "Philosophy."

21. I discuss these matters at greater length, with references to many texts, in chapter 9 of *The Therapy of Desire: Theory and Practice in Hellenistic Ethics* (Princeton University Press, 1994).

22. See the Plutarch passage cited above; for discussion see Schofield, *The Stoic Idea*.

23. Although Cicero in book III comes close to asserting that our obligation to humanity takes priority over all other obligations, he is far less confident in book I, and indeed makes many more concessions to local affiliation than other Stoic thinkers. On his view of our diverse obligations, see Christopher Gill, "The Four *Personae* in Cicero's *De Officiis*," *Oxford Studies in Ancient Philosophy*. On these issues I am also indebted to an unpublished dissertation chapter by Eric Brown.

24. See also Marcus I, 14 in *The Meditations* (Hackett, 1983): he thanks his teachers for giving him a grasp of the idea of a polity "with the same laws for all, governed on the basis of equality and free speech." See also V, 16.

25. See also VI, 44: "My city and my country, as I am Antoninus, is Rome; as I am a human being, it is the world."

26. See Schofield, *The Stoic Idea*, for an excellent discussion of Stoic attitudes to sex equality. In the Stoics' ideal city, men and women would be citizens on an equal footing; even distinctions of dress would be abolished (Diogenes Laertius VII, 33).

27. For a good discussion of Stoic impartiality see Julia Annas, *The Morality of Happiness* (Oxford University Press, 1993), pp. 262–276.

28. See also Cicero, *De Officiis* I, 107, according to which we have two characters: one universal, arising from our rationality, and one individual, deriving from our particular talents and abilities.

29. For the Hierocles fragment, see Annas, pp. 267–268, and Long and Sedley, p. 349. For Cicero's use of the circle metaphor, see *De Officiis* I, 50ff. (See the fine annotated translation *Cicero: On Duties*, ed. M. Griffin and E. Atkins (Cambridge University Press, 1991).)

30. Terence, *Heautontimoroumenos*, paraphrased in *De Officiis* (I, 30) and quoted by Kant on p. 460 of *Metaphysics of Morals* (*Kant's Ethical Writings* (Hackett, 1983), p. 125). Kant criticizes malicious delight in the misfortunes of another as contrary to our duty according to the principle of sympathy. For the complexities in Cicero's view of our diverse roles and obligations, see Gill, "Four *Personae*."

31. See Diogenes Laertius VII, 32–33, and Schofield, *The Stoic Idea*. Some of the pertinent texts, including much of the Diogenes passage, are translated by Long and Sedley (pp. 429–434).

32. The Stoics debate as to whether the best form of government is monarchical or republican, but they consistently insist that the liberty of action in the citizen is something to be prized. Marcus, for example, speaks of his goal as that of "a monarchy which prizes the liberty of its subjects above all things" (I, 14). Republican conspiracies invoked this idea of *libertas*, as did many Stoics on their death, especially in connection with politically motivated suicide. See, among other texts, Seneca, *On Anger*, 3.15 (discussed on p. 435 of *Therapy of Desire*) and Tacitus's account of Seneca's death (*Annals* 15, 61–63, cited on p. 437 of *Therapy of Desire*). It is beyond the scope of this chapter to investigate debates among the Stoics as to what political institutions and policies this ideal entailed.

33. The central surviving texts are Seneca's *On Anger* and *On Mercy*, tr. J. Cooper and J. Procopé (Cambridge University Press, 1994). For a general discussion of Stoic views, see chapter 11 of *Therapy of Desire*.

34. II, 1. See also VI, 6: "The best method of defense is not to become like your enemy."

35. Diogenes Laertius VI, 49: "When someone spoke scornfully of his exile, he said, 'You poor man—that was how I became a philosopher.'"

36. On this question see Hinrich Fink-Eitel, "Gemeinschaft als Macht: Zur Kritik des Kommunitarismus," in *Gemeinschaft und Gerechtigkeit*, ed. M. Brumlik and H. Brunkhorst (Fischer, 1993). Consider especially this, from p. 315: "Die Gemeinschaftsliebe ist eine notwendigerweise zielgehemmte, libidinöse Beziehung, und darin besteht . . . ihre dauerhaft bindende Kraft. Die gehemmte Libido führt ersatzweise zur Regression der frühesten Gefühlsbindung der Identifizierung mit einem idealisierten Elternteil (zumeist dem Vater), dessen bewundertes Vorbild man sich als Ichideal einst narzisstisch zu eigen gemacht hatte."

37. For a discussion of "mature dependence" and its connections with cosmopolitanism see W. R. D. Fairbairn, *Psychoanalytic Studies of Personality* (Routledge, 1951).

38. Here is an instance in which the influence of the Stoics may have reached Kant indirectly through the mediation of natural-law writers who were ultimately much influenced by Marcus.

39. Kant's friend Ehregott Andreas Christoph Wasianski tells a remarkable story about the importance for Kant of hospitality to the stranger. A week before his death, stricken in both body and mind, Kant received a visit from his doctor, a busy and eminent man. Although he could hardly speak at all, and could express his meaning only in sentence fragments, he struggled to express his gratitude that a man with so many obligations would take the time to call on him. When the doctor asked him to sit down, Kant did not. The doctor asked Wasianski why not, since standing was obviously giving him difficulty. Wasianski conjectured that Kant was standing out of courtesy, unwilling to sit until the stranger and guest had taken a seat first. "The doctor seemed dubious about this reason, but he was quickly convinced of the truth of my statement and moved almost to tears when Kant, having collected his powers with main force, said, 'The sense of humanity has not yet abandoned me.'" (quoted in Cassirer, *Kant's Life and Thought* (Yale University Press, 1981), pp. 412–413)

40. The speeches ascribed to Marcus are collected at the end of the Loeb Classical Library edition of his work (Harvard University Press, 1916).

41. On the equality of women in the Stoic ideal community, see Schofield, *The Stoic Idea*. On the Roman Stoics, see Musonius Rufus's two short treatises, "That Women Too Should Do Philosophy" and "Should Sons and Daughters Have the Same Education?"

42. On Seneca's ambivalence toward slavery see Griffin, *Seneca*.

43. Julia Annas argues in *The Morality of Happiness* that the major moral conclusions of Stoicism are logically independent of their teleology. I am basically in agreement with her. On the other side, see John Cooper's review of Annas (*Philosophical Review*, 1994). It should also be borne in mind that the Roman Stoics may well be less confident of natural teleology than the original Greek Stoics. Epictetus shows little if any concern with such a view of nature, and Musonius Rufus's appeals to design are peripheral to the argument. Seneca's own view of nature (in *Naturales Quaestiones*) bears a complex relation to Stoic views, and he is far more inclined than the Greeks seem to have been to stress the pervasive *disorder* of things. Since the Roman writers influenced Kant more profoundly than the Greek writers, this difference is significant for our purposes.

44. Reiss edition, p. 87.

45. On ways of reading Lucretius that deny the serious force of his anti-religious and anti-teleological ideas, see chapter 5 of *Therapy of Desire*.

46. Is this Epicurean voice in the text one of Kant's own imagining, or is he responding to some contemporary debate between Epicureans and Stoics? No doubt one more knowledgeable than I about the eighteenth-century context could clarify this issue.

47. See also the anti-Epicurean argument on p. 48 of "Idea for a Universal History," where Kant considers Lucretius's hypothesis that the world order was created by a chance swerve of the atoms.

48. See "The Women of Trachis."

49. This is not to deny that the shift from a providential to an evolutionary perspective might change some moral notions in this area—for example, our understanding of our relationship to other animals, and the moral duties we owe them. On this question, Kant unreflectively follows Stoicism in singling out human beings for unique moral importance, though he is not entitled to advance the Stoics' reasons for so doing. On the whole question, see James Rachels, *Created from Animals* (Oxford University Press, 1990).

50. See my discussion in *Therapy of Desire*.

51. This conclusion is by now widely accepted in developmental psychology and anthropology. See, for example, John Bowlby, *Attachment* (Basic Books, 1973); W. R. D. Fairbairn, *Psychological Papers* (Edinburgh, 1952); Jean Briggs, *Never in Anger* (Harvard University Press, 1980). For related primate research, see F. de Waal, *Peacemaking among Primates* (Harvard University Press, 1980), and the article on bonobo society in the March 1995 *Scientific American*.

52. See especially Seneca, *On Anger*, book I (discussed in chapter 11 of *Therapy of Desire*).

53. *On Anger* III, 36 (discussed in chapter 11 of *Therapy of Desire*).

54. This is of course also a love of the divine. On complexities in Stoic attitudes toward love, and its directedness to special individuals, see Nussbaum, "Eros and the Wise: The Stoic Response to a Cultural Dilemma," *Oxford Studies in Ancient Philosophy* 13 (1995): 231–267.

55. See Dan M. Kahan and Martha Nussbaum, Two Conceptions of Emotion in Criminal Law, manuscript, spring 1995.

56. See the discussion of pity in the Doctrine of Virtue of *The Metaphysics of Morals*, which alludes explicitly to the Stoic conception.

57. See especially *Emile*, book IV. On natural goodness, see Joshua Cohen, "The Natural Goodness of Humanity" (forthcoming). Rousseau's views seem close to those expressed by Seneca in book I of *On Anger*.

58. See Nancy Sherman, *Kant and Aristotle* (forthcoming).

59. This is not to deny that there are other forms of the idea that grow out of ethnocentric identity politics; to these the Stoic/Kantian should be energetically opposed.

60. See for example VIII, 34: "If you have ever seen a dismembered hand or foot or a head cut off, lying somewhere apart from the rest of the trunk, you have an image of what a person makes of himself . . . when he . . . cuts himself off or when he does some unneighborly act. You have somehow made yourself an outcast from the unity which is according to Nature; for you came into the world as a part and now you have cut yourself off."

61. "Theory and Practice," p. 89.

2

Kant's Idea of Peace and the Philosophical Conception of a World Republic

Matthias Lutz-Bachmann

In his 1795 work "Toward Perpetual Peace" Immanuel Kant formulated a political philosophy of international politics whose innovative potential has not been exhausted to this day.[1] In that work Kant elucidated the reasons for developing a substantive normative political philosophy from the concept of peace and for making the concept of peace one of the basic concepts of political philosophy, understood as a division of philosophy of right.[2] Among the promises that remain largely unfulfilled are Kant's advocacy of reforming international law [*Völkerrecht*][3] according to the principles of practical reason and his postulate of a peaceful global order that would place nations into legal relations with one another and ban military action from their external relations. There is good reason to see in Kant's idea of a "peaceful law of peoples," which anticipates a global legal community, an outline of the plan for establishing an organization of united nations—a plan that (if one disregards the failure of the League of Nations) would finally be implemented 150 years after the appearance of "Toward Perpetual Peace" with the signing of the charter of the United Nations in 1945.[4]

In this essay I want to discuss the most fundamental thesis of "Toward Perpetual Peace": Kant's idea of a league of free republics. To this end I first present the Preliminary Articles. I then try to point out difficulties in Kant's arguments that lead to a significant problem in the presentation of the Second Definitive Article. The central political thesis of Kant's work—that a league of nations [*Völkerbund*] rather than a world republic should be established in order to bring about peaceful relations among nations—is inconsistent with Kant's own assumptions and therefore proves to be untenable.[5]

1

Kant's "Toward Perpetual Peace" certainly does not belong to the group of texts upon which his reputation and his outstanding position in the history of philosophy rest. It would nevertheless be a mistake of large proportions to classify it as merely an occasional work and thus to assign it only peripheral importance. Despite its programmatic brevity and the ease with which it reads compared to many of his other texts, this text proves to be highly significant, not least for its implications concerning international politics. It also has philosophical significance, because in it the author tries to represent the unconditionedness of a peaceful global order with precise philosophical means. In contrast with the tradition of the Christian ethics of peace, which stretches from Augustine in late antiquity[6] to Erasmus in early modernity,[7] Kant does not hold the imperative to establish peace to be a commandment of Biblical religion over and against the realities of the political practice of states; rather, he justifies the imperative as a postulate of political philosophy. Consequently, Kant dispenses with the construction of a utopian, idealized state of harmonious human relationships[8] as a central condition for the success of international peace. Instead, Kant takes conflict as a given and relates his concept of peace to the unique role of establishing peace through just law: for Kant, only law, the legitimacy of which is established by reason, provides a procedure for resolving the conflicts that continually erupt among people without resorting to violence. It is not a coincidence that Kant presents his proposal for establishing peace among nations in the literary form of a contract; it is not only precisely the form and procedure of a contract reached by free agreement among those affected that is the only basic model of rational law; such an agreement also manifests pure practical reason as the normative basis of intersubjective relations generally.

Any discussion of Kant's conception of peace must recall precisely the kind of war Kant has in mind when he allows "our moral practical reason" to declare "its irresistible veto: there shall be no war."[9] In The Doctrine of Right of *The Metaphysics of Morals* Kant distinguishes two cases of war: the war "between me and you in the state of nature" and the war "between us as states which, though internally in a lawful condition, are nevertheless externally (in relation to one another) in a lawless condition."[10] "Toward Perpetual Peace" discusses its conception of peace with reference to the second case, peace among established states. The peace compact within a state serves Kant here not only as an indication of the demand of modern natural law [*Vernünftrechtlichen Förderung*][11] to leave the state of nature as a state of war but also as a model from which the constitutive moments of a peace compact among states can be determined by analogy. "Toward Perpetual Peace" presupposes in its description of such initial conditions the realities of war in the eighteenth century, a time in which sovereign states, as a rule still without republican forms of government, carried out their localized conflicts by military means which by our standards were quite limited. The occasions for war were mostly restricted to conflicts between the governments of sovereign, individual states which sought to assert their particular interests not through legally structured procedures but through the temporally and geographically restricted use of force. It is clear that Kant's understanding of the occasions and conduct of war cannot be directly applied to contemporary world politics without significant modification.

Nevertheless, even if historical distance makes the direct application of Kant's concepts and their descriptive content to the present impossible,[12] the normative content of his considerations and the systematic construction of his idea of peace still deserve our attention. The six Preliminary Articles, which constitute the first section of Kant's text, formulate six conditions which Kant believes must be fulfilled if a true peace among the nations is to emerge. These conditions define more precisely the negative conditions without which a lasting peace is unthinkable, and they foreshadow a positive idea of peace. The conditions reveal that what Kant means by peace in the strict sense is not the factual absence of war (that is, the silence of weapons) but "the end of all hostilities."[13] For this reason Kant even believes there might be a "suspicious pleonasm" in the title "Toward Perpetual Peace"—"suspicious" for him precisely because normal usage already lightly applies the word 'peace' to situations in which there is a preliminary cease-fire but in which a hidden state of war still prevails. In light of this concept of peace, every peace compact of the past resembles a mere "deferment of hostilities"[14] and all of previous human history resembles a state of war only intermittently interrupted by periods of peace. Now it is the decisive insight of our moral practical reason that such a state of war signifies not only a human misfortune (as in Hegel's philosophy of history) but also a state which must be unconditionally ended. With a peace agreed to unconditionally, which the First Preliminary Article formulates as a condition of the possibility for a "perpetual peace among nations," Kant combines the hope that all causes of future wars are entirely eliminated. He writes without reservation that "the existing reasons for war, even if not yet known to the parties contracting peace, are, in the peace compact, completely nullified even if they are gleaned from archival documents with the most sharp-sighted skill for hair-splitting."[15] The initial peace compact, which the First Preliminary Article demands and which precedes the perpetual peace among states, requires all participants to have the sincere intention to forgo "all claims which one state could have against another up to this time and which could give occasion for hostilities."[16]

Like the commentary on the First Preliminary Article, the remaining Preliminary Articles refer to the political situation of Kant's time. They have two functions in light of the existing international political practice of the absolutistic states: first, to formulate the conditions which must be fulfilled immediately regardless of the circumstances of action, and, second, to outline similarly necessary conditions of peace which nevertheless allow for somewhat delayed implementation, depending upon the situation. Kant calls the first group *leges strictae* [strict laws] and the second group *leges latae* [wide laws]. According to Kant, the "strict" conditions for peace include, besides the already-mentioned First Preliminary Article, the prohibition formulated in the Fifth Preliminary Article on "violent" intervention by a state "in the constitution and government of another state"[17] and the prohibition introduced in the Sixth Preliminary Article of certain ways of waging war which would destroy the minimal level of mutual trust that the First Article sets out as essential for the beginning of a true peace compact. Arguing entirely according to classical international law and its doctrine of "law in war" [*ius in bello*], Kant forbids wars of extermination [*bellum internecinum*][18] and of punishment [*bellum punitivum*].[19] In The Doctrine of Right, Kant adds to this list a further prohibition on wars of subjugation [*bellum subiugatorium*].[20] In the second group, the "wide" conditions for peace, Kant introduces the prohibition formulated in the Second Preliminary Article on the acquisition of states by other states through inheritance, exchange, purchase, or gift-giving; Kant forbids these practices, which were not unusual under absolutism, because they contradict his notion of "the idea of the original contract" and the doctrine of modern natural law that the state is a "moral person."[21] In the Third Preliminary Article Kant cites the further requirement that standing armies [*miles perpetuus*] be disbanded over time. Kant thereby explicitly contradicts not only the military doctrine prevailing since the time of Venetius—"Si vis pacem, para bellum" ["If you want peace, then prepare for war"]—but, even more, the conscription policies of absolutist governments, which appear "to entail the use of people as mere machines and tools in the hands of another (the state), which does not harmonize well with the law of humanity in our own person."[22] Finally, the Fourth Preliminary Article forbids the widespread practice of incurring national debt to conduct war.

2

Thus, the Preliminary Articles not only formulate the conditions without which a peace compact among states would fail on practical grounds; they also, by cataloguing a series of political demands, criticize the politics of all absolutistic states, and especially those of Prussia.[23] Even if we disregard the historically conditioned nature of Kant's demands, most of which have certainly retained a noteworthy practical relevance up to the present, the conspicuous lack of precision in the systematic structure of his argument merits further discussion. The extent to which it indicates specific difficulties that characterize "Toward Perpetual Peace" as a whole will become apparent later. Kant struggles with a fundamental problem in the presentation of the Preliminary Articles. Their function consists of presenting the necessary but negative conditions for a lasting peace compact. However, in order to fulfill this task convincingly, the Preliminary Articles already presuppose the entire systematic weight of the arguments that Kant presents in the main part of his work, the Definitive Articles of the Second Section. However, the Definitive Articles themselves fulfill a different function. They outline the general philosophical principles of law upon which the entire Kantian conception of peace normatively rests. The imprecisions in Kant's Preliminary Articles can be explained, at least in part, by their mediating function between the level of a philosophical construction of the commands of modern natural law in the Definitive Articles and their actual purpose of outlining those conditions prevailing in a state of war among states which must be removed in order that the idea of unconditional peace can be realized in practice, but without being able to recur to the full recognition of the principles of peace of modern natural law. This forces Kant by the logic of his argument to juxtapose various systems of law (without real mediation among them) by appealing to principles of natural law, international law, and modern natural law.

The difficulties presented by this mediating function of the Preliminary Articles emerge in Kant's expositions of articles 2 and 5. In these articles Kant not only repeats the international legal doctrine of the inviolable "sovereignty" of states as the subjects of normative international law which prevailed from Bodin[24] to Vattel[25]; he also utilizes the legal conception of an "original contract,"[26] which he nevertheless first systematically introduces in the First Definitive Article.[27] While the idea of the original contract is portrayed in the First Definitive Article as the decisive criterion for the founding of a republican polity which distinguishes the true constitutional state from the despotic state, Kant uses it in the Preliminary Articles to justify a thesis with a rather different content: the unconditional respect for the sovereignty of *all* states. Such a demand, however, extends even to those despotic states which the idea of the *contractus originarius* should exclude from participation in the principles of modern natural law. Thus the "idea of the original contract" is employed in the Preliminary Articles to justify a thesis for which it is systematically unsuited against the background of the Kantian theory of civil law, from which it arises. This is not to say that there could not be other good reasons to accept the conclusions of the second and fifth Preliminary Articles, such as those of political prudence or recognition of the accepted international law; it is just that Kant's justification, as it stands here, is not convincing. His justification has the objectionable consequence that the inviolability of the sovereignty of all states seems to be required by modern natural law, a thesis which cannot follow systematically for Kant. In the discussion of "Toward Perpetual Peace" that follows, we will see that the ambivalences in Kant's text regarding the demand for a world republic to secure peace are connected with precisely this point at which the argument breaks down.

A further set of problems connected with the above-mentioned difficulty occurs in the Sixth Preliminary Article, which takes up the international legal theorem of a "law in war." In The Doctrine of Right Kant himself characterizes this law as a division "of international law, in which the greatest difficulty is simply making it into a concept."[28] The problems, which Kant himself sensed, emerge during the attempt to answer the question how it is supposed to be possible "to think a law in this lawless state,"[29] when it is also true that *inter arma silent leges*; Kant defines the state of war as lacking precisely any basis for law which alone makes a law rationally binding. Kant offers as a way out of these theoretical problems a practical maxim: if war cannot be prevented, it ought at least be conducted according to rules which make it appear possible "to leave that state of nature of the states (in their external relations to one another) and to enter a legally constituted condition."[30]

In "Toward Perpetual Peace" Kant also pursues a practical solution to these theoretical aporias. It originates from the rough and idealizing separation Kant adopts between the state of nature and a legal order, and thus between war and peace as two not simply separate but mutually opposed spheres of validity. Consequently, he cannot avoid using the concept of a "law in war" [*ius in bello*] handed down in the traditional international law. At the same time, however, a weaker concept of legal validity need not be abandoned in a state of war; it becomes apparent that the effects of international law, namely pacification and the restriction of war and its consequences, cannot simply be denied.[31] Nevertheless, for Kant the grounds which speak for a limitation on ways of waging war cannot be of a legal nature; they cannot be taken from a positive legal order, because the state of war excludes all law by its very definition, nor can they be taken from any sort of natural law, because this is an expression of the state of nature among human beings, not of a common will produced through a rational agreement, corresponding to Kant's systematic argument that law must be understood as "the totality of conditions under which the will of the one can be united with the will of the other according to a universal law of freedom."[32] The insight into the necessity of the limits on ways of waging war must be derived from the practical insight of reason itself. It is revealing that Kant does not rely at this point upon an argument that he had already used in the commentary on the Third Preliminary Article, namely upon the practical insight of reason that forbids instrumentalizing human beings as mere means for one's own strategic goals.[33] Kant seems not yet to believe that war, or at least offensive war, is a context of action which in principle injures the dignity and rights of the people it affects and therefore ought to be unconditionally forbidden. At this point Kant does not appeal to the importance of individual persons or consider the legal relationships between states and individuals. Remaining consistent with the systematic structure of his argument, he considers the relations among states and, according to the highest moral insight of reason that there should be no war among states, proposes the practical maxim that, even in the war of the state of nature, hostile actions that "make mutual trust impossible during future peace" are not permitted.[34]

Against wars of extermination[35] [*bellum internecinum*], also forbidden by the maxim regarding mutual trust, Kant can nevertheless present another argument that confronts us with a further problem in his position. The wars of extermination Kant wants to see forbidden are those wars in which not the population, as in genocide, but the state as legal-political community is annihilated. It is conceivable that Kant has in mind the division of Poland among Prussia, Russia, and Austria, which led with the third division of Poland to a preliminary settlement in 1795, the year of the first printing of "Toward Perpetual Peace." Be that as it may, Kant refers to the fact—and this is the core of his argument—that with the annihilation of a political entity all law realized by people in this political community disappears. He writes: "From [this] it follows that a war of extermination, because the extermination can affect both sides alike and thus all law, would permit perpetual peace only in the vast graveyard of humanity. Hence such a war, as well as the use of means which lead to it, must be absolutely forbidden."[36]

As convincing as these considerations may be *prima facie*, they lead to two further difficulties. First, Kant appears to presuppose that with every state as such there also exists a system of law which demands continued existence and reason's unconditional recognition, or which in any case may not be abolished from without by means of a war. This presupposition raises difficulties analogous to those we have already seen in light of Kant's claim that the sovereignty of every state has unconditional recognition in accord with the traditional international law. Because Kant does not limit legal recognition to free republics, as the text shows, he seems prepared, at least as a limit case in his theory, to grant despotic states not only protection from violent injury to their sovereignty but also recognition as at least minimally constitutional and worthy of unconditional respect. This is a surprising conclusion, as one would have expected it more from Hobbes than from Kant. In any case, it shows that Kant thought pragmatically in recognizing the great harms to the goal of peace caused by a fundamental lack of recognition of the sovereignty of despotic states by republican polities.

As for the second problem, it becomes clear that Kant must in reality place states at war with one another into two spheres which are mutually exclusive in terms of their normative validity: inwardly Kant takes them to be, as we have seen, at least minimally constitutional, while in their external relations they stand in a state of nature which they are required to leave. It finally becomes clear here that Kant's idealized conception of two sharply separated spheres of validity, membership in both of which he ascribes to every state, generates conceptual difficulties for his argument; he can hold this conception only if it is possible to separate analytically the spheres of domestic and foreign politics from one another, at least with regard to basic principles. One can hardly call such a separation politically realistic. In fact, Kant himself does not appear willing to hold this separation in considering the political realities of the international relations of his time. The Preliminary Articles prove that he sees very clearly that states' domestic and foreign politics constantly intermingle and continuously affect one another, so that one and the same action by a state must be simultaneously placed in two spheres separated in terms of their normative basis. Thus, the philosophical fiction of two spheres of validity that Kant presupposes reasonably and successfully for the enterprise of founding of a free republic becomes decidedly problematic in its further application to the sphere of international politics.

3

Midway through "Toward Perpetual Peace," in the section titled Definitive Articles for Perpetual Peace among Nations, we encounter Kant's demand that the peace among states be secured by a new law of peoples. This new law of peace among the states is supposed to dissolve the classical doctrine of international law from "Hugo Grotius, Pufendorf, Vattel among others (mere tiresome comforters)"[37]; as far as Kant is concerned, with their doctrine of a right to war [*ius ad bellum*] for sovereign states, these theorists have only lengthened the state of war among states and given the conflicting parties justifications for ever new offensive wars. Contrary to the classical international law, the new law of peoples begins with the practical insight of reason, which "from the throne of the highest morally legislating authority absolutely condemns war as a legal procedure and makes the state of peace an immediate duty."[38] Just as peace among individuals requires a contract among them by which they constitute a republic, so this peace among states also requires a "contract among peoples"[39]; this contract has the task, as a *contractus originarius* among states, of founding the new peaceful law of peoples. However, unlike the *contractus originarius* among individuals, this contract is supposed to found not a republic of peoples, that is, not a "world state unifying all peoples [*Völkerstaat*]," but only a "league" among them, "which one can call a league of peace, which would differ from a peace treaty in that the latter seeks to end only *one* war, while the former seeks to end all wars forever."[40] Kant thus expressly excludes from this contract among states the constitution of a new political entity; it has the more modest function of "simply maintaining and securing the freedom of a state for itself and simultaneously of other confederated states."[41] Kant denies this league all legislative, executive and judicial power; according to Kant, no state entering the league would have to "submit to public laws and a compulsion under them."[42]

Only republics are eligible for membership in this league of states, because only they are constitutionally organized and can protect the freedom and equality of their citizens before the law through their republican constitutions. It is this political program of a federation [*Föderation*] of free republics which do not surrender their sovereignty as states but only their questionable right to war against one another according to classical international law that Kant pursues at the beginning of his Second Definitive Article: "The new law of peoples is to be founded upon a federalism of free states."[43]

However clearly these assertions outline the guiding political goal of "Toward Perpetual Peace," Kant's justification of the proposal entails difficulties and contradictions which call into question the usefulness of his suggested model for international peace. Kant's central argument in support of a league of sovereign states and in opposition to a world republic does not demonstrate what it is supposed to. Kant demonstrates his proposal's conformity to reason by arguing by analogy: just as individual human beings following the demand of reason [*exeundum ex statu naturali*] are to leave the state of nature through the *contractus originarius* and establish a republic in which each can realize his or her own freedom without diminishing the freedom of other citizens, so states are to enter legal relationships with one another through a contract that can end the state of war among them once and for all. Of course, it is surprising that Kant employs the idea of an "original contract," which gives the republic its legitimating power, because the analogy to political right [*Staatsrecht*] he is at pains to draw would, when applied to the case of a new peaceful law of peoples, correspond strictly to the demand that all the states party to the treaty enter into a compact that constitutes a new political entity common to them with a minimum level of constitutional separation of powers. In order to be legally constituted, this new political entity would have to ensure, by analogy to the republic, that each individual free state could realize its freedom (that is, its self-determination as a state) without diminishing the freedom of other states. From this criterion, which emerges from the analogy with political right, it would follow for the "state of peoples" that only through an at least possible free agreement of all affected states could any common resolution attain force of law and thus be binding for all. Of course, Kant does not draw this conclusion, even though his analogy to the peace-securing role of the republic demands it. Instead, he explicitly rejects the idea of a "republic of states," as we have seen, and puts in its place the idea of a "league of free states" that is to lack precisely the feature of statehood, namely, the system of civil law, which more than anything else in the case of his doctrine of political right could secure peace among individuals. What convincing reasons does Kant present for deviating from the structure of his own argument? In the text of the Second Definitive Article, Kant presents three arguments in support of the league of peace and in opposition to the "republic of states."

The first argument refers to a "contradiction" supposedly contained in the proposal of a "republic of states" (Kant himself speaks in this passage of a "state of peoples"): "Therein, however," he argues, "would be a contradiction: because every state contains the relation of a legislating ruler to an obeying subject (namely, the people), but many peoples in one state would constitute only one people, which contradicts the requirement (since we are considering here the right of people against one another, insofar as they constitute several different states and should not be combined into one state)."[44] The further justification of this thesis nevertheless reveals that Kant cannot discover a self-contradiction in the concept of the "state of peoples"; rather, there is only a contradiction between the main task of the law of peoples, namely to provide a foundation for the "right of peoples against one another," on the one hand, and the proposal of a "state of peoples" or a "republic of states," on the other.

Kant's objection against a "republic of states" or a "state of peoples" would be justified if a "republic of states" entirely superseded all existing legal relationships among the states which constituted it and transposed domestic law onto a global level. However, this condition is not necessary for peace. It assumes that all the states in the world have actually joined this "republic of states" after they have reformed domestically and become legally constituted republics, and that the individual republican states fuse with one another so that a new cosmopolitan law entirely supersedes all existing legal relations and replaces them. The emerging "unified world state" would in fact dissolve all sovereign rights of liberty of the existing individual states in their internal and external relations. Now such a "unified world state" is not even up for debate given Kant's initial conditions; it cannot be derived from the analogy between the *contractus originarius*, through which human beings as individuals form a republic, and the contract among free republics, because it conflicts with the central condition Kant formulated in the doctrine of political right for individual republics to be constitutional, namely that they not diminish or entirely abolish the freedom of their citizens. From this condition for the individual republic, the correctly formed analogy demands that the "republic of states" also not be organized in opposition to its members' rights of liberty and equality. This implies that the "republic of states" would have a mandate for action only in those political spheres individual states could not regulate on their own. Apparently, Kant believes that the analogy to the contract establishing a republic requires the contract among states to establish a unified world state; he thus rejects a conclusion that does not really follow from his own argument by analogy.

The second objection against the proposal for a "republic of states" concerns not the conclusions but the argument by analogy itself. According to Kant, "that cannot be valid for states, according to the law of peoples, which is valid for human beings in the lawless state according to the natural law, namely, 'to be obliged to leave this state.'"[45] It is clear that this assertion contradicts Kant's preceding argument; he had only shortly beforehand emphasized the analogy between states and human beings when he wrote that "peoples organized as states can . . . injure one another in their state of nature (that is, in independence from external laws) simply by their coexistence, and each of them, for the sake of its security, can and should demand the others to enter with it into a single, republic-like constitution in which the right of each can be protected."[46] How does Kant justify the distinction he apparently believes exists between the lawless relation of the states at war with one another and the lawless relation of human beings at war with one another, a distinction which is supposed to explain why the analogy sought after earlier may not be pressed any further? Kant justifies this important difference by appealing to the fact that states, or at least republics, "already have internal legal constitutions"[47] which are altogether absent from individual human beings as such. Moreover, it is decisive for Kant that in the state of nature human beings live in conditions of freedom without universal laws, while states, besides their internal legal constitutions, also already stand under conditions "according to the international law" that grant them inviolable sovereignty; for this reason Kant can say that states "have outgrown the compulsion of others to bring them under a wider legal constitution according to the conceptions of law of the others."[48] While freedom is due human beings on the basis of nature, "sovereignty" is a legal title which international law confers upon a state. Thus, the internal organization according to the rule of law (at least in the case of the republican state) and the sovereignty granted by international law distinguish states from individuals; it must follow, then, that the contract reason demands of each must also be different.

Now it cannot be denied that Kant's original analogy compares elements which are quite different but which correspond to one another when seen from a particular perspective. What common element enables an analogy to succeed between "republic" and "human being," which in and of themselves are highly different entities? It cannot be found in their characteristics "observed in and of themselves." Rather, it lies in the fact that both can be thought as capable of founding a new sphere of legal validity through a collective act of the will, a sphere into which they transfer rights by free contractual agreement which beforehand were due each one only individually and independently of the others. According to Kant's doctrine of political right, law instituted in this way is legitimate because it neither limits nor destroys the freedom of its constituents. What Kant concedes as both possible and necessary according to modern natural law for the original contract that founds a republic is to be applied analogously in the other case of the "republic of states" or the "state of peoples": the constitution and original freedom (or sovereignty) each republic has individually and independently from the others is not necessarily abolished through the transfer of legal titles; instead, if certain principles are heeded, it is confirmed and more fully realized through the creation of a new law. However, like the sphere of law of the republic, the new sphere of law of the "republic of states" must guarantee the original rights of freedom and self-determination of its members through fundamental rights and democratic procedural rules, that is, through well-ordered and equal rights of co-determination. Thus, the republic of states normatively and obligatorily receives constitutional rules for its internal structure.

The third argument in "Toward Perpetual Peace" clearly reveals Kant's wavering on the legitimacy of the "republic of states." At the end of the Second Definitive Article, Kant advocates anew the federal league of states, but he characterizes it as a "*negative* substitute" which must take "the place of the positive idea of *a world republic*,"[49] because existing states persist in the existing international law and are not in fact prepared to surrender their sovereignty and institute a new law that founds the *civitas gentium*. Because existing states "in no way want" the "republic of states" (or the "state of peoples") "according to their idea of the international law, . . . consequently, what is correct in thesi, they repudiate in hypothesi"[50]; therefore, instead of a "world republic" ("if all is not to be lost"[51]), a federal league of free states must be formed in order to secure peace. With this argument, Kant not only withdraws the fundamental objections he made earlier against conforming the "republic of states" to the laws of reason; he also abandons the level of the justification of the idea of a contract and appeals to arguments regarding the extent to which actions can actually be expected. This breaking off of further justification makes his argument against the "state of peoples" seem implausible. However, at the same time Kant's arguments do suggest a direction for political practice. Whether a reasonable conception of peace can be realized will depend upon political practice. From Kant's perspective, the federal league of peace is a demand of reason in light of the existing realities of states and their actual propensity not to relinquish any degree of sovereignty. Of course, in light of the analogy to the idea of the republic and the possibility of founding a "republic of states" Kant requires of the republics and their new league of states that they try to produce relations which correspond to the "republic of states," or "the positive idea of a world republic," as demanded by modern natural law. At this point in the text Kant turns from political considerations to a philosophical perspective which shows the idea of an original peace contract among peoples to be an obligatory norm of the cosmopolitan action of every people organized as a state [*Staatsvolk*].

What follows from these reflections on the basic propositions of "Toward Perpetual Peace"? Obviously, Kant provides no basis for rejecting the concept of a world republic or a new cosmopolitan structure discussed today in terms of the need for a new global political order. We can establish that the arguments Kant uses against the "state of peoples" are not convincing and moreover that they contradict the premises of his own theory of modern natural law. Instead, these premises provide insights that doubtless help formulate conditions which lead to the founding of new cosmopolitan structures and a supporting form of law for contemporary international politics. A new cosmopolitan law should further develop those legal principles which underlie the Charter of the United Nations and which are an expression of the existing international legal order in the direction of a republican world constitution with strong legislative, executive, and judicial elements, like those which already stand available to the United Nations and its related organizations, as, for instance, the International Court.

—*translated by David W. Loy*

Notes to Chapter 2

1. Immanuel Kant, *Zum Ewigen Frieden. Ein philosophischer Entwurf,* 1. Auflage 1795 (A), 2. Auflage 1996 (B), in Werke VIII. [This is available in English as "Perpetual Peace: A Philosophical Sketch," in *Kant: Political Writings,* second edition, ed. H. Reiss (Cambridge University Press, 1970).—translator]

2. For recent literature on "Toward Perpetual Peace" see H. Saner, *Kants Weg vom Krieg zum Frieden* (Munich, 1967); H. Williams, *Kant's Political Philosophy* (Oxford, 1983); G. Geismann, Kants Rechtslehre vom Weltfrieden, *ZfPF.* 37 (1983): 362–388; O. Höffe, *Kategorische Rechtsprinzipien* (Frankfurt am Main, 1990), pp. 249–284; G. Cavallar, *Pax Kantiana* (Wien, Köln, Weimar, 1992); P. Laberge, Das radikal Böse und der Völkerzustand, in *Kant über Religion,* ed. F. Ricken and F. Marty (Stuttgart, 1992); W. Kersting, Kant und die politische Philosophie der Gegenwart, in *Wohlgeordnete Freiheit* (Frankfurt, 1993); O. Höffe, ed., *Kant, Zum ewigen Frieden* (Berlin, 1995); V. Gerhardt, *Immanuel Kants Entwurf Zum ewigen Frieden* (Darmstadt, 1995).

3. I have translated translated *Recht* as 'law' except when the context requires 'right' or when parting with convention would lead to confusion. I have also distinguished two

Kant's Idea of Peace and a World Republic

senses of *Völkerrecht*: the "international law" Kant criticizes ("Toward Perpetual Peace," 103; 355 (BA 33)) and the new "law of peoples" he proposes.—translator

4. On the legal constitution of the United Nations Organization founded in 1945 see G. Unser, ed., *Die Uno, Aufgaben und Strukturen der Vereinten Nationen* (Munich, 1992), 5. Auflage.

5. The distinction here is between *Völkerbund* and *Weltrepublik*.—translator

6. Cf. Augustine, *De Civitate Dei* XIX 10–13, 26–28.

7. Cf. Erasmus, *Dulce bellum inexpertis* (1515), ed. B. Hannemann (München, 1987); Erasmus, *Querela pacis undique gentuim ejactae profligataeque* (1517).

8. A. Neusüss, *Utopie. Begriff und Phänomen des Utopischen* (Frankfurt and New York 1986), 3. Auflage, esp. pp. 471–515.

9. Kant, *Metaphysik der Sitten* VI, 354 (A 233). [The relevant portions of the text are available in English as *Metaphysics of Morals*, in *Kant: Political Writings*, 131–175. This passage is on p. 174.—translator]

10. Kant, "Doctrine of Right," in *Political Writings*, p. 165.

11. I have translated *Vernunftrecht* and related words as "modern natural law."—translator

12. For a more detailed account of the historical differences that separate us from Kant's concepts of war and peace see Jürgen Habermas, Kants Idee des Ewigen Friedens—aus dem historischen Abstand von 200 Jahren [translated in this volume].

13. Kant, "Toward Perpetual Peace," 93; 343 (BA 5).

14. Ibid.

15. Ibid., 93–94; 343–44 (BA 5f.).

16. Kant, Refl. 7837, Werke XIX, 530.

17. Kant, "Toward Perpetual Peace," 96; 346 (BA 11).

18. Ibid. (BA 12).

19. Ibid., 96; 347 (BA 13).

20. "Doctrine of Right," in *Metaphysics of Morals*, 168; 347 (A222).

21. Kant, "Toward Perpetual Peace," 94; 344 (BA 7).

22. Ibid., 95; 345 (BA 8f.). [In this context, *Recht* has the meaning of both right (on the moral level) and law (on the political level). I have translated it 'law' because of the political thrust of the paper.—translator]

23. Cf. Hans Saner, "Die Negativen Bedingungen des Friedens," in Höffe, *Kant, Zum ewigen Frieden,* 53, 61–66.

24. Cf. J. Bodin, *Les sex livres de la république* (1583) I, cap. IX.

25. Cf. E. de Vattel, *Le droit des gens* (1758) I, ch. I, § 4.

26. Kant, "Toward Perpetual Peace," 94; 344 (BA 7).

27. Cf. ibid., 99–100; 350 (BA 20).

28. Kant, *Metaphysics of Morals,* 168; 347 (A 221).

29. Ibid.

30. Ibid.

31. Volker Gerhardt (*Immanuel Kants Entwurf Zum ewigen Frieden*) is to be wholeheartedly supported when he sharply rejects Carl Schmitt's dangerous and impudent talk of the "preservation" of war by international law (in *Der Nomos der Erde in Völkerrecht des Jus Publicum Europaeum*).

32. Kant, *Metaphysics of Morals,* 133; 230 (A 33).

33. Kant, "Toward Perpetual Peace," 95; 345 (BA 8); cf. on this point *Grundlegung zur Metaphysik der Sitten* IV, 429 (BA 66f) [*Groundwork of the Metaphysics of Morals*].

34. Kant, "Toward Perpetual Peace," 96; 346 (BA 12).

35. Ibid.

36. Ibid., 96; 347 (BA 13).

37. Ibid., 103; 355 (BA 33).

38. Ibid., 104; 356 (BA 34).

39. Ibid., 104; 356 (BA 35).

40. Ibid. [In this section, the terms "republic of states" [*Staatenrepublik*], "state of peoples" [*Völkerstaat*], "world republic" [*Weltrepublik*], and "republic of peoples" [*Völkerrepublik*] all refer to a worldwide state encompassing all peoples which Kant rejects in favor of the league of nations [*Völkerbund*].—translator]

41. Ibid.

42. Ibid.

43. Ibid., 102; 354 (BA 30). "New" is my addition.

44. Ibid., 102; 354 (BA 30f).

45. Ibid., 104; 355 (BA 34).

46. Ibid., 102; 354 (BA 30).

47. Ibid., 104; 355 (BA 34).

48. Ibid., 104; 355–356 (BA 34).

49. Ibid., 105; 357 (BA 38).

50. Ibid.

51. Ibid.

3

Kant's "Toward Perpetual Peace" as Historical Prognosis from the Point of View of Moral Duty

Karl-Otto Apel

1 The Problem of a Critical Reconstruction

The somewhat complicated title of my essay indicates that my theme is the specifically Kantian conception of the metaphysical and epistemological connections between philosophy of history and practical philosophy. Once again of interest today, this conception does not merely prefigure the speculative and dialectical conception of progress that comprises the common "meta-narrative" of the *maîtres penseurs* of the nineteenth century (especially Hegel and Marx). Such a criticism of Kant has been suggested by thinkers as diverse as Hans Jonas, Andre Glucksmann, and Jean-François Lyotard. In order to make the specificity and practical relevance of the Kantian conception of history more apparent, it seems to me necessary to take off the disguise of Kant's two-world metaphysics, and thus to think with Kant against Kant.

It hardly needs to be remarked that Kant's "Toward Perpetual Peace" now once again merits great attention. The failure of the League of Nations was, according to Kant's expectations, a "pathologically compelled" result of World War I. The analogous project that followed World War II became the United Nations. Having survived the Cold War, the UN now faces a new test that will confirm its staying power. As a federation of nearly all the sovereign states on Earth, including a large portion of the former colonies of the Northern major powers, the UN faces the new task of effectively preventing national wars. Such territories include the areas in which the post-colonial differentiation of sovereign states is not yet settled, such as the Near and the Far East (Palestine and Taiwan), as well as in the territory of the former Soviet Union and Yugoslavia.

As a matter of fact, the UN still lags behind the Kantian presupposition of a legal community made up of "externally equal" and "inwardly republican" states. Rather, it must still tolerate not only de facto differences in government within its member states but also deviations from the "republican" constitution and even what Kant calls "despotic" states. Instead of the "equality" of all members, the political distinction is made between the members of the General Assembly and the members of the Security Council, whose permanent members (the United States, Great Britain, France, Russia, and China) are even provided with veto rights over all substantial decisions.

Nontheless, these elements of the "pathologically compelled" compromise at the end of World War II could, in Kant's view, nonetheless be entirely suitable for making possible the next phase in approximating the ideal order of peace and law founded on a federation of free peoples. It has become clear that the causal efficacy of conflict resolution and the prevention of war in the transitional phase between the international "state of nature" and cosmopolitan law can be established only through the cooperation of the major powers. But the desired peaceful order cannot be achieved through a factual consensus formation among all people of good will alone. Rather, it is for Kant far more the result of a natural "mechanism" of the inclinations of human self-interest, in that it must (at first, anyway) result from an intention of nature that makes use of this mechanism.

In sketching these vague hints of the relevance of the Kantian project at this moment in world history, I have also brought to light a few of the methodologically relevant characteristics of Kant's "philosophical sketch." Kant oscillates between, and sometimes combines, arguments employing juridical or even deontological-ethical postulates in fashioning an international legal contract and arguments employing a naturalistic and teleological "quasi-prognosis." The latter aspect of this project becomes much clearer when one interprets Kant's 1795 "sketch" in the context of the preceding writings in philosophy of history, above all, the renowned 1784 essay "Idea for a Universal History with a Cosmopolitan Purpose."[1]

If one is prepared to take seriously the current efforts to secure institutional stability and functional efficacy for the United Nations as a possible illustration of the Kantian sketch (that is, if one is prepared not to discredit them from the start—with Machiavelli or with Hegel—out of disappointment in utopian hopes or out of *realpolitik* skepticism), then the very combination of heterogeneous viewpoints lends Kant's project renewed relevance and even plausibility. In any case, this mixture has its own fascination. But from this fascination grows, more than ever, an urgent need for epistemological and methodological clarification and for a reconstruction of the systematic presuppositions of Kant's "sketch" that might transcend the architectonic of Kant's system.

It is well known that discussions in philosophy, social science, and history between Kant's time and the present—that is, between the Enlightenment and its postmodern critics—have put nearly every presupposition of the Kantian sketch into question. Its normative ideals and its epistemological presuppositions concerning history are all seen as components of a dogmatic version of modern Western metaphysics that must be overcome. This criticism uses arguments that could radicalize the Kantian critique of reason but which are now turned against the historical Kant, especially his historical teleology.

The best-known and most prima facie plausible of these arguments consists of the critique of historical determinism as the secularization of divine providence, a criticism that Karl Popper leveled primarily against Comte, Hegel, and Marx. This criticism, given new currency by Karl Löwith, Hans Jonas, the Nouvelle Philosophes, and the postmodernists, is now directed against Kant, the alleged predecessor of the speculative-dialectic historical philosophy of the nineteenth-century *maîtres penseurs*. It seems at least prima facie plausible that this criticism effectively challenges an interesting element of the Kantian philosophy of history that operates in the background of "Toward Perpetual Peace": the supposition of a teleological "intention of nature," which might also be called "cunning of nature" in anticipation of Hegel. This supposition concerns the idea that the wisdom of nature (which Kant, like Hegel, sometimes refers to as 'Providence') utilizes the "antagonism" of the "unsocial sociability" of humanity, so that the lengthy, apparently senseless, but nonetheless purposive dialectical process ultimately achieves the condition of a just external, legal order of human coexistence. This same end is also postulated by the moral autonomy of a priori reason; however, because of the dependence of human beings on their sensible inclinations, it can never by realized by the capabilities of reason alone.

It has to be conceded that the sort of practical interpretation still advanced by the early-twentieth-century neo-Kantian Marxists Max Adler and Karl Vorländer[2] (that Kant's philosophy of history is an anticipation of the dialectical insights of Hegel and Marx) is untenable. As is clearly the case with Hegel and Marx, it becomes a form of (causal and teleological) historical determinism. This conception of the cunning of nature should not merely be dismissed as so much dogmatic metaphysics. It is useful for pointing out a crucial aporia in Kant's architectonic from a contemporary perspective. It shows that the central presupposition guiding Kant's theoretical philosophy (namely, that the world of experience is characterized by the seamless causal determinism) is in direct conflict with his practical and political aims: the possibility of realizing a moral political order through interventions in social-political reality by autonomous reason. In the case of the ultimate end of history, it is not only that the presumed collaboration between the cunning of nature and moral reason can no longer be considered convincing. Rather, it is that realization of the intention of nature in the long run must be predictable in a specific sense: as an "unconditional prognosis" concerning the future historical process. Popper has shown that such an "unconditional prognosis" stands in sharp contrast with a "conditional prognosis," in that only the former belongs to the realm of the causal-analytic sciences as Kant understood them.[3]

But if historical determinism is primarily a teleological certainty about the future, then this teleology conflicts with the moral justification for every moral obligation. As Popper has shown, a scientific-dialectical version of an unconditioned historical prognosis collapses into an "ethical historicism" or a "futurism."[4] It replaces the authority of the moral ought with the authority of the "dialectical science" of "historical necessity" and necessarily leads to the political perversion of morality.

It seems quite clear that this latter interpretation, found in orthodox Marxism-Leninism, deeply contradicts the spirit of the Kantian project. The arguments on which "Idea for a Universal History with a Cosmopolitan Purpose" is based clearly lead to the conclusion that knowledge of historical necessity could not provide the foundation of morality. Rather, the opposite is true: a morally grounded ought demands that we think hypothetically and fallibly about progress in history—that is, in terms of a possible historical process to which morally informed practice can be tied. One can then, as the title of my essay implies, speak of a historical prognosis from the point of view of moral duty.

The following passages are perhaps the most important for demonstrating Kant's own emphasis on both the role of actively bringing about "perpetual peace" as "duty" or "task" of practical reason on the one hand and, on the other hand, the role of the quasi-prognosis of a guarantee of achieving of "perpetual peace" through the teleology of a natural mechanism: (1) In the conclusion of the chapter discussing Cosmopolitan Right in "The Doctrine of Right" Kant states: "Now, moral-practical reason within us pronounces the following irresistible veto: *There is to be no war*, either war between individual human beings in the state of nature, or war between separate states, which, although internally law governed, still live in a lawless condition in their external relationships with one another. . . . Thus it is no longer a question of whether perpetual peace is really possible or not. . . . On the contrary, we must simply act as if it could really come about (which is perhaps impossible), and turn our efforts towards realizing it and establishing that constitution which seems most suitable for this purpose (perhaps that of republicanism in all states, individually and collectively). By working towards this end, we may hope to abolish the disastrous practice of war." (Ak[5] VI, 360: 174) (2) In contrast, in the First Supplement to "Toward Perpetual Peace," under the heading On the Guarantee of a Perpetual Peace, Kant asserts: "Perpetual peace is *guaranteed* by no less an authority than the great artist Nature herself (*natura daedala rerum*). The mechanical process of nature visibly exhibits the purposive plan of producing concord among men, even against their will and indeed by means of their very discord. . . . In this way, nature guarantees perpetual peace by the actual mechanism of human inclinations. And while the likelihood of its being attained is not sufficient to enable us to *prophesy* the future theoretically, it is enough for practical purposes. It makes it our duty to work our way towards this goal, which is more than an empty chimera." (Ak VIII, 360-8: 108-14)

In the last lines that I have just quoted, Kant himself indicates how the glaring contradictions between the duty to bring about this end and the presumption of the natural guarantee of its achievement could perhaps be resolved.

But we must also state categorically what such a solution would entail. A consistent and coherent interpretation of the Kantian texts in terms of the conception of a practical mediation such as the one implied above demands a complete reconstruction of the architectonic of the Kantian system that makes up the background for his historical philosophy. It should be noted that the many passages in which Kant appears to speak entirely of the teleological intention of nature (in the manner of the pre-Kantian and hence dogmatic metaphysics), must be reinterpreted with the help of those few passages in which he reminds himself and the reader that "critical philosophy" can speak of a teleological structure of natural processes only in terms of the "regulative idea" of "reflective judgment." More than that, Kant's vague suggestion must be fully spelled out: that the regulative idea of the theoretical reconstruction of history corresponds to a postulate of practical reason. As opposed to the three classical postulates of the *Critique of Practical Reason*, such a postulate would not only claim to be a transcendent "hope"; it is indeed precisely demanded by the a priori moral-political duty to work toward the long-term realization of progress.

In light of this critical reconstruction of "Toward Perpetual Peace," one could in fact connect the practical and theoretical philosophy through the expectation of the historical consequences of moral action, even starting from a hermeneutical justification in light of Kant's own specific suggestions. Above all, this reconstruction requires a deep revision of the fundamental presuppositions of the Kantian conceptual system at one central point. The distinction between the unknowable *Dingen an sich* and the mere appearances of the world of experience that is essential to Kant's critical epistemology, which is identical to the one between the intelligible world of human freedom and the autonomy of reason and the causally determined world of the experiential externality of human action, has to be radically transformed. This transformation, informed by a critique of meaning and

by transcendental pragmatics,[6] is also the basis for a critical reconstruction of the argument by which Kant unifies the philosophy of
history and practical philosophy in *Idea for a Universal History with a
Cosmopolitan Purpose* and "Toward Perpetual Peace."

The need for this reconstruction can be seen in the way in which
Kant wanted to link the "cosmopolitan intent" of practical reason with
the historical sciences, the causal analysis of which he expected to develop into an equivalent to the natural sciences (VIII, 5). Moreover,
Kant also sought to determine the relationship between the merely
"external order of freedom of a republican legal state" and the "inwardly motivated freedom of morality." In terms of the metaphysical
dualism of the two-worlds doctrine that pervades his entire critical
philosophy, Kant's expectation that in principle it must be possible to
establish a republican constitutional state (even "for a nation of devils
so long as they possess understanding" (VIII, 112)) is consistent with
his principles. This expectation is absurd in light of the demand that
an internally consistent practical reason must not only will such a
legal order but also participate in its establishment on a global scale.
This *reductio* applies also to a "game-theoretical" conception of a legal
order, which works even though the rulers and the ruled in this order
obey only the egotistic-strategic rationality of devils.[7]

One must certainly concede to Kant that one can never know with
certainty whether human beings (others or even oneself) are guided
in their actions by moral motives (thus "from duty"). Therefore, the
legal state only enforces the "legal duties" of its citizens (in the sense
of actions conforming to duties) rather than "duties of virtue." But it
in no way follows (if one does not include the two-worlds doctrine as a
further premise) that a legal order could emerge in the world of intelligible experience by means of self-interested action alone. (This is
indeed the task that Kant sets for himself in the philosophy of history.) Rather, such an order presupposes the willingness of human beings to act morally and to be committed to justice.[8]

Kant only appears to have considered how moral-political engagement is actually possible in such passages as the one, in an appendix to
"Toward Perpetual Peace," in which he appealed to politicians not to
take a step "without first paying tribute to morality" (Ak VIII.380:125).
Even those obligations that Kant's "moral politicians" incorporate into
their maxims of action do not result from some "purpose" derived

from the interests of the state as the "highest *empirical* principle of political wisdom." Rather, such obligations "should be influenced only by
the pure concept of rightful duty, i.e., by an obligation whose principle is given a priori by pure reason . . . whatever the physical consequences may be" (Ak VIII.379:123-4). In the same way as the contrary
expectation that it is possible for "a nation of devils" to establish a
state, these maxims correspond to the dualism of the two worlds of
Kant's metaphysics, which completely separates the world of practical
experience from the world of moral responsibility. As opposed to this
separation, a more relevant and plausible conception suggested by
Kant to his like-minded readers can be found between the lines of his
historical philosophical works, in that in the long run it is possible to
use actions that are both strategically clever and morally responsible
to take advantage of the constellations of political power and opportunities resulting from the antagonism of human interests in order to
achieve of the goals of a cosmopolitan order of peace and law.
However, the metaphysical dualism of the two-worlds doctrine clearly
cannot be unified with such a practically relevant reinterpretation of
"the intention of Nature" entirely in terms of the goals of reason. The
Kantian vision of convergence in history requires two assumptions:
first, that experiential natural processes and the "external actions" of
history, on the one hand, are not completely inaccessible to the interventions and motivations of freedom and moral reason on the other;
and, second, that the moral autonomy of reason is not thereby eo
ipso corrupted by the empirically oriented means-ends rationality.[9]

Instead of taking this route, Kant stubbornly follows his metaphysical dualism and uses his "ethics of conviction" (in Weber's sense) to
confront both the "political moralist" and the "moral politician" in
the appendix of "Toward Perpetual Peace." This leads into the objective problem of the "disunity of morality and politics," the recognition
of which constitutes the basis for the conception of the historical-
dialectical "cunning of nature." This cunning ultimately reduces the
objective problem to one of the subjective motivation of actors: "Thus
in objective or theoretical terms, there is no conflict whatsoever between morality and politics. In a subjective sense, however (i.e. in relation to the selfish disposition of man, which, since it is not based
on maxims of reason, cannot however be called practice), this con-

flict will and ought to remain active, since it serves as a whetstone for virtue." (Ak VIII.379:124)

Consistent with the way this moralism completely loses sight of the demand for the empirically oriented political responsibility for consequences, Kant went so far as to affirm the principle *Fiat justitia, pereat mundus*, which he made less odious by translating it as "Let justice reign, even if all the rogues in the world must perish." (Ak VIII.378:123) Just before this passage, Kant's purely negative characterization of the maxims of the "empirically" oriented politician (*Fac et excusa!*, *Si fecisti, nega* and *Divide et impera*) (Ak VIII.374:120) made clear that he could not even conceive of the basic problem of the moral politician: even when he acts for the sake of the ideal of the just order, he must also be aware that it is possible for many more than the "rogues" to perish when, according to Kant, the "knot is broken asunder." Indeed, this impossibility of the moral politician to act positively represents the objective problem of "combining politics and morality" (Ak VIII.380:125).

With these critical remarks I have in no way disavowed the relevance of a possible convergence of the empirically conditioned passage of history with the aim of pure practical reason that emerges for the first time with Kant. Rather, my purpose is to expose Kant's incompatible systemic presuppositions. In what follows I will attempt to think with Kant against Kant, indicating the transformations of Kant's architectonic that give maximum plausibility to the project of a philosophy of history with a practical intent.

2   History and the Practical Presuppositions of the Kantian Project

A Critique of the Kantian Solution to the Problem of Unifying the Freedom of Action with Causal Necessity

Under the rubric of a of philosophy of history with practical intent (or, more precisely, the hypothetical representation of the historical process as converging toward the goal of practical reason in a social system that maintains a legal and peaceful order), the locus of Kantian solution to the problem of freedom is found at his architectonic's deepest point. Kant anchors his solution to the problem of human freedom in the distinction between the noumenal and the phenomenal world. This is the starting point for a transcendental pragmatic transformation of the philosophy of history, which is grounded in the analytically anchored and critical theory of meaning. This is because Kant thought he had already uncovered such a solution in the transcendental dialectic's Third Antinomy. In other words, in light of the causally determined order of nature presumed by Kant and the natural sciences of his time, salvaging the possibility of the morally relevant freedom of will and action became the main practical motivation for his dualistic distinction between the "intelligible world of the unknowable thing in itself" (including the "intelligible I") and the world of mere appearance. In his solution of the Third Antinomy, Kant argues that this distinction proves to him the possibility of the co-establishment of freedom and causal necessity in two worlds seen independent of each other (the solutions of the First and Second Antinomies, by contrast, kept both sides of the antinomy tied to the "mere" world of appearances).

For the sake of argument, assume that the concept of an unknowable yet necessarily existing intelligible world of *das Ding an sich* is internally consistent.[10] It is necessary to note that Kant's two worlds are still not capable of solving the problems of conceptualizing free human actions as purposive and responsible interventions in the experienceable world of nature or history. That is, the world of experience is always based on a continuous causal determinism. If this is so, then it must at least be presumed to be independent of any subsequent determination through a "causality of freedom" in space and time (of the sort Kant presupposed). It is also therefore in principle impossible to bring about a causally ordered calculable effect in the world of experience through an action determined by reason. However, that some intervening action A is able to bring about an experienceable effect B that would not have occurred without A is the transcendental pragmatic (although not only in a mentalistic sense) presupposition of experimental physics.[11] Furthermore, the instrumental utilization of opportunities for the reaching of practical goals (whether these are in agreement with practical reason or not) is presupposed in every political intervention in historical-social reality.

The Kantian system's presuppositions lead to quite different conclusions: every achievement of human goals through phenomenally real intervening actions is possible only through the metaphysical connection of a pre-established harmony between the intelligible human "causality from freedom" and the predicted consequences of action in the causal nexus of the world of experience. Ultimately, this connection establishes the convergence of the historical process and the actualization of the morally derived goals of a cosmopolitan order of law and peace it implies. That is, people would not even have the opportunity to choose among the multiplicity of possible relations of cause and effect available for the realization of these goals; even if this is so, they do not even have the chance to effect the realization of the ultimate end of the historical process. (N. Hartmann thought that human freedom of action was indeed compatible with the causal determination of nature, but not with the achievement of the final end of history by the intention of nature.[12]) Otherwise, people must be able to generate the actual effectiveness of a new cause (from freedom) introduced through the intervening action A, which has B as its effect, and with this be able to give the process of history a new and causally attributable direction. According to the Kantian system, this is unthinkable. Human attempts to realize the goals of reason can be achieved only to the extent that they are predetermined through some causal mechanism within the continuous causal chain of the determination of nature.

This latter interpretation, however, would still be compatible with the Kantian vision of convergence the orthodox interpretation of the Kantian system also suggests as the pre-established harmony of the intelligible intervening actions (caused by freedom) and the empirically predictable causal effects by presuming that the "natural intention" of "Providence" guides the historical process towards its final end and thus replaces the goals of human reason. This interpretation is unsatisfying not only because it is based on a "dogmatic" and "excessive" metaphysics. In terms of the human orientation toward freedom presupposed in Kant's own philosophy of history and in his practical philosophy, this interpretation is also deeply counterintuitive, precisely because it makes it possible to think of freedom of the will and freedom of action only as intelligible "quasi-origins," as it were, of certain causal effects in the world of experience. This interpretation thereby eliminates the possibility of conceiving of humanity as having a causal responsibility for even a part of the historical process. (In addition, it should also be noted that this conception of responsibility is, unfortunately, in harmony with Kant's neglect of moral responsibility for consequences in his moral philosophy of the formal good will.)

Attempting to understand the Third Proposition of *The Idea for a Universal History with a Cosmopolitan Purpose* without the aid of the architectonic of Kant's system shows why the presupposition of a freedom of action without possible responsibility for successful consequences is unsatisfactory on Kant's own terms. The thesis states: "Nature has willed that man should produce entirely by his own initiative everything which goes beyond the mechanical ordering of his animal existence, and that he should not partake of any other happiness or perfection than that which he has procured for himself without instinct and by his own reason. . . . It seems as if nature had intended that man, once he had finally worked his way up from the uttermost barbarism to the highest degree of skill, to inner perfection in his manner of thought and thence (as far as is possible on earth) to happiness, should be able to take for himself the entire credit for doing so and have only himself to thank for it." (VIII 20:43)

These most deeply speculative concepts of the Kantian philosophy of history, anthropology and (implicitly) theodicy are clearly incompatible with the achievement of a cosmopolitan order of law and freedom solely by causal mechanisms or the intention of nature. It seems that for Kant this "intention of nature" or "Providence" also implies that it is human beings who ultimately attain this state through the intentions of reason.[13] In the following, we will attempt to follow this practical heuristic rather than the architectonic of Kant's system.

The Transcendental Pragmatic Transformation of the Kantian Architectonic: Freedom and Causal Necessity

In the following I shall briefly discuss a transformation of the Kantian two-worlds metaphysics informed by transcendental pragmatics, especially with regard to its application in the relationship between freedom and causality. According to a strict interpretation of the basic concepts of the *Critique of Pure Reason*, the concepts of understanding and reason can only meaningfully be applied to possible experience, in contrast to the Platonic forms which refer directly to *das Ding an sich* independent of all experience. Following these basic critical concepts strictly, these same methodological devices can also be applied to the concept of reality. Accordingly, objects that can actually be known are not *Dinge an sich* (which, according to Kant and the prior Christian-Platonic tradition, refer to the divine *intellectus archetypus*, the basis for thinking of things in a formal-generative rather than an objective way). Rather, they are experienceable or knowable by us in terms of a regulative idea to which nothing factually experienced or known can fully correspond.[14] Although actually knowable reality is also independent from every factual and realizable result of the knowledge, it is not independent of all possible knowledge in general. Otherwise, reality could not be conceived as something known by us: nor could we give any meaning to the conception of reality that has practical relevance for us (as is in fact the case for the concept of the unknowable *Dinge an sich*).

This transformation of Kant's two-worlds theory through a critique of meaning was first articulated by C. S. Peirce: in it, the fundamental critical conception articulated in the *Critique of Pure Reason* is fully preserved but now given a postmetaphysical form: in place of the more or less dogmatic-metaphysical distinction between the intelligible and phenomenal worlds, we now distinguish between the potentially infinite task of knowledge as a practice of research (which cannot be attained by any single person or particular community) and all conceivable factual results of the knowledge of experience. Such a distinction, first formulated by Peirce, again forms the basis of the fallibilistic principle of the knowledge of experience.[15]

Even after this critical dissolution of the two worlds doctrine, the question remains: how can the causal necessity of experienceable consequences of events coexist with the freedom of human will and action? On the one hand, given the Kantian presupposition shared by all his scientifically trained contemporaries, that the causal necessity of the connection of events is a priori valid for all conceivable knowledge of experience, a solution to this key problem of metaphysics hardly seems possible once we set aside the two-worlds theory. On the other hand, if one applies the principle of fallibilism to the concepts of understanding and the categories that for Kant constitute the object of possible experience, and hence apply them a priori to all possible experience, it is at least conceivable to relegate the use of the principle of causal necessity and limit its use to a particular realm of possible experience.

In the twentieth century, one such limitation on causal necessity has been suggested in two distinct ways: The first such attempt emerges in the philosophy of science. In Kantian terms, the mentalistic-transcendental presupposition of causality as a category of understanding is not sufficient for achieving any distinction between the expectations of causally necessary consequences of events and the mere regularity of consequences of events in the neo-Humean sense. For example, causality as a category of understanding cannot distinguish between the expectation that iron expands when it is heated from the expectation that the earth rotates when iron is heated. Nonetheless, the category of causal necessity suggests that the first expectation can be distinguished from the second through the structure of possible experience as it is related to human action. This was actually predicted by Kant in the well-known preface of the second edition of the *Critique of Pure Reason*, according to which the inventions of physicists compel nature to answer their questions through experimentation.[16] In this way, it now appears that the physicist is justified in presuming the causal necessity of the consequences of events rather than their mere regularity. They are justified in accepting that through the completion of some (intervening) action A, they can bring about the subsequent event B, which without A would not have occurred. Following this line of Kantian reflection, I see the possible transcendental pragmatic transformation of the mentalistic-transcendental justification of the a priori of the expectation of causal necessity for consequences of events.

The second, notable version of this transformation of Kant's problem lies in considering how the possibility of real, practical freedom of action no longer seems incompatible with the acceptance of the causal necessity of the consequences of events. Rather, the opposite is true: the practice of the real freedom of action is now seen as the very condition of the possibility of causal necessity. This transcendental pragmatic concretization of both concepts makes the "Copernican turn" in philosophy more fully visible by showing that the presupposition of necessary causal connections among events derives from the intervening causality of the successful experimental practice, thus proving another possible limitation of the a priori justification of the presumption of causal necessity. The justification of the presumption of causal necessity comes to a halt when we extrapolate beyond the classical self-understanding of physics, and thus beyond the relationships of the manipulable objects found within the world of experimental experience to the possible world of experience in general. In the framework of a protophysics,[17] the argument that it is necessary to presuppose that the relationships of the successful causal intervention is tied to a valid causal determinism, its universalization is shown to be mere dogmatism in light of the transcendental pragmatic transformation of the Kantian philosophy.[18]

At this point the paradigmatic innovations of twentieth-century physics come into play: foremost is the transformation of the experimental situation in microphysics, in which the Kantian categories of substance and causality no longer apply as a schemata to the relation of elementary particles.[19] The results of synergetic and chaos theory also compel us to question any presupposition of the constancy of the laws of nature themselves.[20]

Without venturing any further into this issue, let us establish the following claim: it is now no longer necessary to presume a form of a causal determination underlying experienceable nature in general, to which we oppose "causality of freedom" relevant for how actors affect the experienceable world as nature and history. Rather, the weight of the scientific evidence implies, following Schelling and Peirce, that we ought to grant the priority of the spontaneity of *natura naturans*, such that the structure of its order and of its laws can better be understood as analogous to "habits" and other regularities which reveal themselves as a "quasi-nature"[21] in the context of human history. They are, so to speak, sedimentations of that very creativity, by virtue of which, Kant argued, human beings could derive everything out of themselves. Thus, many of the difficulties that stood in the way of Kant's working out a historical philosophical conception of a progress of natural evolution toward the goals of practical reason have recently been removed to a great extent.

The Positive Heterogeneity of the Consequences of Social Action: Freedom of Action versus "Cunning of Nature"

The transformation sketched above could still leave the Kantian conception open to serious objections, especially if it were to try to reconstruct and make intelligible the point of Kant's philosophy of history that I have called the "cunning of nature." Have we not ignored or at least defused in a harmonistic way the dualistic tension between what human beings can achieve through conscious freedom of action and what according to Kant could be achieved only by nature or providence? Is not the final goal achievable only without conscious intentionality, and even when related to consciousness only through quite heterogeneously motivated actions?

Any postmetaphysical reconstruction of those speculative intuitions must begin with the speculative intuitions that constitute the kernel common to the social and economic philosophical ideas of Mandeville's Fable of the Bees, Adam Smith's theory of the invisible hand, and the conception of cunning used by Kant and Hegel in the philosophy of history. In contemporary terms, playing off the functional "systems rationality" against the good or evil intentions of "actor's rationality" in sociological systems theory[22] belongs to the same speculative topos. I am not suggesting that the whole topos is speculative in a suspect way; rather, it is already the insight of action theory that the consequences of actions are essentially heterogeneous as soon as the controllable frame of experimental actions is transgressed. This heterogeneity is already present in planned strategic cooperation between differing action subjects, and even more so in complex historically and socially conditioned situations.[23] The deviation of the consequences of actions from their intended goals can be assessed either from the point of view of the actors or from that of a distantiated observer. If value judgments are involved, such consequences can be assessed as negative (for example, from the point of view of an acting politician as being frustrating, or from the point of view of a historian as the tragic failure of a politician) or as positive (for example, as expedient or functional in relation to the goals of a social system, or for the purpose of a philosophy of history in its practical intent).

Furthermore, the negative deviations reassert the old problem of learning from history. Certainly Hegel and the proponents of nineteenth-century historicism had good reason to call into question this possibility presumed by the goals of the practice of historiography since the time of Thucydides. In fact, the frustrations of political planning cannot simply be removed by avoiding long-term planning and assimilating the conditions of political actions to those of observable experiments. This sort of alignment of conditions becomes obstructed through the irreversibility of the historical interactions of people and their consequences. (This holds for Popper, whose proposal to pursue an experimentally controlled politics of the "piecemeal social engineering" is based on the "conditional predictions" of the social sciences.[24] Popper cannot meet the objection that a strict repetition of the initial conditions for social experiments in a historical framework is not possible, one reason being that under conditions of free communication one cannot predict the behavior of agents (such as the consumer or the voter) without becoming ensnared by Merton's paradox of the self-fulfilling or self-defeating prophecy. The tendential removal of the heterogeneity of the social consequences of action through the "conditional predictions" of controlled social experiments is itself still subject to the heterogeneity of consequences, because the predictions alter the initial conditions of the quasi-experiment in an irreversible way.)

In relation to the positively assessed heterogeneities of the consequences of social action, however, such speculative extrapolations have been taken further. Such extrapolations are characteristic of Kant's philosophy of history, of those of Hegel and Marx, and of the secret metaphysics of functionalistic theories of social systems. The most efficacious paradigm of the latter sort had already been founded in the eighteenth century in Adam Smith's doctrine of the invisible hand, which is supposed to guarantee to participants in the capitalistic market economy the social benefits of profit-oriented competitive action. This paradigm remains convincing today, especially if it is not used to lend support, as in Hayek, to a Social Darwinistic theory of cultural revolution but rather is complemented by the economic ethic of a social market economy on a global scale.[25] In this version, the objection that a section of society (today a part of humanity) will be unavoidably impoverished by the effects of the capitalistic economic order could perhaps be met and refuted. First suggested by Hegel and then by Marx, the problem of the heterogenity of action is sublated by a shift to the social dialectical paradigm of the "cunning of reason," which leads to a total historicism and ultimately to the "sublation" of practical reason itself.

The Kantian vision of the cunning of the "intention of nature," which makes use of the "antagonism" of "unsocial sociability" in order to reach the telos of human society required by practical reason, is now even closer to a point of departure free of metaphysics—provided that one removes all implications of a causal and/or teleological determinism. Here emerge not only the problem of negative consequences but also the effects of the positive heterogeneities of the social consequences of our actions. This much has already been made clear: from the very outset it would contradict the spirit of Kant's mediation between the theory of history and practical reason if at this point one would only recommend a position of pure passive "hope" regarding the course of history. Rather, the positive heterogeneities of the social consequences of our actions offer the possibility of reinterpreting those presuppositions, which in the Kantian system are apparently inconsistent: the freedom of action under the imperative of practical reason and the cunning of nature in its practical intent. But what we experience in the case of the negative heterogeneity of the consequences of action again and again as frustration becomes the impetus for learning from history, as we try to eliminate it from our attempts at progress. Precisely this structure of our social action also opens up to positive heterogeneity as an opportunity to think about and to make use of the results of history which came about without or against our intention as the means, or at least the starting point, for the actualization of the goals of reason imposed upon us. In fact, it is possible to unify the goal of a cosmopolitan order of law and peace as postulated by practical reason with Kant's historical philosophical presuppositions without contradictions: with the presupposition that the actualization of the demands of reason is not to be brought about merely through the good will of those who explicitly advocate it. In other words: the unintended course of things—represented by the positive heterogeneities of the consequences of action—meets the project of practical reason halfway.

Kant's Justification of the Possibility of Moral Progress

At this point a more genuine Kantian conception could be developed, even though it is not to be found in the main works of Kant's moral philosophy or in his philosophy of history; rather, it is a way to mediate among his main works, as a whole. Kant's Critical Philosophy distinguishes between the questions "What can I know?" "What ought I do?" and "What may I hope?" However, the problem here is to discover an answer to a question that is not contained in any one of these questions but is found in all three: How ought we to think about the possibility of moral progress in history?

Indeed, Kant considers this question in all his writings on the philosophy of history which allude to the possibility of the cunning of nature aiding attainment of the goals of practical reason. One answer, which he had suggested in part III of the section of "Theory and Practice" on international law is convincing in light of my previous critique of his metaphysical system. Its emergence here could be connected with the way Kant defends the roles of various "theories" with regard to morality, law, the state, and finally international law. By grounding such theories in the concept of duty, Kant answers objections raised by "practical experience" to their usefulness (VIII, 62). The treatment of these issues in the section Theory and Practice focuses on the foundation of a practically plausible mediation between a theory of international law based on duty (that is, the theory of a cosmopolitan order of law and peace which ultimately has a moral justification) and the conceptual possibility of actualizing the presupposed progress in world history.

The theme of the third part of the 1793 essay mediates between "Idea for a Universal History with a Cosmopolitan Purpose" and "Toward Perpetual Peace"—that is, between the philosophy of history, in which the quasi-dialectical idea of a cunning of nature is introduced, and the practice-related idea of a contract that forms the basis of the law of peoples. The answer to the question of the mediation between the duty-grounded theory of the law of peoples and its historical application is not given directly through the introduction of the speculative idea of a helpful "intention of nature." Instead it is accomplished through a development belonging to Kant's ethics, which makes it possible to distinguish Kant's approach rather clearly from nineteenth-century speculative historical philosophy.

The development that is relevant here is found in Kant's reply to Moses Mendelsohn's rejection of all speculation on progress, even a hypothetical one:

> I do not need to prove this assumption [that progress toward the end of the moral improvement of humanity is possible]; it is up to the adversary to prove his case. I am a member of a series of human generations, and as such, I am not as good as I ought to be or could be according to the moral requirements of my nature. I base my argument upon my inborn duty to influence future generations in such a way that they will make constant progress (and I must thus assume that progress is possible), and that this duty may be rightfully handed down from one member of the series to the next. History may well give rise to endless doubts about my hopes, and if these doubts could be proved, they might persuade me to desist from an apparently futile task. But so long as they do not have the force of certainty I cannot exchange my duty (as a *liquidum*) for a rule of expediency which says that I ought not to attempt the impracticable (i.e. an *illiquidum*, since it is purely hypothetical). And however uncertain I may be and may remain as to whether we can hope for anything better for mankind, this uncertainty cannot detract from the maxim I have adopted, or from the necessity of assuming for practical purposes that human progress is possible. (VIII, 88–89)

Kant then further specifies the relation of this practical postulate to moral hope:

> It is quite irrelevant whether any empirical evidence suggests that these plans, which are founded only on hope, may be unsuccessful. For the idea that something which has hitherto been unsuccessful will therefore never be successful does not justify anyone in abandoning even a pragmatic or technical aim. . . . This applies even more to moral aims, which, so long as it is not demonstrably impossible to fulfil them, amount to duties." (VIII, 89)[26]

Certainly Kant connects this decree of moral duty (that historical progress is possible) with the reflection that "this immeasurably long undertaking [of progress] will depend not so much upon what *we* do (e.g. the education we impart to younger generations) and upon what methods we use to further it; it will rather depend upon what human *nature* may do in and through us, to *compel* us to follow a course which we would not readily adopt by choice" (VIII, 90).

Of course, this special presupposition must not contradict the overall a priori grounding of the conceptual possibility of progress in moral duty. Rather, for Kant, it follows from the morally justified duty to explore through a philosophy of history with practical intent all the possibilities that offer ways to approach the realization of the purpose of reason—here the cosmopolitan order of law and peace. This interpretation offers finally an undogmatic (postmetaphysical) justification of speculative hypotheses and appears to express what Kant means by his historical philosophical idea of the "aim of nature": ". . . it is not inappropriate to say of man's moral hopes and desires that, since he is powerless to fulfil them himself, he may look to *providence* to create the circumstances in which they can be fulfilled. The end of *man* as an entire species, i.e. that of fulfilling his ultimate appointed purpose by freely exercising his own powers, will be brought by providence to a successful conclusion, even although the ends of *men* as individuals run in a diametrically opposite direction." (VIII, 91).

The point of these speculative global hypotheses is not their quasi-theological supposition of an "aim" of Providence or of Nature. Rather, these hypotheses open up the space for connecting my actions to the factual course of history, given that progress is a moral task to all humanity. Kant interprets the possible consequences of human "unsocial sociability" in these terms: "For the very conflict of individual inclinations, which is the source of all evil, gives reason a free hand to master them all; it thus gives predominance not to evil, which destroys itself, but to good, which continues to maintain itself once it has been established." (VIII, 91) Seeing such a condition as presenting a moral task would ultimately depend on the recognition of the "pathologically compelled" results of war as the opportunity (*occasioni*, in Machiavelli's terms) for the emergence of a self-maintaining order of law and peace; going beyond Kant, this interpretation also depends on recognizing the consequences of unsocial sociability as presenting the opportunity to participate in the realization of the final end of history.

Kant expresses the difference between such a conception and the recognition of the necessity of the historical process typical of Hegel or Marx clearly when he remarks that "the distress produced by the constant wars in which the states try to subjugate or engulf each other must finally lead them, even against their will, to enter into a cosmopolitan constitution, is no more than a personal opinion and hypothesis; it is uncertain, like all judgments which profess to define the appropriate natural cause of an intended effect which is not wholly within our control" (VIII, 91).

Once we rethink teleology in terms of opportunities to realize the cosmopolitan order of law and peace in history, it is also possible to reevaluate Kant's assessment of the positive means that help realize these goals. I have in mind the expectations that Kant connected with the "spirit of commerce" (VIII, 114), with the republican constitution (VIII, 100), and with the "publicity" of all the demands and the claims (VIII, 126) connected with law.

If by "the spirit of commerce" one understands all the tendencies which had led to the formation of a capitalistic world economic order in the nineteenth and twentieth centuries, then, from an ethical perspective, one may arrive at very ambivalent conclusions regarding these developments. For example, they are connected with the process of colonization that was introduced by Iberian trade capitalism and continued in the Third World by the European trade and industrial capitalism and the imperialism of the North. From the long-term perspective, it appears to be unmistakable that economic interests in overcoming all trade obstacles through an international order of law and peace have at least (as Kant thought) opened space for the moral regulation of this order, say, through human rights. In the current global situation the strongest potential for preventing war does appear to be tied to the institution of a world economic order and the regional economic alliances (for example, the European Union, NAFTA, Mercosur, ASEAN).

The estimation of the global political achievements of the republican constitutional states since the French Revolution is also extremely ambivalent, if one thinks, on the one hand, of how the princely wars of sovereigns were replaced by the national wars of the nineteenth and twentieth centuries, and, on the other hand, of how republics and representative democracies are not primarily responsible for the emergence of nationalism, which produced total, nationalistic, and the ideologically driven world wars. Quite to the contrary, republics and democracies have provided a model of a legal order based on the type of positive rights and constitutions that point toward their development in a cosmopolitan order.

One should not simply equate the model of the republican "principle of democracy" and its principle of "national sovereignty" with the global realization of the "principle of law" postulated by Kant. In the current global situation, that would be tantamount to misunderstanding the basic tension underlying domestic and foreign affairs—the tension between the plurality of particular states as self-maintaining systems and universal "principles of law" such as human rights whose moral justification and legal positivization directs us to a cosmopolitan legal order. To this extent even the realization of the republican constitutional state only opens up a world-historical opportunity to act on the "moral duty" to realize a cosmopolitan order of law and peace.

Finally, we should consider the possible global political consequences of the internal connection that Kant draws between the principle of law and the principle of "publicity." The consequence Kant counts on here could hardly have anything to do with the "mechanism of nature" functioning behind our backs. Rather, Kant equates the demands of publicity, which he opposes to the politics of revolutionary conspiracy and secret diplomacy (VIII, 126–127) with the a priori valid criterion of law (VIII, 125) based on a metaphysical justification of morality and its moral rigorism, something along the lines of "Fiat justitia, pereat mundus." To this extent, because of the ethics of responsibility must be applicable to the realm of politics, one cannot expect an unconditional compliance with the principle of publicity.

But how do mere pretensions to adhere to the principle of publicity affect Kant's insight that the realization of justice is internally connected with its claim to publicity? Are there not countless claims to represent matters capable of such consensus? Is it not true today, in the age of mass media and of thousands of conferences, that such public appeals merely conceal strategic interests which one could not openly avow?

In fact, all this is true. In view of these historical facts, the putting into practice of the principles of publicity always was, and is today more than ever, burdened with the risk of rhetorical manipulation. The progressive effect of the pressures to give at least the appearance of compliance with the principle of publicity and its connection to the principle of justice more than compensates for the risk of rhetorical manipulation. In the interests of their strategic success, all politicians must now support the principle of publicity in Kant's sense. That is, that they must at least create the impression that they have opened their concerns to a test of discursive consensus formation.

3 A Transcendental Pragmatic Reconstruction of Kant's "Fact of Reason": Political Opportunities and Historical Responsibility

After the reconstruction of the mediation between the moral demand of a cosmopolitan order of law and peace and the assumption of a morally relevant progress in history, it is necessary next to provide a critical reconstruction of the justification of the moral demand of reason itself. The demand to bring about through politics a law of peoples by taking advantage of historically conditioned opportunities obviously transcends the "duty" expressed in the formal rule of the "categorical imperative." How does Kant show the normative cohesion of the three theories grounded in duty: morality, civil law, and the law of peoples? Can the political process of bringing about the civil and cosmopolitan order of law and freedom be justified as moral duty?

It seems to me that such a justification is at least required by the subject matter and that this is also suggested by Kant's use of the term 'duty'. Nonetheless, Kant himself could not actually accomplish such a justification for two main reasons.

The first reason is that the presuppositions of Kant's two-worlds doctrine make it impossible to justify a responsibility for the actualizing of goals in the experiential world through the interventions of our free actions. Strictly speaking, Kant believes that duty expresses the "pure intention" to follow the "moral law": to act according to maxims that accord with the moral law, "regardless of the physical consequences." In this way Kant can postulate the existence of a legal order in terms of the coercive civil laws of particular states and of the law of peoples, both of which, analogous to the categorical imperative, generalize the external laws of freedom through the reciprocal limitation of each other's free will. Nonetheless, he cannot actually justify a duty in the sense of the moral responsibility to bring about such a legal order at the level of institutions. This limitation of Kant's ethics is also mirrored in the fact that he does not translate the postulate of the consensus of all citizens constitutive of a republican constitution into a duty to actually bring about the "original contract," which remains a regulative ideal. Thus, Kant argues there is no right to rebel against a "despotic" constitution and government.

The second reason why Kant cannot actually justify the moral duty to bring about a civil or cosmopolitan order is linked to the first (especially in its presupposition of the two-worlds doctrine). Nevertheless, it is the more fundamental objection, simply because in the *Critique of Practical Reason* Kant had to abandon the idea of providing the ultimate justification of the categorical imperative through a "transcendental deduction" of "a priori synthetic practical judgments." Although still provided in *The Groundwork of the Metaphysics of Morals* (IV, 392, 425, 444, 449; V, 33–34, 47–48, 51), this ultimate justification had to be replaced with the somewhat dogmatic declaration of the self-evident "fact of (practical) reason" (V, 46, 48). The reason for giving up on the transcendental deduction in the realm of practical reason lies again in the fact that the metaphysical presuppositions of his two-worlds doctrine, as Kant himself notes (V, 46–48), trap him in an inescapable aporia: He must view the existence of freedom qua autonomy of reason as the "ratio essendi" of the validity of ethical law, while at the same time presupposing as the only thinkable "ratio cognoscendi" of the existence of freedom that the moral law is already justified. The distinction between a *ratio essendi* and a *ratio cognoscendi* can be seen at best as a metaphysical explanation of the "reality" of the autonomously legislating reason. Nonetheless, as the justification of the validity of the moral law, it is a *circulus vitiosus*.[27]

By thinking with Kant against Kant, we can at this point begin a radical reconstruction of his form of the transcendental argument for the validity of the demands of practical reason. Kant's talk of a non-empirical "fact of reason" can be understood in the a priori perfect tense and therefore points toward a presupposition of all rational thought that has "always already" and necessarily been made.[28] The argument proceeds in the following manner: We have always already recognized the validity of the moral law as a necessary condition for the possibility of intersubjectively valid thought and to that extent already recognized the "self-determination of reason." This interpretation opens up the possibility of understanding Kant's laconic answer as a transcendental-reflexive ultimate justification of the validity of the moral law. "Rational thought" (as "the thinking which necessarily accompanies all my intuitions") is already that which cannot methodologically be analyzed further in the *Critique of Pure Reason*. It is the "highest point," from which the "transcendental deduction" of the "principles" can and must always already presuppose "synthetic a priori statements."

But a further difficulty presents itself for the ultimate transcendental justification of the validity of the moral law, a difficulty which is found in the transition from the *Critique of Pure Reason* to the *Critique of Practical Reason*. The presupposition of a "transcendental solipsism" (Husserl), which has been predominant since Descartes, has a justificatory function only for "consciousness in general," taking the subject-object relation as the condition of the possibility for thinking and knowing. An argument on this basis lacks the simultaneous, complementary transcendental function for the subject-cosubject relation of intersubjective communication. With such a role for intersubjectivity, the necessary recognition of moral law cannot be understood as the condition of the possibility of reasonable thought. (For this reason, neither Descartes nor Husserl is able to provide an ultimate justification of ethics.)

Nonetheless, Kant avoids these difficulties in the *Groundwork* before he offers any transcendental justification by introducing the metaphysical presupposition of an "intelligible realm of ends," which posits all rational beings (including gods and human beings as finite rational beings) as ends in themselves (IV, 39–40). The presupposition of intersubjectivity, indispensable for ethics, is thus secured in an ad hoc fashion. An adequate transcendental-reflexive analysis of the necessary and transcendentally-reflexively incontestable presupposition of intersubjectivity for rational thought is thus never achieved. This failure is apparent in the fact that Kant can only refer the valid moral law to the concept of an ideal community of all rational beings, which is not even justified in a transcendental-reflexive fashion. He cannot at the same time relate valid moral laws to the socio-cultural and historically conditioned presupposition of the contingent yet incontestable a prioris of the facticity of membership in a particular society's tradition of "substantial ethical life" (Hegel). In its place Kant introduces his two-worlds metaphysics and juxtaposes the abstract unconditioned demands of reason to all empirical motivations of means-ends rationality. Consistent with his dualism, they are all causally determined and relegated to mere inclination or interest. Under these presuppositions, the form of moral responsibility, presupposed in Kant's philosophy of history, becomes unthinkable: the responsibility for bringing about the ends of reason under historically contingent circumstances.

At this point a decisive, transcendental pragmatic transformation of the Kantian justification of ethics radically renews the form of justification in transcendental philosophy. Such a transformation presupposes that the "highest" point of transcendental analysis necessary for the theory of knowledge and for the transcendental critique of reason in general cannot be represented as a solipsistic and hence pre-communicative "I think." Rather, it is represented through a linguistically expressible strictly performative "I argue" that applies reflexively to itself and can be made convincing in discourse. These conditions, together with the appropriate existential and rule presuppositions of the consensual understanding of validity claims in argumentative discourse, cannot be denied without the pain of performative self-contradiction.

According to strictly transcendental reflection,[29] an intersubjective a priori assumed as a necessary presupposition in argumentative discourse can be shown to be the dialectical a priori of a communication community that cannot be gotten behind by further analysis. Not only is this a priori of the communication community distinct from Kant's metaphysically assumed a priori of the ideal community of rational beings, it is also distinct from the a priori of a substantial ethical life[30] that is now widely presupposed by Heidegger, Gadamer, Wittgenstein, and the communitarians. Nonetheless, both intersubjectivity assumptions are still contained within it. In actual philosophical discourse we presuppose membership in a factual communication community (an a priori overlooked by Kant) and the transcendental a priori of an unlimited ideal communication community (an a priori anticipated in Kant's metaphysics). We presuppose the former a priori as the lifeworld background for our contingent pre-understanding of the world as well as for the pre-given agreements with others over conventional norms of morality. The first a priori also constitutes our preunderstanding of possible maxims of action in Kant's sense. The latter a priori (which, generally speaking, the representatives of contemporary philosophy can no longer establish, because they take it to be mere metaphysics or utopian eschatology) is presupposed in the philosophical discourse about the lifeworld. We presuppose such an a priori along with the universal validity claims (including intelligibility, truth, truthfulness, and moral correctness) necessary for serious argumentation, which can only be redeemed counterfactually in an ideal communication community.[31] At the same time, it is important to remember that the ideal communication community is a transcendental pragmatic and not a metaphysical assumption, and that the ideal consensus on the validity claims is only a "regulative ideal" in the Kantian sense. Nothing empirical can ever correspond fully to such ideals; hence, they can never be taken to be an empirical fact, although they are inextricably tied to the possibility of redeeming validity claims.

Although it is important to distinguish the two opposite facets of the dialectical a priori of the communication community just drawn, they are also complementary to one another. Within argumentation a tension is presupposed between the empirical a priori and the ideal a priori, together with the (potentially infinite) task of resolving the tension in the long run. In theoretical discourse, one seeks to resolve the tension between an actually possible consensus and an ideal, unrevisable consensus about truth. In practical discourses of law and morality, one seeks to resolve the tension between the norms actually agreed to by participants and the norms that would be agreed to under ideal conditions. The latter consensus applies not only to those participants actually present but also to all those conceivably affected—and, indeed, to any conceivable judge of their validity.

Still more important than the long-term resolution of the tension between reality and ideality within the framework of already-constituted theoretical and practical discourses is a radical tension between the real and the ideal. This tension is exhibited, on the one hand, by the possibility of settling differences of opinion and practical conflicts by means of argument rather than through force or strategic bargaining, and, on the other hand, by the predominant global reality of human interaction and communication in which discursive solutions are not yet possible. This tension in the communication a priori grounds the moral duty, to attempt to achieve adequate institutional possibilities to solve practical conflicts through argumentative discourse in the lifeworld. This duty, together with the principle of equal entitlement of all, is already recognized in the a priori of philosophical discourse. In principle, it is a coresponsibility shared with all possible discourse partners for the determination and solution of morally relevant problems. To this extent, the transcendental-pragmatic justification of discourse ethics also establishes the justification for an ethics of coresponsibility for human institutions.[32]

This final step in the transcendental reflexive reconstruction of Kant's discourse on the "fact of pure (practical) reason" supplies the basis for an ultimate justification of the ethics of reason, which shows the moral duty to bring about a legal system in both its national and cosmopolitan forms. It also shows that there is a duty to adopt the hypothetical orientation in notions of the philosophy of history toward the idea of progress. As oriented to such ends, these duties transcend the formal obligation of the categorical imperative and thus also transcend the formal obligation to resolve all conflicts of norms through consensus formation in practical discourse. From the perspective of discourse ethics, however, such duties do not belong with those norms which are found capable of consensus in practical discourse. Rather, they concern bringing about the institutional conditions for both legal and moral practical discourse on the global scale. In this context it is important not only to consider what Kant already saw— that what is at stake is not only the realization of an international order of law and peace (VIII, 24, 47), as a presupposition of the realization of the "perfect civil constitution" for an individual state. Moreover, the fully realized order of law and peace is the presupposition for the unburdening of human beings from the forms of strategic action that are institutionalized in self-maintaining systems at all levels, so that we can actually expect that they will act according to their morality.[33]

These reflections justify the practical application of normative theories (VIII, 61–92) in the following way: the normative coherence of all three theories based on the Kantian conception of duty (including moral, national and international law) is not only found in the degree to which there are well-warranted differences and similarities between the theories. In addition, the practical realization of the object domain of all three theories can and must become the object of a moral duty understood as demanded by the coresponsibility of all finite rational beings to bring about their realization in appropriate institutions. Only in this way—through practical reason—can we completely retrieve the presupposition of "Toward Perpetual Peace": it turns out to be a transcendental-pragmatic presupposition that is not compatible with Kant's two-worlds metaphysics.

—translated by Stephen Synder

Notes to Chapter 3

1. Quotations and citations are from Immanuel Kant, *Political Writings* (Cambridge University Press, 1991). Sources of translations of passages include *Critique of Practical Reason* (Macmillan, 1993) and *The Grounding for a Metaphysics of Morals* (Hackett, 1993).

2. Compare Max Adler, "Kant und der ewige Friede," in *Immanuel Kant zu ehren*, ed. J. Kopper and R. Malter (Suhrkamp, 1974). See also Karl Vorländer, "Kant und Marx," in *Materialien zu Kants Rechtsphilosophie*, ed. Z. Batscha (Suhrkamp, 1976).

3. See Karl Popper, *The Poverty of Historicism* (Routledge & Kegan Paul, 1957); Karl Popper, *Open Society and Its Enemies*, volume II (Routledge & Kegan Paul, 1945).

4. See Popper's *Poverty of Historicism* and volume II of his *Open Society and Its Enemies*.

5. Ak: Akademie Ausgabe.

6. See Karl-Otto Apel, *Understanding and Explanation: A Transcendental-Pragmatic Perspective* (MIT Press, 1984), p. 232ff. See also *Charles S. Peirce: From Pragmatism to Pragmaticism* (University of Massachusetts Press, 1981) and "Transcendental Semeiotic and Hypothetical Metaphysics of Evolution: A Peircean or Quasi-Peircean Answer to a Recurrent Problem of Post-Kantian Philosophy," in *Peirce and Contemporary Thought*, ed. K. Ketner (Fordham University Press, 1995).

7. See Karl-Otto Apel, "Diskursethik vor der Problematik von Recht und Politik: Können die Rationalitätsdifferenzen zwischen Moralität, Recht und Politik selbst noch durch die Diskursethik normativ-rational gerechtfertigt werden?" in *Zur Anwendung der Diskursethik in Politik, Recht und Wissenschaft*, ed. K.-O. Apel and M. Kettner (Suhrkamp, 1992).

8. What is meant by "intelligible experience" is a theme of the hermeneutical social sciences; it was recognized in the nineteenth century as a proper theme of the empirical sciences according to Hegel's conception of "objective spirit." Because of the metaphysical dualism between the causally determined world of natural science and

the metaphysically postulated "intelligible world" of the relations of freedom, these sciences were not recognized in Kant's work.

9. Compare A. Dorschel, *Die idealistische Kritik des Willens. Versuch über die Theorie der praktischen Subjektivität bei Kant und Hegel* (Felix Meiner, 1992).

10. Compare my works introduced above in note 5.

11. Compare G.-H. von Wright, *Explanation and Understanding* (Cornell University Press, 1971), chapter 2. See also *Understanding and Explanation*, p. 83ff.

12. Compare N. Hartmann, *Ethik* (Berlin, 1935).

13. This problematic also is found in the philosophy of G. Vico. While Vico would like to understand history as a human product, he would like to attribute the reality of the unintentional consequences of human action to divine Providence. See Karl-Otto Apel, *Die Idee der Sprache in der Tradition des Humanismus von Dante bis Vico* (Bouvier, 1980), p. 327ff.

14. Compare *Charles S. Peirce*, p. 25ff.

15. See Charles Sanders Peirce, "Fallibilism, continuity, and evolution," in *Collected Papers of Charles Sanders Peirce*, ed. C. Hartshorne et al. (Harvard University Press, 1931–1935, 1958), volume 1, pp. 141–175. Also see Karl-Otto Apel, "Fallibilismus, Konsenstheorie der Wahrheit und Letztbegründung," in *Forum für Philosophie Bad Homburg*, ed. W. Köhler et al. (Suhrkamp, 1987).

16. See the preface to the second edition of *Critique of Pure Reason* (St. Martin's Press, 1965), where Kant states: ". . . a light broke upon all students of nature. They learned that reason has insight only into that which it produces after a plan of its own. . . . Reason, holding in one hand its principles, according to which alone concordant appearances can be admitted as equivalent to laws, and in the other hand the experiment which it has devised in conformity with these principles, must approach nature."

17. See *Protophysik*, ed. G. Böhme (Suhrkamp, 1976).

18. See G.-H. von Wright, *Causality and Determinism* (New York, 1974).

19. See C. F. von Weizsäcker, "Das Verhältnis der Quantenmechanik zur Philosophie Kants," in *Zum Weltbild der Physik* (Hirzel, 1945), p. 83 ff.

20. See H. Haken, *Erfolgsgeheimnisse der Natur. Synergetik: Die Lehre vom Zusammenwirken* (Deutsche Verlags-Anstalt, 1981), especially chapter 11. See also E. Jantsch, *Die Selbstorganisation des Universums* (Hanser, 1979).

21. *Understanding and Explanation*, p. 204ff.

22. See Niklas Luhmann, *Zweckbegriff und Systemrationalität* (Suhrkamp, 1973).

23. Here I am not making the usual reference to Wilhelm Wundt's "heterogeneity of goals" (see volume I of the third edition of his *Ethik* (Stuttgart, 1903), p. 274ff.). Following Kant, I assume that the construction of a cosmopolitan order of law and peace is an ethically justifiable goal of reason, to be sought with an appropriate

flexibility needed for contingent strategies of political action necessary to make the transition to this new order possible.

24. See Popper, *Poverty of Historicism.*

25. See K. Homann and F. Blome-Drees, *Wirtschafts- und Unternehmensethik* (UTB (Vandenhoeck), 1992). See also Karl-Otto Apel, "Institutionsethik oder Diskursethik als Verantwortungsethik? Das Problem der institutionellen Implementation moralischer Normen im Falle des Systems der Marktwirtschaft," in *25 Jahre Diskursethik. Anwendungsprobleme der Diskursethik,* ed. J. Harpes (forthcoming).

26. In "Welches sind die wirklichen Fortschritte, die die Metaphysik seit Leibnizens und Wolfs Zeiten in Deutschland gemacht hat?" (a work in which he addresses the question of progression in theology), Kant states: "The acceptance of fact that the world as a whole is always progressing for the better is not justified by any theory, but rather by pure practical reason, which demands dogmatically that we act in accordance with such a hypothesis."

27. See Karl-Heinz Ilting, "Der naturalistische Fehlschluß bei Kant," in *Rehabilitierung der praktischen Vernunft,* Vol. I, ed. M. Riedel (Rombach, 1972).

28. See Karl-Otto Apel, "The a priori of the communication community and the foundations of ethics: The problems of a rational foundation of ethics in the scientific age," in *Towards a Transformation of Philosophy* (Routledge & Kegan Paul, 1980), p. 271ff. Reprinted in *Ethics and the Theory of Rationality* (Humanities, 1996).

29. For the difference between "theoretical" and "strict" reflection (where the latter means a full account of the presuppositions of acts of argumentation), see Wolfgang Kuhlmann, *Reflexive Letztbegründung: Untersuchung zur Transcendentalpragmatik* (Alber, 1985), p. 76ff.

30. See Karl-Otto Apel, "Das Anliegen des anglo-amerikanischen 'Kommunitarismus' in der Sicht der Diskursethik," in *Gemeinschaft und Gerechtigkeit,* ed. M. Brumlik and H. Brunkhorst (Fischer, 1993).

31. See Jürgen Habermas, "What Is Universal Pragmatics?" in *Communication and the Evolution of Society* (Beacon, 1979); Habermas, *Theory of Communicative Action,* volume I (Beacon, 1979), chapter III. See also Karl-Otto Apel, "Normatively Grounding 'Critical Theory' through Recourse to the Lifeworld? A Transcendental-Pragmatic Attempt to Think with Habermas against Habermas," in *Philosophical Interventions in the Unfinished Project of Enlightenment,* ed. A. Honneth et al. (MIT Press, 1992).

32. See Karl-Otto Apel, *Diskurs und Verantwortung. Das Problem des Übergangs zur postkonventionellen Moral* (Suhrkamp, 1988); Apel, "How to Ground a Universalistic Ethics of Co-Responsibility for the Effects of Collective Actions and Activities?" *Philosophica* 52 (1993), no. 2: 9–29.

33. See Apel, "Diskursethik vor der Problematik von Recht und Politik."

II

Human Rights, International Law, and the Global Order: Cosmopolitanism Two Hundred Years Later

4

Kant's Idea of Perpetual Peace, with the Benefit of Two Hundred Years' Hindsight

Jürgen Habermas

First espoused by the Abbé St. Pierre, "perpetual peace" is for Kant an ideal that lends intuitive force to the idea of a cosmopolitan order. In this way, Kant introduces a third dimension into his "Doctrine of Right." Along with the civil law of states and in place of international law, he now introduces an innovation with broad implications: the idea of a cosmopolitan law based on the rights of the world citizen. The republican order of a democratic constitutional state, founded on human rights, demanded more than a weak binding of states in their foreign affairs through international law. Rather, the legal order within each state was supposed to lead ultimately to a global legal order that unites all peoples and abolishes war. "All forms of the state are based in the idea of a constitution which is compatible with the natural rights of man, so that those who obey the law should act as a unified body of legislators. And if we accordingly think of the commonwealth in terms of the concepts of pure reason, it may be called a Platonic ideal [*respublica noumenon*], which is not an empty figment of the imagination, but the eternal norm of all civil constitutions whatsoever, and a means to abolish all wars."[1] It is the concluding phrase, "and a means to abolish all wars," that surprises us. It points toward the norms of international law which regulate war and peace, if only peremptorily; they are valid only until pacification through law shows the way to a cosmopolitan order that abolishes war, the possibility of which Kant develops in "Toward Perpetual Peace."

Of course, Kant developed this idea using the concepts drawn from the debates concerning modern natural law and the specific historical experiences of his times. Differences in conceptual framework and temporal distance now separate us from Kant. With the superior and undeserved knowledge of later generations, we see today that his proposals suffer from conceptual difficulties and that they are no longer appropriate to our historical experiences. In the following, I will therefore first sketch out the premises that constitute Kant's starting point. These premises affect all three steps of his argument: the definition of the goal, namely, perpetual peace; the description of the actual project, which takes the legal form of a federation of nations; and, finally, the solution to this problem posed by this project in the philosophy of history, the gradual realization of the idea of a cosmopolitan order. Following upon this analysis, in the second section I examine how Kant's idea of peace fares in light of the historical experience of the last 200 years. In the third section, I turn to the question of how it must be reformulated with a view to the contemporary global situation. The alternatives to the return to the state of nature proposed by legal scholars, political scientists, and philosophers have evoked strong objections to the universalism of the proposed cosmopolitan law and its politics of human rights, objections which lose their force once we draw the appropriate distinction between law and morality within the concept of human rights. Such a distinction also offers the key to a metacriticism of Carl Schmitt's influential arguments against the humanistic foundation of legal pacificism.

1

Kant defines the *goal* of the achievement of a "legal order" among peoples negatively, as the abolition of war: "There shall be no war," proclaiming that the "disastrous practice of war" must be brought to an end.[2] Kant justifies the desirability of such a peace through the evils of those forms of warfare which the princes of Europe were waging at that time with their mercenary armies. In discussing its evils, Kant mentions first and foremost not the victims of war but rather the "horrors of violence," the "devastation," and, above all, the plundering and impoverishment of a country resulting from the considerable burdens of debt that arise from war, as well as other possible consequences of war, including subjugation, the loss of liberty, and foreign domination. Added to them is moral decline brought about when subjects are induced to such criminal acts as spying and spreading of false information or reduced to the maliciousness of snipers or assassins. Here Kant has in mind the panorama of limited war as it had been institutionalized in the system of the balance of power as a legitimate means to solve conflicts by international law ever since the Peace of Westphalia. The end of such a war defines the conditions of peace. And, as a specific peace treaty ends the evil of an individual war between nations, so the peace compact among all peoples "puts an end to war forever" and does away with the evils of war as such. This is the meaning of Kant's phrase "perpetual peace." But it is a peace as limited as the model of war upon which it is based.

Kant is thinking here of spatially limited wars between individual states or alliances, not of world wars. He is thinking of wars conducted between ministers and states, but not yet of anything like civil wars. He is thinking of technically limited wars that still permit the distinction between fighting troops and the civilian population, and not yet of anything like guerrilla warfare and the terror of bombardment. He is thinking of wars with politically defined aims, and not yet of anything like ideologically motivated wars of destruction and expulsion.[3] Given the premises of limited warfare, the normative regulation of international law extends only to rules for the conduct of war and for the settlement of peace. The "right to go to war" [*ius ad bellum*] is the basis for legal regulation both "during" and "after" war; it is, strictly speaking, no right at all, for it merely expresses the arbitrary freedom accorded the subjects of international law in the state of nature, that is, in the lawless condition that characterizes their external relations to each other.[4] The only criminal law backed by sanctions that can intervene into this lawless state relates to the conduct of war itself, and even then it is only carried out by the courts of those states that are currently waging war. War crimes are merely those crimes committed *during* war. Now that wars are unlimited, the concept of peace has also been correspondingly expanded to include the claim that war itself, in the form of a war of aggression, is a crime that deserves to be despised and punished. For Kant, however, there is not yet a crime *of* war.

While a perpetual peace provides one of its more important characteristics, it is only a symptom of a cosmopolitan order. Kant must still solve the *conceptual problem* of how this order could be thought of from the viewpoint of law. He must find the proper difference between cosmopolitan law and classical international law, and thus what is specific to *ius cosmopoliticum.*

Like all rights in the state of nature, international law is only provisionally valid; by contrast, cosmopolitan law resembles state sanctioned civil law in that both definitively end the state of nature. When describing the transition to the cosmopolitan order, Kant therefore repeatedly draws on the analogy to the first act of leaving the state of nature, through which the establishment of a particular state makes it possible for citizens of a particular area to live in legally guaranteed freedom. Just as the social contract ended the state of nature between individuals who are otherwise left to their own devices, so too, Kant suggests, the state of nature between warring states now comes to an end. In "Theory and Practice," published two years before "Toward Perpetual Peace," Kant draws strict parallels between these two processes. There he still speaks of a "universal state of all peoples, to whose powers all states shall freely submit themselves."[5] Here, too, he mentions the destruction of human well-being and the loss of freedom as the greatest evils of war, and then continues: "There is no possible way of counteracting this except a state based on the law of peoples, upon enforceable public laws to which each state must submit (by analogy to the civil state among individual human beings). For a lasting universal peace by means of the so-called European balance of power is nothing but an illusion."[6] Kant speaks here of a "universal state of all peoples, under whose authority all states should freely submit themselves." But only two years later, in "Toward Perpetual Peace," Kant carefully distinguishes between "a federation of nations" and "a state of all peoples."

From now on a distinctly "cosmopolitan" order was to be distinguished from the legal order within states by virtue of the fact that, unlike individual citizens, states do not subject themselves to the public coercive laws of some supreme power; instead, they retain their existence as individual states. In the federation of free states that forgo war in their external relations, the sovereignty of each member remains inviolable. The states associated with one another in this way preserve their sovereign powers and jurisdiction and do not dissolve into a world republic modeled after a state writ large. In place of the "positive idea of a world republic" is put the "negative substitute of an enduring and gradually expanding federation likely to prevent war."[7] Such a federation emerges through sovereign acts of will exercised in many different contracts under international law, which are now no longer to be thought of on the model of the social contract. For these contracts do not establish any claims to enforceable rights by the parties over and against each other, but rather bind members to an alliance whose continued existence depends on an "enduring and voluntary association." But this act of association goes beyond the binding power of the international law of peoples only in virtue of its feature of "permanence." Hence, Kant compares the federation of nations to a "permanent congress of states."[8]

The contradictory character of this construction is quite apparent. In other passages, Kant asserts that a congress "merely signifies a voluntary gathering of various states that can be dissolved at any time, not an association which, like the American states, is based on a political constitution."[9] Kant never explains just how this union is to be permanent, the feature on which a civilized resolution of international conflict depends, without the binding character of law based on the establishment of something analogous to a constitution. On the one hand, Kant wants to preserve the sovereignty of its members by the proviso that they may dissolve their compact; this is what makes possible the comparison the federation with congresses and voluntary associations. On the other hand, a federation that creates the conditions of peace in the long run must differ from merely provisional alliances to the extent that its members must feel *obligated* to subordinate their own *raison d'etat* to the jointly declared goal of "not deciding their differences by war, but by a process analogous to a court of law." Without this element of obligation, the peaceable congress of nations cannot become "permanent," nor can its voluntary association become "enduring"; instead, it would remain hostage to an unstable constellation of interests that is likely to degenerate and fall apart, much as the League of Nations did years later. Kant cannot have any *legal* obligation in mind here, since his federation of nations is not organized around the organs of a common government that could acquire coercive authority. Rather, he is forced to rely exclusively on each government's own *moral* self-binding. But such trust is hardly compatible with Kant's own soberly realistic descriptions of the politics of his times.

Kant is thoroughly aware of this problem, but he covers it over with a simple appeal to reason: "If a state says: 'There shall be no war between myself and other states even though I do not recognize any supreme legislative power which could secure my rights and whose rights I should in turn secure,' it is impossible to understand what justification I can have for placing any trust in my rights, unless I can rely on some substitute for the union of civil society, namely, on the free federation. If the concept of a law of peoples is to have any significance, reason must connect it with a federation of this kind."[10] This assurance leaves open the decisive question: How is a permanent self-binding of states which continue as sovereign to be ensured? This is not even the empirical issue of how to approximate the idea; it is a conceptual problem with the idea itself. If the union of peoples is not a moral but a legal arrangement, then all the qualities of a "good constitutional state" that Kant enumerates some pages later would be present and would make it possible for such an organization to do more than rely on the "good moral culture" of its members; it now could, when appropriate, make its own binding demands.

Viewed historically, Kant's reticence concerning the project of a *constitutionally* organized community of peoples is certainly realistic. The democratic constitutional state, which had just emerged from the American and French Revolutions, was still the exception rather than the rule. The existing system of the balance of power functioned on the assumption that only sovereign states could be the subjects of the law of peoples. Under these conditions, external sovereignty designates the capacity of states, each acting independently in the international arena, to defend the integrity of its borders by military means when needed. Internal sovereignty refers to the capacity, based on the state's monopoly over the means of violence, for maintaining peace and order by means of administrative power and positive law. *Raison d'etat* is thus defined according to the principles of a prudential power politics that includes the possibility of limited wars, whereby domestic policy is always subordinated to the primacy of foreign policy. The clear separation of foreign and domestic policy stems from a narrow and politically well-defined concept of power according to which, in the final analysis, power is measured in terms of the degree to which those in power have command over the means of violence stored in the barracks of the military and the police.

As long as this classical-modern world of nation states remains an unsurpassable conceptual limit, any attempt at a cosmopolitan constitution that does not respect the sovereignty of states necessarily appears unrealistic. This explains why Kant never considers the possibility of a community of peoples under the hegemony of a powerful state as a viable alternative; indeed, he always presents it with the image of a "universal monarchy."[11] Under such premises, such supreme political power would result in "the most terrible despotism."[12] Because Kant does not escape the limited horizon of his historical experience, it becomes equally difficult to establish any moral motivation for creating and maintaining a federation among free states that are all still dedicated to power politics. In order to provide a solution to this problem, Kant proposes a philosophy of history with a cosmopolitan intent, which is supposed to make plausible the improbable "agreement between politics and morality" through a hidden "intention of nature."

2

Kant identifies three naturally occurring tendencies which meet reason halfway and which explain why a federation of nations could be in the enlightened self-interest of states: the peaceful nature of republics, the power of world trade to create communal ties, and the function of the political public sphere. It is informative to cast a historical glance back at these arguments in two respects. On the one hand, they have been falsified by developments in the nineteenth and twentieth centuries. On the other, they refer to historical trends that betray a peculiar dialectical quality. These very same trends reveal that the premises on which Kant based his theory reflect the conditions he perceived at the close of the eighteenth century that no longer hold. Yet these trends would seem to support the claim that a conception of cosmopolitan law that was properly reformulated in contemporary terms might well find support in a constellation of forces that meets it halfway.

(1) Kant's first argument claims that international relations lose their bellicose character to the extent that the republican form of government is achieved within states; this is because the population of democratic constitutional states demand that their governments pursue peaceful policies out of their own self-interest. "If, as is the case under such a constitution, the consent of the citizens is required to decide whether or not war is declared, it is very natural that they will have great hesitation in embarking on so dangerous and costly a game."[13] This optimistic assumption has been disproved by the mobilizing power of an idea, the ambivalence of which Kant was in no position to perceive in 1795. Nationalism was certainly a vehicle for the desired transformation of subordinated subjects into active citizens who identify with their state. However, its existence makes the nation state no more peaceful than its predecessor, the dynastic absolutist state.[14] From the viewpoint of nationalist movements, the classical self-assertion of sovereign states gains the connotations of freedom and national independence. Therefore, the republican convictions of citizens create the willingness to fight and die for nation and fatherland. With some justification, Kant considered the mercenary armies of his day to be instruments for "the use of human beings as mere machines . . . in the hands of someone else" and called for the establishment of the citizen militia. But he was not able to foresee that the mass mobilization of young men obligated to military service would stir nationalist passions and produce an age of devastating, ideologically unlimited wars of liberation.

At the same time, the idea that a democratic state domestically encourages a pacifistic stance toward the outside world is not completely false. Historical and statistical research shows that states with democratic constitutions do not necessarily conduct fewer wars than authoritarian regimes (of whatever kind), but that they are less likely to be warlike in their relations toward one another. This finding can be given an interesting interpretation.[15] To the extent that the universalist value orientations of a population accustomed to free institutions also influence foreign policy, the republican polity does not behave more peaceably as a whole; however, this orientation does change the character of the wars which it conducts. The foreign policy of the state changes according to the motivations of its citizenry. The use of military force is no longer exclusively determined not only by an essentially particularist vision of *raison d'etat* but also by the desire to promote the international proliferation of non-authoritarian forms of state and government. More important, if value preferences transcend preserving national interests and extend rather to the implementation of democracy and human rights, then the very conditions under which the balance of power operates have changed irrevocably.

(2) The history we now survey also permits us to understand Kant's second argument in a similarly dialectical manner. Kant's direct assertions were certainly wrong, but in a more indirect way he also turns out to have been correct in a crucial respect. Indeed, Kant considered the growing interdependence of societies produced through the exchange of information, persons, and commodities, and especially through the expansion of trade, to be favorable to the peaceful association of peoples.[16] Trade relations expanded in early modernity into the dense network of a world market, which according to Kant "provides the basis for an interest in the security of peaceful relations through mutual gain." As Kant puts it: "The spirit of commerce cannot coexist with war."[17] However, Kant had not yet learned, as Hegel would from the English economists,[18] that capitalist development would lead to an opposition among classes that would in turn threaten both peace itself and the presumed readiness to live in peace in politically liberal societies. He could not foresee that the social tensions that only increased with accelerating process of capitalistic industrialization would both strain domestic politics with civil wars and lead foreign policy down the path toward imperialist wars. Throughout the nineteenth century and the first half of the twentieth, European governments repeatedly drew on the force of nationalism in order to divert social conflicts outward and to neutralize them with foreign-policy successes.

It was only after the catastrophes of World War II led to the depletion of integrating nationalist energies that the successful pacification of class antagonisms by means of the welfare state was possible. Only then did the internal situation of the industrialized nations change to such an extent that, at least within the OECD countries, economic interdependence led to the very "economization of international politics"[19] that Kant had rightly hoped would have a pacifying effect. Today globally dispersed media, networks, and systems necessitate a density of symbolic and social relationships, which bring about the constant reciprocal influence between local and quite distant events.[20] These processes of globalization rendered complex societies, with their delicate technological infrastructures, ever more vulnerable. As military confrontations between the nuclear-armed great powers became more and more improbable because of the huge risks, local conflicts piled up comparably numerous and terrible sacrifices. At the same time, globalization put into question the presuppositions of classical international law, namely, the sovereignty of states and the sharp distinction between domestic and foreign policies.

Non-governmental actors such as multinational corporations and internationally influential private banks render the formal sovereignty of nation states increasingly hollow. Even the governments of the economically most powerful countries today are keenly aware that they are caught on the horns of a dilemma: on the one hand, their scope for action is limited by the structures of the nation state; on the other hand, they must respond to imperatives based not entirely on world trade but also on increasingly global networks of productive relations. Sovereign states could profit from their economies so long as they were "national economies" that could be influenced by political means. With the denationalization of the economy, in particular with the interdependencies in the world financial markets and in industrial production itself, national politics loses its control over the general conditions of production[21]—and with it any leverage for maintaining its standard of living.

At the same time, there is a blurring of the boundaries between domestic and foreign policy that are constitutive of state sovereignty. The classical image of power politics is being changed not only by additional normative features such as a politics of democratization or of human rights, but also through a peculiar diffusion of power itself.

With the growing pressure for cooperation, more or less indirect influence is becoming more important than direct implementation of one's own goals through the exercise of administrative power or threats of violence. Instead, power is now exerted indirectly in the structuring of perceived situations, in the creation of contacts, in the interruption of flows of communication, or in the definition of agendas and problems; in short, it is exercised on the boundary conditions within which actors make their decisions.[22] "Soft power" forces "hard power" aside and robs the subjects Kant had counted on in his association of free states of the very basis for their independence.

(3) Similar tendencies emerge once again in considering Kant's third argument, which he puts forward in order to blunt the suspicion that the projected federation of nations is a "mere chimera." In a republican polity, constitutional principles become the standards by which policies must be publicly measured. Such governments do not dare try to "justify their policies publicly through clever slights of hand alone,"[23] even though they may need principles only to pay lip service to them. To this extent, criticism in the civic public sphere can prevent the execution of intentions that neither can withstand the light of day nor are consistent with publicly defensible maxims. On Kant's view, public criticism also has a programmatic function to the extent that philosophers, in their capacity as public teachers of the law or as public intellectuals, are permitted to "talk freely and publicly about the maxims of waging war and creating peace" and to convince the public of all citizens of the validity of their basic principles. Kant probably had the example of Voltaire and Frederick II in mind when he wrote the following moving sentence: "It is not to be expected that kings will philosophize or that philosophers will become kings; nor is it to be desired, however, since the possession of power inevitably corrupts the free judgment of reason. Kings and sovereign peoples who are govern themselves by egalitarian laws should not, however, force the class of philosophers to disappear or to remain silent, but should allow then to speak publicly. This is essential in both cases in order that light may be thrown on their affairs and . . . beyond suspicion."[24]

As the atheism controversy involving Fichte would show only a few years later, Kant had every reason to fear censorship. We may also forgive his trust in the power of philosophy to convince others and in the sincerity of philosophers; historical skepticism about reason belongs more to the nineteenth century, and it was not until the twentieth century that intellectuals engaged in the gravest betrayals. What is more important is that Kant obviously counted on the existence of a transparent and surveyable public sphere formed by literary means and open to arguments, the membership of which would be borne by a small class of educated citizens. He could not foresee the structural transformation of the bourgeois public sphere in the future: a public sphere dominated by the electronic mass media, semantically degenerated, and taken over by images and virtual realities. He could hardly even imagine that the milieu of an Enlightenment of "speech and discussion" could be so utterly transformed into forms of indoctrination without language and linguistic deception.

This veil of ignorance probably explains why Kant dared to anticipate something so far in the future that it is only now actually coming about: namely, his brilliant anticipation of a global public sphere. The existence of the world public sphere emerges in the wake of global communication: "The process by which all the peoples of the earth have entered into a universal community has come to the point where a violation of rights in one part of the world is felt everywhere; this means that the idea of cosmopolitan law is no longer a fantastical or overly exaggerated idea. It is a necessary complement to civil and international law, transforming it into public law of humanity (or human rights [*Menschenrechte*]); only under this condition (namely, the existence of a functioning global public sphere) can we flatter ourselves that we are continually advancing toward perpetual peace."25

The first events that actually drew the attention of the world public sphere, and polarized its opinion on a global scale, were the wars in Vietnam and the Persian Gulf. It was only very recently that the United Nations organized in rapid succession a series of conferences on global issues, including ecology (in Rio de Janeiro), population growth (in Cairo), poverty (in Copenhagen), and global warming (in Berlin). These "world summits" can be interpreted as so many attempts to bring some political pressure to bear on governments simply by making the problems of human survival themes for the global public—that is, by appealing to the force of world opinion. One should not overlook the fact that this temporary public attention is still issue-specific and channeled through the established structures of national public spheres. Supporting structures are needed to stabilize communication between spatially distant participants, who exchange contributions at the same time on the same themes with equal relevance. In this sense there is not yet a global public sphere, let alone a European one, as urgently needed as it is. However, the central role played by a new type of organization, namely non-governmental organizations such as Greenpeace or Amnesty International, is not confined to conferences, but more generally concerns creating and mobilizing transnational public spheres. Their role is at the least an indication of the growing impact on the press and the other media of actors who confront the states from within the network of international civil society.[26]

The important role that Kant gives to publicity and to the public sphere raises the question of the relationship between the legal constitution and the political culture of a polity.[27] A liberal political culture forms the ground in which the institutions of freedom put down their roots; at the same time, it is also the medium through which progress in the political process of civilizing a population takes place.[28] Certainly, Kant speaks of the "growth of culture" that leads toward greater agreement over principles[29]; he also expected that the public use of communicative freedom would be transformed into processes of enlightenment that would affect the attitudes and ways of thinking of the populace in political socialization. In this context, Kant speaks of "the heartfelt sympathy which any enlightened person inevitably feels for anything good as he comes to understand it fully."[30] However, such remarks lack any systematic importance, because the dichotomous conceptual frame of transcendental philosophy separates internal from external conditions, morality from legality. In particular, Kant does not recognize the relationship in a liberal political culture between prudential pursuit of one's interests and moral insights and habits, between tradition and critique. The practices of such a culture mediate between morality, law, and politics and at the same time form the suitable context for a public sphere that encourages political learning processes.[31] Kant did not really need to retreat to some metaphysical "intention of nature" in order to explain how a "pathologically enforced social union can be transformed into a moral whole."[32]

As these critical reflections show, Kant's idea of a cosmopolitan order must be reformulated if it is not to lose touch with a world situation that has fundamentally changed. The long-overdue revision of Kant's basic conceptual framework is made easier by the fact that the cosmopolitan idea itself has not remained fixed. Ever since Woodrow Wilson's initiative and the founding of the League of Nations in Geneva, the idea of a cosmopolitan order has been repeatedly taken up and implemented in politics. After the end of World War II, the idea of perpetual peace was given more tangible form in the institutions, declarations, and policies of the United Nations (as well as in other transnational organizations). The challenge of the incomparable catastrophes of the twentieth century has also given new impetus to Kant's idea. Against this somber background, the World Spirit, as Hegel would have put it, has jerked unsteadily forward.

European societies confronted the horror of a spatially and technologically unlimited war during World War I. World War II brought home the mass crimes of an ideologically unlimited war. Behind the veil of the total war contrived by Hitler, the breakdown of civilization was so complete that a shaken world accelerated the transition from international law to cosmopolitan law based on the rights of the world citizen. First, the outlawing of war initially mentioned in the 1928 Kellogg-Briand Pact was transferred into the war-crimes tribunals of Nuremberg and Tokyo. These tribunals did not limit themselves to crimes committed during war, but rather incriminated war itself as a crime. From this point onward, the "crime *of* war" could be prosecuted. Second, criminal law is now expanded to include "crimes against humanity"—that is, crimes carried out by legally empowered organs of the state with the assistance of countless members of organizations, functionaries, civil servants, businessmen, and private individuals. With these two innovations, governmental subjects of international law lost their general presumption of innocence in a supposed state of nature.

3

Any fundamental conceptual revision of Kant's proposal ought to focus on three aspects: (1) the external sovereignty of states and the changed nature of relations among them, (2) the internal sovereignty of states and the normative limitations of classical power politics, and (3) the stratification of world society and a globalization of dangers which make it necessary for us to rethink what we mean by "peace."

(1) Kant's concept of a permanent federation of nations that respects the sovereignty of each is, as I have shown, inconsistent. The rights of the world citizen must be institutionalized in such a way that it actually binds individual governments. The community of peoples must at least be able to hold its members to legally appropriate behavior through the threat of sanctions. Only then will the unstable system of states asserting their sovereignty through mutual threat be transformed into a federation whose common institutions take over state functions: it will legally regulate the relations among its members and monitor their compliance with its rules. The external relationship of contractually regulated international relations among states, where each forms the environment for the others, then becomes the internally structured relationship among the members of a common organization based on a charter or a constitution. The Charter of the United Nations has precisely this significance in that it prohibits offensive wars (with the prohibition of violence in article 2.4) and empowers the Security Council to use appropriate means, including military action, "whenever a threat or violation of peace or an attack is present." At the same time, the UN Charter expressly forbids the intervention in the internal affairs of a state (in article 2.7). Each state retains the right to military self-defense. In December of 1991, the General Assembly reaffirmed this principle: "The sovereignty, territorial integrity, and national unity of a state must be fully respected in accordance with the Charter of the United Nations."[33]

With these ambiguous regulations, which both limit and guarantee the sovereignty of individual states, the Charter makes allowances for its own transitional status. The UN does not have its own military forces, or even any which it could deploy under its own command, much less any by means of which it might enjoy a monopoly over the means of violence. It is dependent on the voluntary cooperation of its members. The missing power base is supposed to be compensated for by the Security Council, in which the superpowers are bound to the world organization in return for veto rights and permanent membership. As everyone knows, this structure led to the consequence that the superpowers blocked each other's moves for decades. And when the Security Council does take the initiative, it makes highly selective use of its capacities for judgment through a disregard for the principle of treating similar cases similarly.[34] This problem once again become relevant through the events of the Gulf War.[35] Although not unimportant in this regard, the World Court in The Hague possesses only a symbolic significance. It is not always in session, nor can it as yet obligate governments to abide by its judgments (as was shown once again in the case of Nicaragua versus the United States).

(2) Because Kant believed that the barriers of national sovereignty were insurmountable, he conceived of the cosmopolitan community as a federation of states, not of world citizens. This assumption proved inconsistent, insofar as Kant derived every legal order, including that within the state, from a more original law, which gives rights to every person "qua human being." Every individual has the right to equal freedom under universal laws (since "everyone decides for everyone, and each decides for himself"[36]). This founding of law in human rights designates individuals as the bearers of rights and gives to all modern legal orders an inviolable individualistic character.[37] If Kant holds that this guarantee of freedom—"that which human beings ought to do in accordance with the laws of freedom"—is precisely the essential purpose of perpetual peace, "indeed for all three variants of public law, civil, international and cosmopolitan law,"[38] then he ought not allow the autonomy of citizens to be mediated through the sovereignty of their states.

The point of cosmopolitan law is, rather, that it goes over the heads of the collective subjects of international law to give legal status to the individual subjects and justifies their unmediated membership in the association of free and equal world citizens. Carl Schmitt grasped this point and saw that this conception implies that "each individual is at the same time a world citizen (in the full juridical sense of the word) and a citizen of a state."[39] The higher-level legal power to define authority itself [*Kompetenz-Kompetenz*] now falls to the unified world state, giving individuals a legally unmediated relation to this international community; this transforms the individual state into "a mere agency [*Kompetenz*] for specific human beings who take on double roles in their international and national functions."[40] The most important consequence of a form of law that is able to puncture the sovereignty of states is the arrest of individual persons for crimes committed in the service of a state and its military.

Even in this respect, current developments have outstripped Kant. Based on the 1941 North Atlantic Charter, the UN Charter imposes the general obligation on its member states to observe and attempt to realize human rights. The General Assembly made these rights precise in an exemplary fashion in the General Declaration of Human Rights, which has been further developed by means of numerous resolutions.[41] The United Nations does not simply leave the protection human rights to the nation states; it also possesses its own instruments for *establishing* that human-rights violations have occurred. The Human Rights Commission possesses various observer functions and reporting procedures that concern themselves with basic social, economic, and cultural rights (although under the "proviso of what is possible"); further, there are procedures for bringing complaints about violations of civil and political rights. In theoretical terms (although not in terms recognized by all signatory states), the rights of individuals to bring formal complaints, which give all citizens the legal means to challenge their own governments, are more significant than the complaints brought by states. But there has been no criminal court that can test and decide upon well-established cases of human-rights violations. Even the proposal to institute a United Nations High Commissioner for Human Rights could not be implemented in the recent Vienna conference on human rights. Ad hoc war-crimes tribunals on the model of the Nuremberg and Tokyo international military tribunals are still the exception.[42] Certainly the General Assembly of the United Nations has recognized the guiding principles on which the judgments of these tribunals were based as the "principles of international law." Nonetheless, this assertion is false to the extent that these trials against leading Nazi military figures, diplomats, ministers, doctors, bankers, and industrial leaders have been treated as "unique" events without the force of legal precedent.[43]

The weak link in the global protection of human rights remains the lack of any executive power that could secure, when necessary, the General Declarations of Human Rights through interventions into nation states, despite their "supreme power" over their territory. Since human rights must in many cases be implemented against the will of the governments of nation states, the prohibition against intervention in international law must be revised. In cases where functioning state power has not disappeared entirely (as it did in Somalia), the world organization undertakes intervention only with the agreement of the affected governments (as in Liberia or in Croatia and Bosnia). Without a doubt, the United Nations took the first steps down a new path during the Gulf War with Resolution 688 in April of 1991, de facto if not de jure. The United Nations based its right of intervention in cases of "threats to international security" on chapter VII of its charter. To this extent, the UN did not, from a juridical point of view, intervene in "the internal affairs" of a sovereign state. But the US-led coalition did precisely this, as the allies certainly knew, when it instituted no-fly zones in Iraqi airspace and deployed ground troops in northern Iraq in order to secure safe areas for Kurd refugees, thus protecting the members of a national minority against their own state.[44] The British Foreign Minister spoke on this occasion of an "expansion of the limits of international action."[45]

(3) The revisions necessary in light of the changed character of international relations and the need to limit the actions of sovereign states relate most directly to the conception of the federation of peoples and cosmopolitan order. Both are the locations in which very demanding norms are put in practice, norms which to some degree already exist. However, there is still, as much as ever, a discrepancy between the letter and the execution of these norms. The contemporary world situation can be understood in the best-case scenario as a period of transition from international to cosmopolitan law, but many other indications seem to support a regression to nationalism. How one assesses the situation depends in the first instance on how one

estimates the effects of the dynamic processes at work in history that meet cosmopolitanism halfway. We have followed out the dialectic of these tendencies, which Kant had in mind under the headings of the peaceful character of republics, the unifying power of global markets, and the normative pressure of liberal public spheres. Today such tendencies join together in an unprecedented and unforeseeable constellation.

Kant imagined the expansion of the association of free states in such a way that more and more democratic states would crystallize around the core of an avant-garde of peaceful republics: ". . . if by good fortune one powerful and enlightened nation can form a republic, this will provide a focal point for a federal association among other states . . . and gradually spread through associations of this kind."[46] As a matter of fact, a world organization has today united *all* states under one roof, and indeed independent of whether they have already established republics or whether they respect human rights. The political unity of the world finds its expression in the General Assembly of the United Nations, in which all governments are represented with equal rights. In this way, the world organization abstracts not only from the differences in legitimation among its member states but also from their status differences within a stratified world society. I speak of a world society because communication systems and markets have created a global context; at the same time, it is also important to speak of a stratified world society, because the mechanism of the world market couples increasing productivity with increasing impoverishment, development with underdevelopment processes. Globalization both divides the world and forces it to cooperative action as a community of shared risks.

From the perspective of political science, the world has since 1917 disintegrated into three worlds. The terms "First World," "Second World," and "Third World" have different meanings since 1989.[47] The "Third World" today consists of those territories where the state infrastructure and monopoly of the means of violence are so weakly developed (Somalia) or so decayed (Yugoslavia) and where the social tensions are so high and the tolerance levels of political culture so low that indirect violence of a Mafia or fundamentalist variety disrupts internal order. These societies are also threatened by processes of nationalist, ethnic, and religious fragmentation. Indeed, the wars that have occurred here in the last few decades are mostly civil wars, which have often gone unnoticed in the world public sphere. The "Second World" is shaped by the heritage of power politics that individual nation states that have emerged from decolonization have taken over from Europe. Internally these states balance their unstable relations through authoritarian constitutions and obstinately insist on sovereignty and non-intervention from the outside (as in the Persian Gulf region). They emphasize military violence and exclusively obey the logic of the balance of power. Only the states of the "First World" can to a certain degree succeed in bringing their national interests into harmony with the normative claims established by the United Nations, an organization that has come at least part of the way toward achieving the cosmopolitan level.

As indicators of belonging to the First World, Richard Cooper lists the decreasing relevance of external boundaries and the toleration of a legally flourishing internal pluralism; the influence of states on one another's traditionally domestic concerns, with a increasing fusion between domestic and foreign policy; the sensitivity to the pressures of a liberal public sphere; the rejection of military force as a means of solving conflicts; the juridification of international relations; and the favoring of partnerships that base security on transparency and trust in expectations. The First World thus constitutes the temporal meridian of the present, as it were, by which the political simultaneity of economic and cultural nonsimultaneity is measured. As a child of the eighteenth century, Kant thought unhistorically, ignored these facts, and thereby overlooked the *real abstraction* that must be accomplished by the organization of the community of nations and which it must also take into account in its policies.

The politics of the United Nations can take this real abstraction seriously only if it works to overcome social divisions and economic imbalances. This aim could, in turn, succeed in the face of the stratification of world society only on the condition that a consensus forms in three areas: a historical consciousness shared by all members concerning the nonsimultaneity of the societies simultaneously related by peaceful coexistence; a normative agreement concerning human rights, the interpretation of which remains disputed between the Europeans and the Asians and Africans; and a shared understanding concerning the meaning of the goal of peace.[48] Kant was satisfied with a purely negative conception of peace. This is unsatisfactory not only because all limits on the conduct of war have now been surpassed but also because of the new global circumstances that link the emergence of wars to specifically societal causes.

According to a proposal made by Dieter and Eva Senghaas,[49] the complexity of the causes of war requires a conception that understands peace as a *process* accomplished by nonviolent means. However, its aim is not merely to prevent violence per se but also to satisfy the real necessary conditions for a common life without tensions among groups and peoples. Such a strategy of nonviolent intervention works in favor of processes of democratization[50] that take into account the fact that global interconnections have now make *all* states dependent on their environment and sensitive to the "soft" power of indirect influence, up to the point of explicitly threatened economic sanctions.

With the increasing complexity of these goals and the burdensome character of these strategies, it must also be admitted that increasing difficulties are holding the leading powers back from taking the initiative and bearing its costs. I want to conclude this section by mentioning the four most important variables in this regard: the composition of the Security Council, which has to always act in concert; the political culture of the leading powers, the governments of which can adopt a "selfless" policy only for the short term, and only then if they are forced to react to the normative pressures of a mobilized public sphere; the formation of regional regimes, which would for the first time provide the world organization with an effective substructure; and the gentle compulsion to globally coordinated action that starts with an undistorted perception of current global dangers. The threats are obvious: ecological imbalance; asymmetries of standards of living and economic power; powerful technologies of an unprecedented scale; the arms trade, especially the spread of atomic, biological, and chemical weapons; terrorism and the rise of drug-related criminality; and so on. In light of this growing list, those of us who do not doubt the capacity of the international system to learn have to place our hopes in the fact that the very globalization of these dangers has already objectively brought the world together into an involuntary community of shared risks.

4

On the one hand, the contemporary reformulation of the Kantian idea of a cosmopolitan pacification of the state of nature between states has inspired energetic efforts to reform the United Nations and, more generally, to create effective supranational organizations in various regions of the world. Such efforts aim at the improvement of the institutional framework necessary for a feasible politics based on human rights, which has suffered serious setbacks since it was first attempted during the presidency of Jimmy Carter (1). On the other hand, this form of politics has evoked a strong opposition that sees any institutional implementation of human rights as a self-defeating moralization of politics. Such policies are, however, based on an unclear conception of human rights that does not sufficiently distinguish between politics and morality (2).

(1) The "rhetoric of universalism" against which this critique is directed finds its most intelligent formulation in proposals to reconstruct the United Nations in the form of a "cosmopolitan democracy." These proposal for reform concentrate on three points: establishing of a world parliament, developing a more complete world court system, and beginning the long overdue reorganization of the Security Council.[51]

The United Nations still clings to features of a "permanent congress of states." If it is no longer to be a mere assembly of government delegations, the General Assembly must be transformed into a kind of parliament that shares its powers with a second chamber. In such a parliament, peoples will be represented not by their governments but by the elected representatives of the totality of world citizens. Countries that refuse to allow representatives to be elected by democratic procedures (procedures that also give special consideration to their national minorities) could be represented in the meantime by non-governmental organizations that the World Parliament itself selects as the representatives of oppressed populations.

The World Court in The Hague currently lacks the power to press charges and make claims; it cannot make binding decisions, and thus it is limited to the function of an umpire. Its jurisdiction is now restricted to the relations among states; it does not extend to conflicts between individual persons or between individual citizens and their governments. In all these respects, the powers of the World Court must be expanded along the lines of proposals made by Hans Kelsen in 1944.[52] International criminal prosecution, which has up to now only been established on an ad hoc basis for specific war-crimes trials, must be permanently institutionalized.

The Security Council was conceived to be a counterweight to the egalitarian General Assembly. It is supposed to reflect the de facto relations of power in the world. Some five decades later, this reasonable principle must be altered to fit the changed world situation; such an adaptation should not be limited to simply expanding the representation of the most influential states (for example, by accepting Germany or Japan as a permanent member). Instead, it has been proposed that, along with the world powers (such as the United States), regional regimes (such as the European Union) should also be given a privileged vote. It is also necessary that the requirement of unanimity among the permanent members be abolished in favor of an appropriate form of majority rule. Following the model of Brussels ministry of the European Union, the Security Council as a whole could be reformed into an executive power capable of carrying out policies. States will adjust their traditional foreign policies according to the imperatives of world domestic policy only if the world organization possesses a military force under its own command and exercises its own policing functions.

These reflections are conventional, in the sense that they are oriented to the organizational components of national constitutions. The implementation of a properly clarified conception of cosmopolitan law demands somewhat more institutional imagination. In any case, the moral universalism that guided Kant's proposals remains the structuring normative intuition. Beginning with Hegel's criticisms of Kant's morality of humanity, an argument directed against this moral-practical self-understanding of modernity has been especially influential in Germany and has left deep traces.[53] Carl Schmitt has given this argument its sharpest formulation, based on reasoning that is incisive and confused at the same time.

Schmitt turns the slogan "he who says humanity wants to deceive" into the powerful formula "Humanity, Bestiality." According to Schmitt, "the deception of humanism" has its roots in the hypocrisy of a legal pacificism that wants to conduct "just wars" in the name of peace and cosmopolitan rights. "When a state fights its political enemy in the name of humanity, it is not a war for the sake of humanity, but rather a war in which a particular state tries to usurp a universal concept in its struggle against its enemy, in the same way that one can misuse peace, justice, progress and civilization in order to vindicate oneself and to discredit the foe. The concept of 'Humanity' is an especially useful ideological instrument. . . ."[54]

Schmitt later extended this argument (directed in 1932 against the United States and the other victors of Versailles) to the actions of the League of Nations and the United Nations. The politics of a world organization inspired by Kant's idea of perpetual peace and oriented to the creation of a cosmopolitan order obeys the same logic: its pan-interventionism necessarily leads to a pan-criminalization and with it to the perversion of the goal it is supposed to serve.[55]

(2) Before I consider the specific context of these reflections, I would like to deal with the argument at a general level and uncover its problematic core. Its two basic propositions are that the politics of human rights leads to wars that are disguised as police actions to lend them a moral quality and that this moralization stamps the enemy as an inhuman criminal and thus opens the floodgates. "We are acquainted with the secret law behind this vocabulary and know today that the most terrible wars are conducted in the name of peace and that the worst inhumanity is committed in the name of humanity."[56] These two statements are justified with the aid of two further premises: (a) that the politics of human rights serves to implement norms that are a part of universalistic morality and (b) that, in accordance with the moral code of "good" and "evil," these negative moral evaluations of an enemy (or a political opponent in war) destroy the legally institutionalized limitation of military conflict (or of political struggle more generally). Whereas the first premise is false, the second

premise suggests a false presupposition with regard to the politics of human rights.

On premise (a): Human rights in the modern sense can be traced back to the Virginia Bill of Rights and to the 1776 American Declaration of Independence, as well as to the 1789 Declaration des droits de l'homme et du citoyen. These declarations are inspired by the political philosophy of modern natural law, especially that of Locke and Rousseau. It is no accident that human rights first take on concrete form in the context of these first constitutions precisely as basic rights guaranteed in the context of the legal order of the nation state. However, they have a double character: as constitutional norms they enjoy a positive validity (of instituted law), but as rights that are attributed to each person as a human being they acquire a suprapositive validity.

In the philosophical discussion of human rights, this ambiguity has provoked much irritation.[57] According to one interpretation, human rights are supposed to have a status between moral and positive law; according to the other interpretation, they appear with identical content in the form of both moral and juridical rights [*Rechte*]; that is, "as a law [*Recht*] valid [*gültig*] prior to any state, but not for that reason already in force [*geltend*]." Human rights are then "not actually preserved or rejected, but nonetheless guaranteed or disrespected."[58] These formulas reflect philosophical embarrassment and suggest that the constitutional legislator only disguises already given moral norms in the form of positive law. This recourse to the classical distinction between natural and instituted law sets up the lines of debate in the wrong way. The conception of human rights does not have its origins in morality; rather, it bears the imprint of the modern concept of individual liberties and is therefore distinctly juridical in character. What gives human rights the appearance of being moral rights is neither their content nor even their structure but rather their form of validity, which points beyond the legal order of the nation state.

The historical texts of various constitutions appeal to "innate" rights and have the form of "declarations": both are supposed to militate against what we now call a positivist misunderstanding and express the fact that human rights are "not under the control of any legislator."[59] But this rhetorical proviso cannot save human rights from the fate of all positive law; they, too, can be changed or even abolished with the change of regimes. As a component of a democratic legal order, they share with all other legal norms a dual sense of "validity": not only are they valid de facto and implemented by the sanctioning power of state violence; they can also claim normative legitimacy (that is, they are capable of being rationally justified). It is in their justification that basic rights do indeed have a remarkable status.

As constitutional norms, human rights have a certain primacy, shown by the fact that they are constitutive for legal order as such and by the extent to which they determine a framework within which normal legislative activity is possible. But even among constitutional norms as a whole, basic rights stand out. On the one hand, liberal and social basic rights have the form of general norms addressed to citizens in their properties as "human beings" and not merely as members of a polity. Even if human rights can be realized only within the framework of the legal order of a nation state, they are justified in this sphere of validity as rights for all persons and not merely for citizens. The more one explores the content of the German Basic Law [Germany's constitution] from the viewpoint of human rights, the more the legal status of resident noncitizens living in Germany resembles that of citizens. It is this universal validity, applied to every human being as such, that basic rights share with moral norms. As can be shown in the recent controversy in Germany over the right of resident aliens to vote, this same point applies to basic political rights too. This points to a second and even more important aspect: Basic rights are equipped with such universal validity claims precisely because they can be justified *exclusively* from the moral point of view. Other legal norms can certainly *also* be justified with the help of moral arguments, but in general further ethical-political and pragmatic considerations play a role in their justification—considerations that have to do with the particular concrete form of life of a historical legal community or with the concrete goals of particular policies. Basic rights, on the contrary, regulate matters of such generality that moral arguments are *sufficient for their justification*. These arguments show why the guarantee of such rules is in the equal interest of all persons qua persons, and thus why they are equally good for *everyone*.

This mode of justification in no way undermines the juridical quality of basic rights, nor does it turn them into moral norms. Legal norms—in the modern sense of positive law—retain their legal form even if their claim to legitimacy can be justified with the help of this further sort of reason. This character is due to their structure, not to their content. According to this structure, basic rights are enforceable individual rights, the meaning of which is to unbind legal persons in very specific ways from moral commands by creating a sphere of action in which each person can act according to his or her own preferences. Whereas moral rights can only be justified as duties that bind the free will of autonomous persons, legal duties are primarily entitlements to voluntary action; indeed, they derive precisely through the legal limitation of these very same individual liberties that they permit.[60]

The conceptual privileging of rights over duties results from the structure of modern coercive law first elaborated by Hobbes. Hobbes introduced a shift in perspective away from pre-modern law, which was still justified from a religious or metaphysical perspective. In a manner quite different from the grounding of duties in deontological morality, law here serves the purpose of protecting the freedom of the individual according to the principle that everything is permitted that is not explicitly forbidden according to those general laws that limit freedom. Certainly, the generality of such laws satisfies the moral point of view of justice, especially if the individual rights derived from them are supposed to be legitimate. The individual rights that protect a sphere of liberty give modern legal order its basic structure. Hence, Kant conceives of law as "the sum of the conditions under which the choices of each can be united with the freedom of others according to general laws of freedom."[61] According to Kant, all special human rights have their justification in the single original right of each individual to equal freedom: "To the extent that it can coexist with the freedom of all in accordance with a universal law, freedom (as independence from being constrained by the arbitrary will of others) is the only original right, belonging to each human being simply by virtue of his or her humanity."[62]

For this reason, Kant has no other place to put human rights than in his "Doctrine of Right." Like other individual rights, as rights they have a moral content. But this content is in no way altered by the fact that human rights structurally belong within an order of positive and coercive law in which claims to individual rights are enforceable. To this extent, it is constitutive of the meaning of human rights that, according to their status as basic rights, they belong within a framework of some existing legal order, whether it be national, international, or global, in which they can be protected. The mistake of conflating them with moral rights results from their peculiar nature: apart from their universal validity *claims*, these rights have had an unambiguously positive form only within the national legal order of the democratic state. Moreover, they possess only weak validity in international law, and they await institutionalization within the framework of a cosmopolitan order which is only now emerging.

On premise (b): If the first premise of the counterargument (that human rights are by nature moral rights) is false, then the first of the two auxiliary propositions (the statement that the global implementation of human rights necessarily follows a moral logic that would lead to interventions disguised as police actions) is also undercut. At the same time, the second statement (that an interventionist politics of human rights would have to disguise itself as a "struggle against evil") is also refuted. In any case this statement suggests the false presupposition that a classical international law oriented to limited wars would be sufficient to steer military conflicts down a "civilized" path. Even if this presupposition still held, the police actions of a democratically legitimate world organization capable of taking action would better earn the title of the means for "civilizing" international conflicts than would limited war. Establishing a cosmopolitan order means that violations of human rights are no longer condemned and fought from the moral point of view in an unmediated way, but are rather prosecuted as criminal actions within the framework of a state-organized legal order according to institutionalized legal procedures. Precisely such a juridification of the state of nature among states would protect us from a moral de-differentiation of law and would guarantee to the accused full legal protection, even in cases of war crimes and crimes of humanity. Even such cases are protected from unmediated moral discrimination.[63]

5

I would like to develop this metacritical argument further by dealing specifically with Carl Schmitt's objections. I return to these objections because Schmitt did not always link the various levels of his argument in an especially transparent way. Schmitt's criticism of a form of cosmopolitan law that does not stop at the sovereignty of individual states was especially preoccupied with a morally discriminating conception of war. In this way, his argument seems to have a clear legal focus. It is directed against the prohibition of offensive war codified in the United Nations Charter and against the arrest of individual persons for war crimes, both of which were unknown in classical international law before World War I. But this juridical discussion, harmless in itself, is laden with both political considerations and metaphysical justifications. We must unfold the existing theory that lies in the background (1) in order to uncover the critique of morality at the core of the argument (2).

(1) Taken at face value, this juridical argument has the goal of civilizing war through international law (a); and it is connected with a political argument that only appears to be consistent with preserving the existing international order (b).

(a) Schmitt does not reject the distinction between offensive and defensive wars simply because it is difficult pragmatically to operationalize it. Rather, the juridical reason is that only a morally neutral conception of war, which excludes the possibility of personal arrest of war criminals, is consistent with the sovereignty of the subjects of international law. If that is true, then *ius ad bellum*, the right to begin a war for any reason whatsoever, constitutes the sovereignty of states. At this level of the argument, Schmitt is not yet concerned with the supposedly disastrous consequences of moral universalism (as he is in other writings[64]); rather, he is concerned with any limitation on how wars are conducted. Only the practice of not discriminating among types of wars is supposed to succeed in limiting military actions in war and thus to protect us from the evil of a total war, which Schmitt analyzed before World War II with admirable clarity.[65]

Schmitt tries to present the return to the status quo ante of limited war as a realistic alternative to the cosmopolitan pacification of the state of nature among states. In comparison with civilizing it, abolishing war altogether is a much more extensive and apparently utopian goal. Admittedly, the "realism" of this proposal can be doubted for good empirical reasons. The simple appeal to an international law, as it emerged out of the wars of religion as one of the great achievements of Western rationalism, does not point the way toward reestablishing the classical-modern world of the balance of power. The classical form of such international law had already failed in the face of the total wars unleashed in the twentieth century. Powerful forces have already brought about a territorial, technical, and ideological delimitation of war. These forces could more likely be tamed through the sanctions and interventions of an organized community of peoples than through the juridically ineffective appeal to the insight of sovereign governments. Precisely at a time when they ought to change their uncivilized behavior, a return to the classical international legal order would hand back to collective actors an unfettered freedom of action. This argumentative weakness is a first indication that the juridical argument only forms a facade, behind which misgivings of a different sort are hidden.

After World War II, Schmitt could save the consistency of his purely juridical argument only by bracketing the mass crimes of the Nazi period as a sui generis category, in order to preserve at least the appearance of moral neutrality for war. In a brief prepared in 1945 for the Nuremberg defendant Friedrich Flick, Schmitt rigorously distinguished between war crimes and "atrocities," stating that the latter transcend human understanding "as the characteristic expression of an inhuman mentality." He admits that "the commands of a superior cannot justify or pardon such outrages committed by those under him."[66] That Schmitt the lawyer was motivated by purely tactical considerations in making this distinction in the context of the Nuremberg trials became brutally clear in the texts written in his diary a few years later. From his "Glossorarium" it is clear that Schmitt not only wanted to see offensive wars decriminalized but also saw the absolute breakdown of civilization in the extermination of the Jews on the same level. He asks: "Was it a 'crime against humanity'? Is there such a thing as a crime against love?" Furthermore, he doubts whether the Holocaust is to be considered a juridical state of affairs at all, because the "object of protection and attack" of such a crime cannot be sufficiently precisely delimited: "Genocide, the murder of peoples, moving concept. I have experienced an example of it in my own body: the destruction of the German-Prussian civil service in 1945." This rather ticklish understanding of genocide leads Schmitt to an even farther-reaching conclusion: "The concept of 'crimes against humanity' is only the most general of all general clauses for use in exterminating an enemy." In another passage, Schmitt puts it this way: "There are crimes against humanity and crimes for humanity. Crimes against humanity were committed by the Germans. Crimes for humanity were perpetrated on the Germans."[67]

Here yet another argument apparently emerges. The implementation of cosmopolitan law with the consequence of the use of a discriminating conception of war is not only considered a false reaction to the development of total war, but is now its cause. Total war is the contemporary form of "just war" and necessarily encourages an interventionist politics of human rights: "What is decisive is that the total character of the war belongs to its claim of being just."[68] In this way, moral universalism takes on the role of an explanandum, and the argument shifts from the juridical to the moral level. Schmitt seems at first to have recommended the return to classical international law as a way to avoid total war. But it is not at all certain that he truly saw the total delimiting of war and hence the inhuman character of the conduct of war as the real evil, or whether it is much more the case that he mostly feared the discrediting of war as such. In any case, in an addition to *The Concept of the Political* written in 1938 Schmitt describes the totalitarian expansion of war to nonmilitary areas in such a way that he sees total war as a hygienic service for peoples: "The step beyond the purely military view of war not only brings with it a quantitative expansion, it also produces a qualitative jump. For this reason total war does not signify a lessening, but rather an intensification of hatred of the enemy. With the mere possibility of such an increase in intensity, the concepts of friend and foe become political once again and are freed from the sphere of private and psychological forms of speech in which they had become completely drained of their political character."[69]

(b) Although it should come as no surprise that an inveterate foe of pacificism should not be so concerned with the problem of the taming of wars unleashed by totalitarianism, Schmitt could also have something else in mind: the preservation of an international order in which wars can still be waged and used to solve conflicts. The practice suggested by a nondiscriminating conception of war keeps intact the mechanism of unlimited national self-assertion as the basis of order. The evil to be avoided is therefore not total war, but rather the decline of the sphere of the political that rests upon the classical distinction of domestic and foreign politics. This distinction is justified by Schmitt through his own peculiar theory of the political. According to this theory, legally pacified domestic politics must be supplemented by a bellicose foreign policy licensed by international law; with its monopoly over the means of violence, the state can maintain law and order against the virulent subversive power of domestic enemies only if it preserves and regenerates its political substance in struggle against its foreign foes. This substance is renewed in the willingness of members of a nation to kill and be killed, since it is of the essence of the political to be related to "the real possibility of physical death." What is "political" is the capacity and will of a people to recognize its foes and to assert itself against "the negation of its existence" though the "otherness of the foreign."[70]

These scurrilous reflections on "the essence of the political" interest us here only for their usefulness in Schmitt's argument. The vitalistic content loaded into the concept of the political is the background for the assertion that its creative power has to be transformed into a destructive power as soon as it is shut off from the "conquering violence" of the predatory international arena. Supposedly for the sake of world peace, the global implementation of human rights and democracy would have the unintended effect of allowing war to step beyond the limits within which it is held by "formally just" international law. Without being permitted to run free in its hunting ground, war will become autonomous, overwhelm the spheres of civil life in modern society, and thus eliminate the complexity of differentiated societies. This warning against the catastrophic consequences of abolishing war through the pacification of law is explicable only through a metaphysics that is at best a relic of its time and which in the meantime also invokes the somewhat naked aesthetics of war as "the storm of steel."[71]

(2) One can certainly distill and specify a particular viewpoint out of this bellicose *Lebensphilosophie*. According to Schmitt, behind the ideological justification of the call for a "war against war" is the universalism of the Kantian morality of humanity, which transforms the temporally, socially, and technologically limited military struggle between organized "units of peoples" into an unlimited paramilitary civil war.

All indications are that Schmitt would react to the United Nations' peacekeeping and peacemaking efforts in precisely the same way as Hans Magnus Enzensberger: "The rhetoric of universalism is specific to the West. The postulates advanced in this way are supposed to be valid without exception or differences for all. Universalism thus knows no distinctions between near and far; it is unconditional and abstract. . . . But since all our possibilities of action are finite, the gaps between claim and reality opens up wider and wider. Soon the limit of objective hypocrisy is also transgressed; it is then that universalism proves itself to be a moral trap."[72] It is therefore the false abstractions of the morality of humanity, an abstract morality that produces self-deception and a hypocritical overburdening of our moral capacities. The limits which such a morality transgresses are seen by Enzensberger and Gehlen as anthropologically deep-seated conceptions of space and time: a being such as a human, made out of such flimsy materials, functions morally only in the proximate perceptual environment.[73]

Schmitt comes closer to Hegel's criticism of Kant when he speaks of hypocrisy. He furnishes the contemptuous formula "humanity, bestiality" with an ambiguous commentary, which at first glance might have come from Horkheimer: "We speak of the main city cemetery and tactfully keep quiet about the slaughter house. But slaughtering is self-evident, and it would be inhumane, even bestial, to say the word 'to slaughter' out loud."[74] This aphorism is ambiguous to the extent that it seems at first to signify an ideology critique directed against the false and transfiguring abstraction of a Platonic general concept with which we often only cover up the dark side of the civilization of the victors, namely the suffering of marginalized victims. But this reading would nonetheless require a kind of egalitarian respect and universal compassion validated by the very moral universalism Schmitt so vehemently rejects. What Schmitt's antihumanism seeks to affirm (along with Mussolini's and Lenin's interpretations of Hegel[75]) is not the slaughtered calf, but rather the battle [*Schlacht*], Hegel's slaughter bench [*Schlachtbank*] of peoples, the "honor of war." For this reason his commentary states further on that "humanity does not wage war . . . the concept of humanity excludes the possibility of the concept of a foe."[76] According to Schmitt, the morality of humanity falsely abstracts from the natural order of the political, namely the supposedly unavoidable distinction between friend and foe. Because it subsumes political relationships under the categories of "good" and "evil," it turns the enemy in war into "an inhuman monster who can not only be defended against but also must be definitively annihilated."[77] And because the discriminating concept of war derives from the universalism of human rights, it is ultimately the infection of international law with morality that explains why the inhumanity of modern war and civil war occurs "in the name of humanity."

Independent of the context in which Schmitt employs it, this critique of morality has had baneful effects through the history of its reception. It fuses a correct insight with a fatal mistake fed by the friend-foe conception of the political. The true thesis at the core of the argument consists in the fact that an *unmediated* moralization of law and politics would in fact serve to break down those protected spheres that we as legal persons have good moral reasons to want to secure. But it is mistaken in its assumption that such a moralization is hindered only by keeping international law free of law and the law free of morality. Both are false under the premises of the constitutional state and democracy: the idea of a constitutional state demands that the coercive violence of the state be channeled both externally and internally through legitimate law; and the democratic legitimation of law is supposed to guarantee that law remain in harmony with recognized moral principles. Cosmopolitan law is thus a consequence of the idea of the constitutional state. In it, symmetry is finally established between the juridification of social and political relations both inside and outside the state's boundaries.

Schmitt's most informative inconsistency is his insistence upon an asymmetry between a pacified legal order within the state and a bellicose one outside it. Since he also imagines legal peace within the state to consist only in the latent conflict between the organs of the state and the enemies whom the state represses by means of struggle, he hands law over completely to the occupiers of state power and declares representatives of the opposition within the state to be domestic enemies—a practice that has left traces in the Federal Republic of Germany.[78] Quite distinct from the democratic constitutional state in which independent courts and the whole body of citizens (sometimes, in extreme cases, activated through civil disobedience) decide about sensible questions concerning unconstitutional behavior, Schmitt weighs the interests of the current holders of power and criminalizes political opponents into enemies in civil war. This loosening of constitutional controls in the border zones of domestic affairs has precisely the effects that Schmitt fears in the pacification of foreign affairs between states: the thorough penetration of moral categories into the legally protected zone of political action and the stylization of opponents into agents of evil. But it would be entirely inconsistent then to demand that international relations remain immune from regulations analogous to those in the constitutional state.

As a matter of fact, an *unmediated* moralization of politics in the international arena would be just as damaging as the struggle of governments with their domestic enemies—something Schmitt permits because he localizes the damage in the wrong place. In both cases, the damage only occurs in light of the false coding of legally protected political and state actions: such actions are falsely moralized, judged according to criteria of "good" and "evil"; they are then criminalized and thus judged according to criteria of "legal" and "illegal." All the while, Schmitt ignores the decisive moment—the legal presupposition of an authority that judges impartially and fulfills the conditions of neutral criminal punishment.

The politics of human rights undertaken by a world organization turns into a fundamentalism of human rights only when it undertakes an intervention that is really nothing more than the struggle of one party against the other and thus uses a moral legitimation as a cover for a false juridical justification. In such cases, the world organization (or the alliance acting in its name) does engage in "deception," because it portrays what is actually a military confrontation between two warring parties as a neutral police action justified by actual law and by the judgments of a criminal court. "Morally justified appeals threaten to take on fundamentalist features when they do not aim at the implementation of a legal procedure [for the positivization and] for the application and achievement of human rights, but rather seize directly upon the interpretive scheme by which violations of human rights are attributed, or when such moral appeals are the sole source of the demanded sanctions."[79]

Schmitt also defends the assertion that the juridification of power politics outside the boundaries of states (and thus the implementation of human rights in an arena previously dominated by military force) *always and necessarily* leads to such a human-rights fundamentalism. This assertion is false, since it is based on the false premise that human rights have a moral nature and thus that their implementation signifies a form of moralization. The problematic side of the juridification of international affairs already mentioned does not consist in the placing of actions previously understood as "political" under legal categories. Quite different from morality, the legal code in no way requires unmediated moral evaluation according to the criteria of "good" and "evil." Klaus Günther clarifies the central point: "That a purely political interpretation of human rights (in the sense of Carl Schmitt) is excluded does not mean that an unmediated moralistic interpretation should be put in its place."[80] Human rights should not be confused with moral rights.

The difference between law and morality that Günther insists upon does not in any way signify that positive law has no moral content. Through the democratic procedure of the political process of legislation, moral arguments (along with other types of reasons) flow into the justification of relevant norm-making activities and in this way into law itself. As Kant already saw, law is distinguished from morality through the formal properties of legality. This means that some aspects of morally evaluated action (for example, intentions and motives) ought not be the proper subjects of legal regulation. Above all, the legal code makes binding the judgments and sanctions of the agencies authorized to protect those affected through narrowly interpreted, intersubjectively testable conditions of the procedures of the constitutional state. Whereas the moral person stands naked before the inner court of his or her conscience, the moral person remains clothed with the cloak of the rights to freedom that are justified by good moral reasons. The correct solution to the problem of the moralization of power politics is therefore "not the demoralization of politics, but rather the democratic transformation of morality into a positive system of law with legal procedures of application and implementation."[81] Fundamentalism about human rights is to be avoided not by giving up on the politics of human rights, but rather only through the cosmopolitan transformation of the state of nature among states into a legal order.

—translated by James Bohman

Notes to Chapter 4

1. Immanuel Kant, "The Contest of Faculties," in *Kant's Political Writings* (Cambridge, 1970), p. 187; *Werke* XI (Suhrkamp, 1977), p. 364.

2. In the conclusion to "Rechtslehre" in *Metaphysics of Morals* (*Kant's Political Writings*, pp. 173–174); *Werke* VIII, p. 478.

3. Indeed, Kant does mention in his "Doctrine of Right" the "unjust enemy," whose "publicly expressed will, whether in word or deed, displays a maxim that would make peace among nations impossible" (*Metaphysics of Morals*, section 60; *Political Writings*, p. 170). However, the examples he gives, such as breaking an international treaty or the division of a conquered country (e.g., Poland in his own time) illuminate the accidental character of this conception. A "punitive war" against unjust enemies is an idea with no real practical consequences, so long as states are considered entities with unlimited sovereignty. Such a punishment could only be given by a juridical authority which judges impartially in terms of violations of the rules of international conduct; but no state could recognize such an authority without limiting its own sovereignty. Only the outcome of the conflict can decide "who is in the right" (*Political Writings*, p. 96; *Werke* XI, p. 200).

4. Kant, *Political Writings*, p. 113; *Werke* XI, p. 212.

5. Kant, "Theory and Practice," in *Political Writings*, p. 92; *Werke* XI, p. 172.

6. Kant, "Theory and Practice," p. 92; *Werke* XI, p. 172.

7. Kant, "Toward Perpetual Peace," in *Political Writings*, p. 105; *Werke* XI, p. 213.

8. In "The Doctrine of Right," *Metaphysics of Morals*, section 61; *Kant's Political Writings*, p. 171.

9. Kant, *Metaphysics of Morals* in *Political Writings*, p. 171; *Werke* VIII, p. 475.

10. "Toward Perpetual Peace," p. 104–105; *Werke* XI, p. 212.

11. "Toward Perpetual Peace," p. 127; *Werke* XI, p. 225.

12. "Theory and Practice," p. 90; *Werke* XI. p. 169.

13. "Toward Perpetual Peace," p. 100; *Werke* XI, pp. 205–206.

14. H. Schulze, *Staat und Nation in der Europäischen Geschichte* (Munich, 1994).

15. See D. Archibugi and D. Held's "Introduction" to their collection *Cosmopolitan Democracy* (Cambridge, 1995), p. 10ff.

16. See "The Doctrine of Right," *Metaphysics of Morals*, section 62; *Political Writings*, p. 172.

17. "Toward Perpetual Peace," 114; Werke XI, p. 226.

18. See Georg Lukacs, *Der junge Hegel* (Zurich, 1948).

19. Dieter Senghaas, "Internationale Politik im Lichte ihrer strukturellen Dilemmata," in *Wohin driftet die Welt?* (Frankfurt, 1994), p. 121ff; here p. 132.

20. This is Anthony Giddens's definition of globalization in *The Consequences of Modernity* (Cambridge, 1990), p. 64.

21. R. Knieper, *Nationale Souveränität* (Frankfurt, 1991).

22. J. S. Nye, "Soft Power," *Foreign Policy* 80 (1990), 152–171.

23. "Toward Perpetual Peace," p. 121; *Werke* XI, p. 238.

24. Kant, "Toward Perpetual Peace," p. 115; *Werke* XI, p. 228.

25. "Toward Perpetual Peace," p. 108; *Werke* XI, p. 216f. [bracketed words inserted by Habermas —translator]

26. On the theme of a farewell to the world of nation states see E. O. Czempiel, *Weltpolitik im Umbruch* (Munich, 1993), p. 105ff.

27. See the essays by Albrecht Wellmer and Axel Honneth in *Gemeinschaft und Gerechtigkeit*, ed. M. Brumlik and H. Brunkhorst (Frankfurt, 1993), p. 173ff and p. 260ff.

28. See the title essay in my book *Die Normalität einer Berliner Republik* (Munich, 1995), p. 165ff.

29. "Toward Perpetual Peace," p. 114; *Werke* XI, p. 226.

30. *Kant's Political Writings*, p. 51; "Idee zu einer Allgemeinen Geschichte," in *Werke* XI, p. 46ff.

31. On the idea of "a people as a learning sovereign," see H. Brunkhorst, *Demokratie und Differenz* (Frankfurt, 1994), p. 199ff.

32. "Idea of a Universal History," in *Kant's Political Writings*. p. 45; "Idee zu einer Allgemeinen Geschichte," in *Werke* XI, p. 38.

33. J. Isensee defends a qualified prohibition of intervention against the increasing tendency to deviate from the norm with the surprising construction of "basic rights for states" in "Weltpolizei für Menschenrechten," *Juristische Zeitung* 9 (1995): 421–430: "What is valid for the basic rights of individuals is also valid mutatis mutandis for the 'basic rights' of states, including their sovereign equality, their self-determination as the power over persons and territory." Constructing an analogy between the sovereignty of states recognized by international law and the basic guaranteed right to freedom granted to individual persons misses not only the fundamental importance of individual rights and the individualist orientation of modern legal order; it also misses the specifically juridical meaning of human rights as the individual rights of citizens in a cosmopolitan order.

34. See the examples in Charles Greenwood, "Gibt es ein Recht auf humanitäre Intervention?" *Europa-Archiv* 4 (1993), p. 94.

35. For my account of these events, see *Vergangenheit als Zukunft* (Munich, 1993), pp. 10–44.

36. Kant, "Theory and Practice," p. 77; *Werke* XI, p. 144.

37. See J. Habermas, "Struggles for Recognition in the Democratic Constitutional State," in *Multiculturalism*, ed. A. Guttman (Princeton, 1994).

38. "Toward Perpetual Peace," p. 111; *Werke* XI, p. 223.

39. As shown in a treatment of this work by Georges Scelle, *Precis de droit de gens* (two volumes; Paris, 1932 and 1934). See Carl Schmitt, *Die Wendung zum diskriminierenden Kriegsbegriff* (Berlin, 1988), p. 16.

40. Schmitt, *Kriegsbegriff*, p. 19.

41. On the Vienna conference on human rights see R. Wolfrum, "Die Entwicklung des internationalen Menschenrechtsschutzes," *Europa-Archiv* 23 (1993): 681–690. On the status of disputed rights to solidarity see W. Huber, "Menschenrechte/ Menschenwürde," in *Theologische Realenzyklopädie* (Berlin and New York, 1992), volume XXII, pp. 577–602; see also E. Riedel, "Menschenrechte der dritten Dimension," *Europäische Grundrechte-Zeitschrift* 16 (1989): 9–21.

42. In 1993 the Security Council established such a tribunal for the prosecution of war crimes and crimes against humanity in the former Yugoslavia.

43. As argued by H. Quaritsch in his "Postscript" to C. Schmitt, *Das internationalrechtliche Verbrechen des Angriffskrieges* (1945) (Berlin, 1994), pp. 125–247, here from p. 236ff.

44. Greenwood (1993, p. 104) comes to the following conclusion: "The idea that the United Nations can use the powers granted in its Charter to intervene in a state for humanitarian reasons appears now to be much more strongly established."

45. As cited by Greenwood, p. 96.

46. "Toward Perpetual Peace," p. 104; *Werke* XI, p. 211ff.

47. See R. Cooper. "Gibt es eine neue Weltordnung?" *Europa-Archiv* 18 (1993): 509–516.

48. T. Lindholm offers a reasonable proposal for the framework of such a discussion of human rights in The Cross-Cultural Legitimacy of Human Rights (report no. 3, Norwegian Institute of Human Rights, 1990).

49. D. and E. Senghaas, "Si vis pacem, par posem," *Leviathan* (1990): 230–247.

50. E. O. Czempiel has investigated these strategies in light of many different examples in *Sonderheft der Zeitschrift für Politik*, ed. G. Schwarz (Zurich, 1989); see pp. 55–75.

51. Here I am following D. Archibugi, "From the United Nations to Cosmopolitan Democracy," in *Cosmopolitan Democracy*.

52. See Hans Kelsen, *Peace through Law* (Chapel Hill, 1944).

53. Habermas, *The Philosophical Discourse of Modernity* (Cambridge, Mass., 1987, p. 336ff.

54. Carl Schmitt, *The Concept of the Political* (New Brunswick, 1976), p. 52. Isensee ("Weltpolizei für Menschenrechten," p. 429) makes the same argument: "Ever since there have been interventions, they have served ideologies: confessional ones in the sixteenth and seventeenth centuries; monarchical, Jacobin, and humanitarian principles; the socialist world revolution. Now human rights and democracy join the series. In the long history of intervention, ideology has served to disguise the interest in power of those intervening and to impart their effectiveness with the aura of legitimacy."

55. Schmitt, *Glossarium 1947–1951* (Berlin, 1991), p. 76.

56. Schmitt, *Concept of the Political*, p. 36.

57. See the essays in *On Human Rights*, ed. S. Schute and S. Hurley (New York, 1993).

58. O. Höffe, "Die Menschenrechte als Legitimation und kritischer Massstab der Demokratie," in *Menschenrechte und Demokratie*, ed. J Schwardtländer (Stuttgart, 1981), p. 250. See also Höffe, *Politische Gerechtigkeit* (Frankfurt, 1987).

59. S. König, *Zur Begründung der Menschenrechte: Hobbes-Locke-Kant* (Freiburg, 1994), p. 26ff.

60. See Hugo Bedau's analysis of the structure of human rights, (developed in dialogue with Henry Shue's position), "International Human Rights," in *And Justice for All*, ed. T. Regan and D. van de Weer (Totowa, 1983): "The emphasis on duties is meant to avoid leaving the defense of human rights in a vacuum, bereft of any moral significance for the specific conduct of others. But the duties are not intended to explain or generate rights: if anything, the rights are supposed to explain and generate the duties." (p. 297)

61. Kant, *Metaphysics of Morals* (Cambridge, 1991), p. 56 [translation modified]; *Werke* VIII, p. 345.

62. *Metaphysics of Morals*, p. 63; *Werke* VIII, 345.

63. On distinguishing the spheres of ethics, law, and morality, see R. Forst, *Kontexte der Gerechtigkeit* (Frankfurt, 1994).

64. Specifically, in his *Das internationalrechtliche Verbrechen des Angriffskrieges.*

65. In both *The Concept of the Political* (1963) and *Die Wendung zur diskriminerenden Kriegsbegriff* (1988).

66. Schmitt, *Das Verbrechen,* p. 19.

67. Schmitt, *Glossarium,* p. 113, 265, 146, 282.

68. Schmitt, *Die Wendung,* p. 1.

69. Schmitt, *Der Begriff des Politischen* (Berlin, 1963). [This section is not included the English translations. —translator]

70. Schmitt, *Concept of the Political,* p. 33.

71. This is a reference to Ernst Junger's novel *Stahlgewetter,* a model of the aesthetization of war for Heidegger as well. —translator

72. Hans Magnus Enzensberger, *Aussichten auf den Bürgerkrieg* (Frankfurt, 1993), p. 73ff. See Axel Honneth's essay in the present volume. Enzensberger rests his case on an extremely selective description of the current international situation, in which the extraordinary expansion of democratic forms of the state in Latin American, Africa, and Eastern Europe is not considered. On this development see Czempiel, *Welt im Umbruch,* p. 107ff. He quickly converts the complex relationships between fundamentalist opportunism with regard to conflicts within states on the one hand and social deprivations and the lack of liberal traditions on the other into anthropological constants. But it is precisely an expanded conception of peace that has affinities with preventive and nonviolent strategies and makes us aware of the pragmatic limitations which undermine humanitarian interventions, as the examples of Somalia and the former Yugoslavia show. For a casuistry of various types of intervention see Senghaas, p. 185ff.

73. Arnold Gehlen, *Moral und Hypermoral* (Frankfurt, 1969).

74. Schmitt, *Glossarium,* p. 259.

75. Ibid., p. 229; see also *Concept of the Political,* p. 63.

76. *Concept of the Political,* p. 54ff.

77. *Concept of the Political,* p. 36.

78. See Habermas, *Kleine Politische Schriften I–IV* (Frankfurt, 1981), pp. 328–339.

79. Klaus Günther, "Kampf gegen das Böse? Wider die ethische Aufrüstung der Kriminalpolitik," *Kritische Justiz* 17 (1994), p. 144. (Bracketed phrase inserted by Habermas. —translator)

80. Ibid.

81. Ibid.

5

Is Universalism a Moral Trap? The Presuppositions and Limits of a Politics of Human Rights

Axel Honneth

With the peaceful revolutions of the late 1980s and with the collapse of the Soviet Union, the world appeared to have moved a significant step closer to the Kantian project of a perpetual peace. Now that the East-West conflict had come to an end, the moment seemed ripe for states collectively to leave the state of nature and to enter into a societal state of morally regulated cooperation. Under the conditions of military confrontation between the two superpowers, the Hobbesian doctrine of the state of nature was regarded almost self-evidently as the appropriate paradigm for international relations: just like individuals, nations were said to confront one another in a relation of potential war of all against all. Not knowing each other's intentions, the superpowers could secure their own self-preservation only if they knew how to affirm superiority in an emergency by the preventive escalation of power.[1]

The end of the East-West conflict, however, saw the apparent disappearance of the condition that Hobbes had to presuppose in order to explain the permanent willingness of all individuals to engage in conflict: the impossibility of the elementary development of trust between individuals (or, in this case, nations). Thus, there now seemed to be no obstacle to applying the Kantian paradigm of international relations to the situation in world politics: states ought to be able to emerge "from the state of lawlessness, which consists solely of war" by giving up "their savage (lawless) liberty, just as individual persons do, and, by accommodating themselves to public coercive law, form a polity of all peoples (*civitas gentium*) that would necessarily continue to grow until it embraced all the peoples of the earth."[2] In ascribing to nature the intention of morally improving human beings for practical-political reasons, Kant could have easily seen nature's pedagogical masterpiece in the dramatic events of the late 1980s: the protracted, frequently dangerous East-West conflict was, as it were, staged by nature merely to inform definitively—at the moment of its abrupt termination—all the governments that participated in the conflict that only morally regulated cooperation can create international security and social prosperity.

The extensive hopes connected with the commemoration of Kant's "Toward Perpetual Peace" were quickly followed by novel practical action: after 45 years of internal stagnation and blockage, the United Nations Security Council actively adopted for the first time the role originally intended for it in 1945 when it was established as an international institution for securing peace and protecting human rights. Approving the use of force against Iraq signaled the prelude to a phase in which the UN passed resolutions—always with an overwhelming majority—on a series of humanitarian or peace-making measures; in the meantime, the number of these measures now exceeds the sum total of all interventions agreed upon in the preceding decades. Of course, the greater the number of international protective measures, the more the situation in world politics seemed to develop in the contrary direction; each intervention in a conflict situation apparently triggered, as if in a chain reaction, a series of new civil wars and outbursts of violence, and each venture in humanitarian aid was accompanied by shocking information about famines and massacres in other parts of the world. Instead of peaceful cooperation in the spirit of revived international law, war and terror spread quickly between peoples. Meanwhile, images of armed gangs, "ethnic cleansing," fundamentalist terror campaigns, and innumerable refugees and famine victims determine the view of the international situation to such an extent that the mere recollection of the Kantian project must sound for many people like sheer cynicism; seven years after nations were given the chance to enter into a social order, they seem to be all the more deeply and hopelessly ensnared in the state of nature.

This new situation in world politics is seen by quite a few people to provide sufficient reason for a return to a modified form of *Realpolitik*; the orientation provided by the Hobbesian paradigm is now supposed to legitimate not military armament but a rejection of the universalism of human rights. "Security policy directed within, moral withdrawal from the outside world"—this slogan summarizes the conclusions drawn by those who consider any recourse to the Kantian model to be pure idealism in light of the increasing frequency and brutalization of social conflicts. On the other hand, those who resolve to continue the project of a moralization of world politics point to the increased opportunities to exert influence that a "democratic internationalism"[3] has: as a result of the end of the East-West conflict, the possibilities of international consensus formation have increased considerably. Because new democratic movements have developed worldwide and so a multitude of civil actors now co-determine what happens in world politics, a politics of human rights has room for effective action for the first time in history. A foreign policy of the worldwide implementation of human rights as a means of peacemaking—with such a slogan we can summarize the ideas of those who, even in view of recent developments, argue for the Kantian model of international relations. Thus, what is above all in dispute between the two camps is the degree to which human rights ought to become an operative reference point for foreign policy today; it is not, however, easy to decide in favor of either one of the conflicting parties, because disagreement prevails on how the situation in world politics today ought to be defined.

For that reason, as a first step, I would like to contrast two opposing interpretations of the global political situation in order to show that they are fused in a specific manner with political-philosophical paradigms; there cannot be, so the thesis goes, a merely empirical or "pure" representation of our situation, because there are always anticipatory understandings of its practical-political value that guide our perceptions. In section 2 I present the conclusions for the question of human rights to be drawn from the two interpretations that I contrast as the Hobbesian and the Kantian paradigms. In section 3 I discuss to the extent to which today the constraints of *Realpolitik* are appropriate even for the Hobbesian paradigm; it is possible that under current conditions we have no other possibility but to follow the Kantian idea of a juridification of international relations.

1

In "Reflections on the Theory of Class," which was written during the years he was working on *Dialectic of Enlightenment,* Theodor Adorno conjectures about the future of social conflict in highly developed capitalism; his reflections lead to the thesis that, under the pressure of economic barbarization, in the end it will not be social classes that confront each other in the class struggle but rather "gangs and rackets." According to Adorno's typical dialectical solution, the history of class struggle becomes in the future what it has been from the beginning: a "history of gang fights."[4] Precisely as if he had been inspired by this speculative prediction, Hans Magnus Enzensberger begins his polemic against the universalism of human rights with the terrifying image of "marauding gangs": everywhere in the world today, according to his quintessential interpretation of the current situation, groups of bandits and criminals are engaged in a war whose only means is pure violence and whose only goal is "robbery, murder, and plunder."[5] The outbreak of such a new form of civil war has occurred because the disintegration of the bipolar world order led inevitably to a de-moralization of social relations: as long as the East-West confrontation saw to it that local conflicts could always be translated into an ideological interpretive scheme and could in this way be processed politically and quickly at an international level, a certain degree of human aggression could be kept permanently under state control; with the collapse of the Soviet Union, however, this ideological containment of civil war was lost and the long-suppressed elements of hate and rage could be vented explosively. For Enzensberger, the new forms of uninhibited brutality are connected with specific occasions of conflict to such an insignificant extent that he has no difficulty in also locating traces of them in the increase in direct violence in the metropolises of the West: be it drug gangs or neo-Nazis, be it hooligans or those running amok, for him it is always the expression of an aggression that, because it is not ideologically bound, is without purpose or aim. In this way there emerges a horrifying scenario in world politics, the powers of suggestion of which derive from a mode of presentation that fuses TV pictures from Somalia or Bosnia-Herzegovina unnoticeably with glaring shots from American science fiction movies. Scattered groups of heavily armed Rambos traverse the wastelands of American cities or the dunes of the African desert, just looking for the next possibility to rob and murder their former neighbors or clan members.

A close proximity to such images is also displayed by the impressions that Michael Ignatieff collected on his journeys to the front lines of international conflict zones.[6] He shares with Enzensberger the conviction that the disintegration of the Soviet Union introduced a new era of civil wars whose central characteristic is constituted by a hitherto unknown degree of morally uncurbed aggression. Ignatieff and Enzensberger also share the observation that in the warring gangs and cliques a type of young violent criminal is in control—a type without any precedent in the history of modern Europe. Enzensberger relies on Hannah Arendt's analysis of totalitarianism in order to outline the attributes according to which the new belligerent figures are to be characterized: without any foundation whatsoever in a political-moral conviction, they are autistic in their hate-filled activities to such a degree that they are no longer able to distinguish between destruction and self-destruction. For Ignatieff, on the other hand, it is the "warlord" of medieval times who, as the historical model, is the one to represent the personality type that he believes he encounters in the gang leaders and belligerent agents of our day: "They appear wherever nation states disintegrate: in Lebanon, Somalia, northern India, Armenia, Georgia, Ossetia, Cambodia, the former Yugoslavia. With their car phones, faxes, and exquisite personal weaponry, they look postmodern, but the reality is purely medieval."[7] It is from observations of this kind that these authors draw theoretical conclusions concerning the structural transformation of world politics as a whole. Neither of them—Enzensberger even less so than Ignatieff—shies away from anthropological speculations, the evidence for which is not to be found in this stylized method of description. In the civil wars of recent times, it is suggested, something like raw human nature emerges—something that Hobbes may have sensed as he set about drafting the hypothetical construction of the state of nature. In this model, it is believed that social relations have to assume the form of aggressive hostility between neighboring groups whenever they are no longer embedded in an overlapping system of order that could provide them with a foundation and clear orientation. Here, it is an open question whether this interpretation of the state of nature actually agrees with Hobbes's intentions; my point is only that neither Enzensberger nor Ignatieff hesitates to see in the ethnic conflicts and tribal wars of our day a situation in world politics in which the aggressive human nature gains the upper hand in an uncontrollable—indeed anarchic—manner.

Of course, such a form of near-mythological Hobbesianism necessarily leads to seeing local fighting and wars not in terms of the prehistory of their social tensions but merely as the atavism of a return of prehistoric forces; as if there had not been a long history of religious and ethnic conflicts, which were kept under control—but could not be resolved—by the two superpowers' ideological function of keeping order. The history of the postwar period is compressed into a single event: with the decline of the Soviet empire, and in the form of heavily armed warlords and gang leaders, the horrendous state of a war of all against all once again invades the civil order of the world. We are to learn from the civil wars that have since been raging what we should have long known: according to their whole constitution, human beings are disposed toward a destructive aggression that can be defused only if it is ideologically fixated on images of spatially remote enemies.[8]

The upheavals in world politics in recent years appear in a completely different light, however, when they are interpreted not in the anthropological sense of a crude Hobbesianism, as a latter-day return to the state of nature, but in the hypothetical sense of the Kantian philosophy of history as consisting of steps in the laborious process of establishing human freedom. As is well known, for Kant the necessity of ascribing a sense of moral progress to the empirical history of humanity follows from the internal difficulties of his conception of morality. If there is indeed such a large gap between moral duty and external reality (as outlined first in the *Critique of Practical Reason*), then we necessarily lose sight of the empirical ends that can give to the consciousness of duty the very substance that is to be implemented in this world. In order to escape this predicament, Kant proposes a hypothetical construction of natural ends, which he attempts to develop in the *Critique of Judgment*. Out of an interest of reason in itself, we may ascribe to nature not only certain laws and functional organic processes; we can also attribute to it the intention of a moral improvement of the human species. Such a moral teleology represents the empirical course of the historical process in a way that allows living subjects to find the appropriate ends for actions motivated by duty in the concrete world. It is realistic in that it assumes that such moral subjects can contribute to the realization of the moral good even given the evil still present in the world. While this hope does not actually motivate actors, it does give their moral motives the necessary content in the empirical world. However, this construction is rather fragile. In order to justify the hypothetical claim of the progress of civilization, it has nothing more to offer than the thesis that reason requires a certain support in the historical world for its practical purposes. Whether progress is a matter of mere projection or of theory (however weakly justified) remains entirely undecided.

It is the task of Kant's philosophy of history to fill this explanatory gap between moral teleology and the empirical world, to some extent, by testing various approaches that can provide weak evidence for factual progress in human history. It is probably beyond question today that Kant failed in his attempts to give empirical meaning to the idea of the intention of nature—for instance, in the doctrine of war as a natural mechanism of moral progress (developed in "Idea for a Universal History with a Cosmopolitan Intent" and in the idea that all human natural dispositions necessarily develop in the species as a whole in the historical process (developed in "Toward Perpetual Peace"). Proposals of this kind from Kant are decidedly problematic because they, oddly enough, run counter to the objectives he linked to the hypothetical view of progress in civilization: instead of connecting moral action (via a demonstration of the prospects of success) to political ends, these speculations about natural mechanisms and empirical constraints actually render every morality superfluous, as Larry Krasnoff has now shown.[9] Thus, if this evidence proffered by the Kantian philosophy of history is doomed to failure, then in the end there remains only the idea Kant developed in the second essay of

"The Conflict of the Faculties." Kant here interprets the spectators' enthusiastic reaction to the French Revolution as "a sympathetic participation" which reveals empirically that there is a "moral predisposition in the human race."[10] Such a proposal is, of course, not without its problems; it leaves wide interpretive latitude for determining when an affective agreement with events is to be taken to be a sign of moral progress. Kant probably has in mind the unselfishness and courage that such reaction patterns exhibit in their being publicly expressed without any chances of self-advancement or gains in confrontation with the political authorities. If we summarize these underlying reflections, then we can conclude, with Larry Krasnoff, that Kant sees a "fact of politics" present in the enthusiastic reaction in the same manner in which he spoke of a "fact of reason" in the context of his *Critique of Practical Reason*[11]: the affirmative reaction of the nonparticipating public to the revolutionary events in France serves to prove that the goals of a republican renewal of the state can actually be encountered in empirical reality—the goals of a moral teleology that until then had only been supposed hypothetically for the course of history as a whole.

It is only in such a modified sense that the Kantian philosophy of history can be used today as a kind of theoretical foil in order to construe from the current upheavals in world politics an interpretation different from the one present in the new Hobbesianism. The studies undertaken recently by Ernst-Otto Czempiel can be understood as an attempt at an empirical justification of such a perspective; for him, the activities with which civil organizations, as a reaction to 1989, entered the arena of world politics assume the same role in history that Kant glimpsed in the enthusiastic reaction of the nonparticipating public to 1789.[12] Of course, Czempiel does not want to deny that in some regions of the world today we are confronted with a frightening increase in ethnically or religiously determined conflicts, which seem to stand in a causal relationship to the cessation of the order-maintaining function of the Soviet Union; but he ascribes a completely different quality to this process of decline, because he directs attention to a series of historical-political events that neither Enzensberger nor Ignatieff takes into account at all. To highlight only the destabilizing consequences that accompanied the termination of the East-West conflict is one-sided to an extent that is not justified by historical events: as Czempiel clearly points out, the decline of the Soviet Union came about because democratic resistance to repression and foreign rule in most countries of Eastern Europe became so strong that scarcely any of the communist regimes could survive. Hence, what appears in the interpretation inspired by Hobbes as merely the decline of a politically ideological framework for maintaining order is for Czempiel first and foremost the historical prologue to a process of democratization that is almost unique in world history. In a short period of time, a dramatic structural transformation came about within the territory of the former Soviet Union, one that provided the population as a whole with an enormous increase in civil liberties and political rights: ". . . in the first half of 1990, there were elections in thirteen of the fifteen republics in the Soviet Union. . . . In Hungry, Czechoslovakia, and Poland (and somewhat less evidently in Bulgaria and Romania), elections were also held in the first half of 1990, which at least in Czechoslovakia and Hungary, and indeed Poland, brought freely elected governments to power. The League of Communists of Yugoslavia gave up its leadership role in January 1990. Notwithstanding the confusion and its victims, the ensuing process of disintegration has to be understood as a basic increase in self-determination and co-determination. Even the Albanian Communist Party permitted independent political parties in December 1990."[13]

With these transformation processes, all of which transpired within a single year, the countries of a political bloc where neither the rule of law nor opportunities for political participation had previously existed embarked upon the difficult journey to the establishment of liberal democracies; they are in the process of joining the circle of the political communities called "well-ordered liberal societies" by John Rawls.[14] That such an internal process can lead to social tensions, indeed even to civil wars, is due to the way it can liberate the civil forces of a country and thereby provide all interests and opinions with the possibility of political articulation. This fact is also exhibited in the historical formation of Western democracies. To that extent, however harsh this may sound, the brutalization of social relations in Eastern Europe may be the price paid, not for the decline of order-maintaining power, but for the construction of democratic institutions.

The same connection between a liberation of the civil public sphere and an increase in societal conflicts can also be observed in those regions of the Third World where the democratization of Eastern Europe had a kind of trigger effect. It was above all in the developing countries of Africa that a liberating influence ensued from the fall of the Soviet Union to the extent that the governing cliques lost the chance to legitimate their purposes, the dictatorial character of the power that seemed to guarantee the existence of an anticapitalist camp; this sort of ideological justification had scarcely been blocked when a flood of expanding political possibilities for co-determination began and have not ceased to this day. In the course of 1990 alone, as Czempiel convincingly demonstrates, "the number of sub-Saharan African nations that moved toward democracy, or displayed clear tendencies in this direction, increased from four to over twenty."[15] No different than in some regions in Eastern Europe, democratization in a number of countries on the African continent was also promptly accompanied by the outbreak of brutal civil wars; the opening of political institutions to the participation of the population set off tribal feuds or religious conflicts, which very often quickly escalated because they had been suppressed by autocratic rulers for decades. But, as in the territory of the former Soviet Union, the causal connection here is different from the image suggested by a regression to the state of nature: it was not the sudden decline of the formerly stable order-maintaining powers that led to the outbreak of social struggles; rather, it was the inclusion of the civil public sphere in the process of political will formation.

Although a comparable structural transformation did not take place in all the regions of the world during this period, increasing numbers of demonstrations and protests in favor of democracy and human rights have made it clear that the signals from Eastern Europe have not gone unseen. In South Korea and Taiwan, gatherings of that kind have become standard practice; in the People's Republic of China or, recently, in Cuba, they are suppressed by means of force only with great difficulty. From all this Czempiel draws the conclusion that 1989 was a year of upheaval in world politics that must be characterized first and foremost in terms of the increase of civil society's power with respect to the state. In the wake of the democratic revolutions in Eastern Europe, international social forces—citizens' movements, religious groups, environmental organization, church associations—have been liberated from the constraints of state order to such an extent that they can increasingly enter the stage of world politics as independent actors and give effect to their interests there. The causes of this democratization in world politics are identified by Czempiel in two epochal cultural developments. On the one hand, with the internationalization of societal communication by means of the mass media (above all, radio), there has been a drastic increase in the probability that the practices of democratic will formation prevailing in the West can become known in the most remote parts of the world. On the other hand, through the worldwide increase in the level of education, a constantly growing number of individuals have the opportunity to process the pertinent information and apply it to their own political situations. A further contribution may be made by mass tourism, by means of which mutual enlightenment about forms of government and ruling practices come about in an inconspicuous manner on a global basis.

From an interpretive perspective in which a historically unprecedented thrust toward democratization is in the foreground, the events in world politics of the late 1980s acquire a meaning completely different from the one presupposed in the interpretive approach defended by Enzensberger and Ignatieff: the enormous increase in civil wars and violent flareups in many regions of the world is then no longer the historical sign of a regression to the human state of nature, but the social consequence of the value conflicts and collisions of interest that emerge for the first time today in conjunction with the rapid increase in the power of civil society. In contrast to the attempt to trace the new forms of violence back to brutal human nature, this second interpretive perspective is much more modest in its explanatory goals. It cannot establish any plausible connection between the increase in physical violence in Western cities and the horrendous massacres in Bosnia-Herzegovina, because it has lost the mediating belief in anthropological constants. However, it has on its side more than a series of empirical indicators that clearly verify a global process of democratization that does not fit the one-dimensional notion of a sudden barbarization of world politics. Above all, this approach has the advantage of a political orientation that it shares with the Kantian project of a philosophy of history with a practical intent. If the development in world politics is reconstructed, in all its ambivalence, in terms of the hypothetical guidelines provided by the idea of progress toward human autonomy, then political opportunities for extending human freedom present themselves that would otherwise remain undiscovered or unused. In short, the justification of optimism is not purely empirical; it is also normative and practical. What follows from this for the current situation can be tested in terms of the various consequences associated with the two competing interpretive approaches to the question of human rights.

2

A Hobbesian understanding of international relations was always connected with the idea that the rational policies of a nation have the purpose of securing preventive military and strategic superiority; that is why for many years this doctrine served the two superpowers, the United States and the Soviet Union, as a legitimation for justifying military interventions that preventively establish or subsequently reestablish the loyalty of geopolitically important nations. Enzensberger is very far from such an aggressive conception of security policy, even though he does defend a kind of Hobbesianism for world politics. Rather, his argument applies to a type of foreign policy that refrains completely from influencing other nations either for one's own interests or for the sake of human rights. In contrast to classical Hobbesianism's self-interested orientation, Enzensberger employs a different idea of the state of nature in world politics in his first recommendation. Since the end of the East-West conflict, the worldwide war of all against all occurs largely between collective actors who, like Mafia gangs or fundamentalist movements, have already evaded any kind of state control. Government foreign policy no longer has to be primarily oriented toward the goal of military superiority over other nations; the developed countries of the West need, however, security policies that are able to effectively seal off national borders against international banditry. In contrast with this idea of security, the second part of Enzensberger's recommendation—the proposal to refrain from every form of a politics of human rights—does not follow automatically from the new notion of the state of nature in world politics. It is not clear why, for instance, strengthening the basic rights of minorities in a certain country through diplomatic and economic pressure would not help prevent the spread of international terrorism. In order to justify the claim that such a form of "soft" interventionism under current conditions is fruitless, Enzensberger musters arguments that are not at all sufficiently covered by the empirical hypothesis with which he begins; he must also rely on a critique of the universalism of human rights. Although it belongs to the antiquated heritage of the counter-Enlightenment, this critique finds advocates in growing numbers today. Its central argument consists in the suggestive claim that the moral obligations of universalism are too great a burden both for individual subjects and for nations.

The idea that all human beings enjoy a number of "inalienable" or basic rights that are considered to be universally valid independent of a community's positive legal order goes back to the tradition of Christian humanism. On the basis of the belief that every human being is created in God's image, a specific dignity was conferred upon the individual—one that grants him or her a right (which existed prior to the state) to respect of his or her person.[16] Even at this early stage, where it is a matter of the religious roots of the universalism of human rights, Enzensberger's first reservation applies, but only as a gross misunderstanding. The justificatory appeal to God's image, Enzensberger remarks, already indirectly shows in the degree to which the idea of human rights is too great a burden for the single individual; to expect everyone to be "responsible for everyone else" can appear as meaningful only against the excessive demand to become "more like God."[17] In Christian humanism, however, the justification of moral universalism goes in a direction completely opposite to what Enzensberger assumes. Because all human beings (notwithstanding their individual features) are said to be created in God's image, each of them is granted inalienable rights, to which individual duties correspond only to the extent that they are within the sphere of what may reasonably be expected from the individual. Thus, legal prerogatives or rights for every single individual were derived from the religious presupposition of a similarity to God and were mediated by the idea of a universal human dignity. The question of the primary subject of responsibility was left largely undecided.

With the idea of natural law, a new, post-religious justification of human rights was developed that specified the content of universal legal rights in terms of emerging liberalism. However, it, too, generated further unclarities. The justificatory concept of being created in God's image was now replaced by the notion that every human being possessed, by nature, certain rights that protected him against state interference in his individual freedom; thus, to these individual negative liberties corresponded clear duties on the part of the state to ensure that individuals remained undisturbed in their autonomous action. Aside from the question of whether analogous duties on the part of the individual were to correspond to the individual rights, the new conception above all left unanswered the question of the source of the legal rights of human beings; obviously, it did not make much sense to project onto nature itself an authority, similar to the person of God, that grants all individuals a series of inalienable rights.

It was the mounting weight of these unclarified problems that continued to motivate attempts at a justification of human rights even after the waning of the idea of natural law. Such attempts to clarify the claim that human beings have to be granted a certain number of basic rights, independent of any legal order, which developed from the first Enlightenment version of modern natural law based on reason through a return to theological models but which now take the form of moral universalism. Along with insight into the scope of such universal human rights, in the course of the historical development of this ideal there also grew an awareness of its role in all moral practice.[18] Today, in general, "human rights" means rights that human subjects mutually grant one another in order to guarantee a life that meets the necessary conditions of "dignity" and respect; the guiding notion here is that a morality of social existence minimally demands that all others are equally able to lead a human life.

Whatever the broader justification looks like in detail, it is now almost always developed in terms of the necessity of self-respect, the structure of reciprocal recognition, or the outcome of a fictitious contract. Reference to the legitimating authority of God, nature, or reason is no longer required; instead it is assumed that human beings themselves are capable of granting the universal rights that guarantee each other a human life with dignity. The specific rights that take over this function of moral protection and guarantee depend, of course, on the nature of the specific justification offered; but there is no disagreement among the various models that liberal rights to liberty, rights to political participation, and social rights all have to be included. The primary bearer of the corresponding obligations varies according to each type of human rights intended; to the extent that all are intersubjective in character, they apply to all other human beings and thus entail individual duties, but in most cases fulfilling these duties is possible only when they are transferred to the jointly constituted institution of the state. Therefore, individual governments are the primary addressees of the claims that follow from human rights.

Even this brief overview is sufficient to demonstrate that Enzensberger is on the wrong track with his polemical interpretation of the idea of being created in God's image; in extending his objections against Christian humanism, his first argument against the moral universalism of human rights claims that it places too great a burden relative to the possibilities for individual action. This objection is found in a similar form in Arnold Gehlen's book *Moral und Hypermoral.* With a tone that anticipates Enzensberger's critique in many respects, Gehlen describes the anthropological overburdening of human beings through the "tyranny of moral hypertrophy."[19] As if only updating this polemic, Enzensberger also asserts that belief in the universalist content of human rights overburdens those who have to endure daily television broadcasts of massacres or famines: "If the terror of the images doesn't make terrorists out of us, it turns us at least into voyeurs, and subjects each one of us to an enduring moral blackmail. Once we have become eyewitnesses, we are open to accusations: now that we know the situation, what are we going to do about it? Television, the most corrupt of all media, is transformed into a paragon of morality."[20] It is indeed correct that the uninterrupted reception of war scenes transmitted by the media does not lead to a desensitization on the part of the normal viewer; rather, it triggers again and again a barely endurable feeling of empathy or indignation that calls for direct, personal involvement. Spontaneous emotional reactions of this kind—appearing in a genuine form in children, who of course have no knowledge of human rights—may well be an indicator of the fact that our sentiments can accommodate themselves to the demands of moral universalism. Anyone who, after reflecting upon his first reaction, continues to perceive himself as the addressee of the silent requests coming from the faces of the victims of war, famine, or disenfranchisement, simply misunderstands the meaning of the institution of human rights; rather than obligate the individual to become directly morally involved, these requests call upon the individual as a citizen of a state to intercede, as much as is individually possible, with his own government for practical help. A "normative division of labor"[21] of this kind presupposes—as is required in view of individuals' limited abilities—taking one's orientation from one of the other premises that Enzensberger attempts to call into question in his critique: that, if it is not primarily the individual subjects, then it is nations that jointly bear the obligation to protect and, if necessary, also enforce human rights worldwide. Against this moral premise, Enzensberger summons the second overburdening thesis that belongs to the antiquated legacy of the counter-Enlightenment.

Up until the historical moment of the founding of United Nations as a response to German fascism, it was solely within the moral possibilities of individual nations' foreign policy to promote the observance of human rights. The liberal democracies of the West had already largely adopted the substance of human rights in the catalogue of basic rights in their constitutions, so they were obligated to observe them at home; but because interference in the sovereign sphere of other countries is prohibited by international law, there were no legal ways or means to take action against obvious human rights violations beyond national borders. With the Universal Declaration of Human Rights by the General Assembly of the United Nations in 1948, this situation changed considerably insofar as the prohibitions and precepts codified in international law were placed above the basic rights codified in the individual nations; the process initiated an uninterrupted endeavor to make universal human rights legal rights by creating internationally recognized instruments of complaint, control, and sanction.[22] This difficult project of a gradual legalization of human rights finally realizes the high expectation associated with them from the beginning: the innovative decision to recognize the individual person as a subject of international law. The idea is that the legally guaranteed possibility of entering an appeal or taking legal action is to be open to all individuals as the bearers of rights; individual nations continue to be seen as the addressees of the complementary obligations. Of course, the problems associated with the claim to universality raised by the human rights codified in international law are at the center of attention across the world today. Not only in developing countries or in other non-Western legal traditions, but also, more recently, in the women's movement, people have with good reason raised objections that point out that the interests of all have not been considered in an equal way.[23] However, it is not internal problems of this kind that Enzensberger has in mind in the second step of his critique of human rights; he seems to doubt that it is at all meaningful today to accept international responsibility for violations of rights in different parts of the world.

Here again, wild polemics and pertinent objections are confused beyond recognition, just as with Gehlen. "Ethical universalism," which means here the idea of universal human rights, is held responsible for the hopeless overburdening facing the international community of nations today in view of the ever-increasing calls for intervention. Every intervention in a place of extreme distress draws, as in a chain reaction, a further intervention in its wake, because, believing the doctrine of equal treatment thrust upon them, all the groups affected assert their right to help. This reveals, however, that Enzensberger is thinking only of the one type of international intervention which serves the purpose of protecting or saving groups of the population threatened by death or suffering. Such intervention across borders was controversial in international law but is today justified by an extensive interpretation of chapter VII of the UN Charter[24]; it has now indeed assumed proportions that raise questions of legitimate allocation and gradation.

The reasons for the rapidly growing need for intervention, however, are to be found not solely in the spread of civil wars, or in the ideological influence of universalism, but rather in the altered character of the moral relationship between nations and civil actors. Through the closer relations of communication, the world has grown into a moral community since the end of the East-West conflict to the extent that there are no longer any legitimate reasons for the governments of rich countries through their combined efforts not to answer a call for help from a threatened group in any part of the world. In such a case, military intervention or the deployment of a peacekeeping force—as happened in Iraq, Liberia, and Somalia—is not always the appropriate means for humanitarian help, because of a lack of essential knowledge about the internal situation and of contact with the civilian population; in the future, the United Nations would therefore probably be well advised to seek cooperation with civilian groups and nongovernmental relief organizations in order to provide help in the indirect way of financial and logistic support. However, all these measures already presuppose the recognition of an international responsibility that can no longer be meaningfully apportioned according to geographical proximity with the rapid shortening of intergovernmental communication paths; when today a group of people in a remote place of the world get into a situation where there is a danger to life and limb, their appeal for help will reach the world's public in a very short period of time and with the same urgency as the requests for help from threatened groups in highly developed countries a few decades ago.

Kant was prescient in anticipating this globalization of moral responsibility when he concluded from the growing together of the "peoples of the Earth" into one community so that "a violation of rights in one place in the world is felt everywhere."[25] Nor does it help to link the allocation of humanitarian aid to the degree of sympathy we feel toward those affected. If appropriate assistance can only be provided internationally, who is to make the decision on behalf of all other nations as to what degree of affective closeness to particular groups is currently in evidence? Even the suggestions Enzensberger finally makes to solve his dilemma presuppose the validity of the moral norms he contests. If it is not arbitrary, every planned graduation of humanitarian intervention must employ publicly justifiable reasons. This is a difficult problem in applying human rights, not a matter of suspending them. The antipathy to moral universalism motivates both Enzensberger and Gehlen to dismiss a real problem of the gradually developing world society as another exaggeration of the focus on human rights. In light of new developments, however, there will be no course of action that does not, from the outset, grant all groups on earth the basic right to assistance from the international community in the event of extreme danger to life and limb.

The solutions to such problems will come not from the omnipotent projection of Western nations but rather from the very likely historically irreversible process of moralizing international relations. This process might not have escaped Enzensberger so easily if he had directed his attention to other forms of a politics of human rights; but the antipathy to moral universalism is so strong that he limits his focus to proving his thesis of a dangerous overburdening solely to the case of humanitarian intervention. Enzensberger does not mention the international measures that do not attempt to rescue endangered groups but rather attempt to prevent and sanction legal discrimination; there is not a single line that deals with the legal, diplomatic, and economic means for exerting pressure for the sake of enforcing the recognition of human rights through "soft power."[26] The consideration of cases of this kind could have made it clear to Enzensberger that today a politics of human rights is indeed desirable—indeed now imperative—not only for moral universalism but also for the purposes of *Realpolitik*.

3

In his text, Kant linked the possibility of a perpetual peace to the presupposition of the existence of constitutional republics; his central argument is that the tendency of nations to apply military force will cease as soon as the citizens can participate in political will formation because, in anticipation of possible privations and dangers, they will vote against any form of war. The fact that the liberal democracies of the West did not hesitate to apply military force in a brutal manner when conquering and suppressing colonies made a mockery of Kant's expectations; that is why everyone agrees that "Toward Perpetual Peace" is a product of idealism in world politics. A review of Kant's prognosis does, however, turn out somewhat better after the end of the colonial era. No military war of any kind has occurred between democratically constituted nations[27]; furthermore, in the political nerve centers of the world, multilateral security alliances have now been developed in which the "reliability of expectations" in constitutional democracies has made the threat or use of force all but inconceivable.[28] This formulation does, however, make it clear that Kant was greatly mistaken about the reasons why republics are peaceful. It is not, as he assumed, the material interests of the population[29] that, in procedures of democratic will formation, work against the willingness to engage in war; it is the pressure of reflection and the transparency of decision-making processes. The recent uninterrupted wave of democratization presents the nations of the politically privileged and peaceful regions of the world with a completely new challenge. After the collapse of the Soviet Union, a number of nations joined the circle of liberal democracies and therefore became candidates for extending the various peacemaking alliances; the spread of democratization to the peripheral regions of the world has released the power of civil society, which from now on will play an increasingly independent role on the stage of international politics; and, last but not least, the disappearance of the state in regions with hitherto authoritarian governments brings with it the possibility that new forms of civil war will break out and that these will partially define the situation in world politics for years to come. In this complicated and multilayered setting, an active politics of human rights represents the only means with which Western democracies can attempt (in their own self-interest) to continue the project of civilizing world politics envisioned by Kant; for, in complete contrast to what Enzensberger claims in the spirit of his new realism, only extensive but nonviolent intervention in favor of enforcing basic rights can expand the geographical radius of political civility to such an extent that the new violence can be contained and countered by internationally coordinated activities. Of course, such a (for its part, "realistically" oriented) politics of human rights will be successful only if it takes into account the moral transformation that currently characterizes world politics.

Understood correctly, the politics of human rights has never attempted to influence the situation of human rights in another country from the outside, but has always tried cooperate with the internal forces of political and social reform. For years this has been facilitated by the fact that the ideas of moral universalism have also radiated out to other cultures through intensified intellectual exchange, finding more and more political supporters worldwide. There is hardly any region in the world today that does not have church associations, scattered intellectual groups, and organized international groups calling for political support from the outside to help in the struggle for human rights. With the upheavals in world politics since 1989, this situation has become even more important inasmuch as the rapid disintegration of centers of state power in many regions provides the forces of civil society with a legitimation that puts them in a position to negotiate on an international basis. With the Solidarity movement in Poland and the African National Congress in South Africa as forerunners, a number of organizations and movements have emerged to promote the realization of human rights across national borders, with enormous support from local populations. This emancipation of civil society with respect to what Czempiel calls the international system of nations has to be taken into account in the foreign policy of Western democracies: the field of activity and the operational basis of foreign policy must be expanded. The goal of preparing the way, with nonviolent means, for a global recognition of human rights can no longer be pursued only by means of diplomatic influence or economic pressure on certain nations; what is required is direct cooperation with internationally operating civil movements.

Of course, the inclusion of such forces in foreign policy's field of activity has to be accompanied by the objective of giving greater weight to the local organizations of civil society that promote the realization of human rights without using state power. As in the social movements in the peripheral regions of the world, these nongovernmental organizations of the West often have better knowledge about the internal situation in a country, are trusted much more by the local population, and possess more flexible strategies for exerting political and diplomatic influence than formal international institutions; that is why there is no longer any reason not to include them in cooperation with the United Nations or in the drafting of a nation's foreign policy. The task of such an expansion of international relations of cooperation would be to gradually develop stable zones that are politically civilized—zones that, in the long term, could become nodal points in a global network of multilateral security alliances. It is probable that only such a dense system of alliances, including both nations and social organizations, would be in a position to effectively curb the ethnically and religiously motivated violence that seems to represent the dark side of worldwide democratization. The connection between these considerations of security policy and an active politics of human rights that follows from Dieter Senghaas's recent justification of the Kantian prognosis can be expressed in a single sentence: Only those political communities that regard themselves as democratic constitutional states currently provide a sufficient guarantee that conflicts will be settled in a peaceful manner.

As the success of Enzensberger's essay demonstrates, the Federal Republic of Germany is much further from such a politics of human rights than any other Western democracy. It has never had a political culture whose moral sensitivity to the fate of other peoples or countries was so great that the international condition of human rights could become a topic of public discourse. Neither the struggle against apartheid in South Africa (which filled whole pages in the daily newspapers of England) nor Solidarity's struggle in Poland (which engrossed large sections of the population in France) aroused much attention in Germany, where public reflection and debate on the defense of human rights is restricted to the question of the legitimacy of deploying the German army. In Germany the political imagination is still confined within the normative horizons of an unquestioned Hobbesian primacy of the military.[30] It would certainly improve the normalizing united Germany if it were to catch up with the lessons of the international significance of human rights, which grew productive roots in the other Western democracies a long time ago.

—*translated by John Farrell*

Notes to Chapter 5

1. My initial idea of setting Kant's text on peace over against Enzensberger's model of international relations as a generalization of Hobbes came from an article by Hans Joas: "Der Traum von einer gewaltfreien Moderne," *Sinn und Form* 2 (1994): 309ff. On the contrast between the two models, see above all Janna Thompson, *Justice and World Order: A Philosophical Inquiry* (Routledge, 1992), chapters 1 and 2.

2. Immanuel Kant, "On Perpetual Peace: A Philosophical Sketch," in *Kant's Political Writings* (Cambridge University Press, 1970), p. 105.

3. See Alan Gilbert, "Must Global Politics Constrain Democracy? Realism, Regimes, and Democratic Internationalism," *Political Theory* 20 (1992): 8–37.

4. Theodor W. Adorno, "Reflexionen zur Klassentheorie," in *Gesammelte Schriften*, volume VIII (Suhrkamp, 1972).

5. Hans Magnus Enzensberger, *Civil Wars: From L.A. to Bosnia* (New Press, 1994).

6. Michael Ignatieff, *Blood and Belonging: Journeys into the New Nationalism* (Farrar, Straus & Giroux, 1993).

7. Ibid., p. 40.

8. On the wider context of this shift in Enzensberger, see Andreas Kuhlmann, "Saddam Hussein ist überall. Die neuen Szenarien der Gewalt und die Etablierung einer schwarzen Anthropologie," in *Extremismus der Mitte. Vom rechten Verständnis deutscher Nation*, ed. Hans-Martin Lohmann (Fischer, 1994).

9. Larry Krasnoff, "The Fact of Politics: History and Teleology in Kant," *European Journal of Philosophy* 2 (1994): 22ff.

10. Immanuel Kant, "An Old Question Raised Again: Is the Human Race Constantly Progressing?" in *On History*, ed. L. White Beck (Bobbs-Merrill, 1963), at p. 144.

11. Krasnoff, "Fact of Politics," pp. 32–33.

12. Ernst-Otto Czempiel, *Weltpolitik im Umbruch. Das internationale System nach dem Ende des Ost-West-Konflikts* (Beck, 1993).

13. Ibid., p. 108.

14. John Rawls, "The Law of Peoples," in *On Human Rights*, ed. S. Shute and S. Hurley (Basic Books, 1993).

15. Czempiel, *Weltpolitik im Umbruch*, p. 110.

16. On this tradition, see above all Wolfgang Huber, "Menschenrechte/Menschenwürde," in *Theologische Realenzyklopädie*, volume XXII, ed. Gerhard Müller (De Gruyter, 1992).

17. Enzensberger, *Civil Wars*, p. 58.

18. In what follows I rely primarily on Hugo A. Bedau's "International Human Rights," in *And Justice for All*, ed. T. Regan and D. van de Veer (Rowman & Allanhand, 1982), and on lecture 17 of Ernst Tugendhat's *Vorlesungen über Ethik* (Suhrkamp, 1993).

19. Arnold Gehlen, *Moral und Hypermoral. Eine pluralistische Ethik* (Athenäum, 1969), especially chapters 10 and 11.

20. Enzensberger, *Civil Wars*, p. 59. [Translation modified slightly.]

21. On this concept and its moral-philosophical presuppositions, see Thomas Nagel, *The View from Nowhere* (Oxford University Press, 1986), chapter 10.

22. See the corresponding article in *Handbuch Vereinte Nationen*, ed. R. Wolfrum (Beck, 1991); at a more personal level, see Karl Josef Partsch, *Hoffen auf Menschenrechte. Rückbesinnung auf eine internationale Entwicklung* (Interform, 1994).

23. On the discussion, see *Human Rights and Cultural Diversity*, ed. W. Schmale (Kiep, 1993); Karen Engle, "International Human Rights and Feminism: When Discourses Meet," *Michigan Journal of International Law* 13 (1992): 517ff.

24. See Christopher Greenwood, "Gibt es ein Recht auf humanitäre Intervention?" *Europa-Archiv* 48 (1993), no. 4: 93–106.

25. Kant, "Toward Perpetual Peace," pp. 107–108.

26. See Joseph S. Nye Jr., "Soft Power," *Foreign Policy* 80 (1990): 153–171.

27. For an impressive account of this, see Michael W. Doyle, "Kant, Liberal Legacies, and Foreign Affairs," *Philosophy and Public Affairs* 12 (1983): 205–235, 323–353.

28. On this and what follows, see Dieter Senghaas, "Internationale Gerechtigkeit. Überlegungen im Lichte des zivilisatorischen Hexagons," in *Probleme der internationalen Gerechtigkeit*, ed. K. Ballestrem and B. Sutor (Oldenbourg, 1993).

29. Kant, "Toward Perpetual Peace," p. 100.

30. See Ulrich Albrecht, "Weltordnung und Vereinte Nationen," *Prokla* 24 (1994): 242–256.

6

The Public Spheres of the World Citizen

James Bohman

While Kant clearly argues in "Toward Perpetual Peace" that a cosmopolitan order among peoples is an attainable ideal, he is surprisingly indirect and modest in justifying this claim. Once a state is properly organized by the principles of right, he claims, it will eventually "unite with other neighboring states and even distant states to arrive at a lawful settlement of their differences by forming something analogous to a universal state."[1] At the same time, Kant admits that various empirical conditions conspire against achieving this ideal of peace at the international level. These social and historical facts include the sheer scale of global relations, which undermines the conditions necessary for a republican constitution; the natural discord among peoples due to persistent linguistic, cultural, and religious differences; the tendency of "civilized" peoples to treat uncivilized peoples in "morally appalling" ways; and the sheer lack of will among nations to limit themselves and their right to go to war through a binding system of international law. Taken together, these persistent conditions disappoint the most obvious possibility for legally binding peace: a universal state modeled on a republic is impossible as the institutional basis for cosmopolitan right. Nonetheless, Kant demanded that cosmopolitan right have some institutional basis if it is to be an attainable ideal rather than a mere moral fiction. In part, it is up to morally motivated political actors to create more favorable conditions for peace within each of their republics.

For this reason, Kant proposes a more modest "negative substitute" for the positive but unrealizable idea of a world republic, in the form of "an enduring and gradually expanding federation which is likely to prevent war" (p. 105). As a negative substitute, this federation is not a regulative ideal, like the perfectly universal state; it is not an Idea of reason at all in Kant's sense, but a mere *means* to bring about the *public* conditions for peace, which become effective once nations are similarly organized and governed. Instead of uniting all legal orders and political authorities into the Idea of one supreme authority, Kant's second-best solution of world federalism accepts the fact of a plurality of sovereign, legally constituted powers.[2] It is, strictly speaking, a confederation of independent states, rather than a federation based on a shared constitution or coercive law. Quite surprisingly, Kant does not assume the ultimate convergence of political ends as a condition of peace, as Hegel and other critics thought he did. Rather, he leaves existing political and legal pluralism in place, along with its underlying potential for conflicting standards of evaluation. A federation permits a pluralistic, but also very weak, political order with no real global governance. But does cosmopolitan right, the most diverse and potentially conflict-ridden political context, have to allow for even more pluralism?

What can this seemingly weak "substitute" of federalism do to bring about the conditions of peace? My thesis here is that its main purpose is to create the institutional conditions necessary for a cosmopolitan public sphere and for an international civil society. Indeed, it is primarily the force of the opinions of world citizens, like the opinions of republican citizens in the state, that will bring about the limitations of military power necessary for peace. The prospect of a united international law emerging out of the current state of nature between nations is remote. For Kant, this means that a federation is required. Since he denies any analogy to the governmental form of the newly formed United States, the pluralism of this cosmopolitan association has no real analogue in the republican form of government. In the cosmopolitan case, the supreme coercive power of public right in the state is replaced by the initially very weak power of the public opinion of world citizens, that is, the power of a *critical* public. Even under the conditions of political pluralism, the formal principle of publicity has a constraining influence, if only an indirect one, upon already-constituted forms of political power and civil authority. I argue that this federation creates the conditions for an international civil society of nongovernmental organizations and a cosmopolitan public sphere, both of which can shape and ultimately reorganize existing republican institutions and political identities.

Although the negative substitute for a universal republic is federalism, a federation of nations is not enough for peace. Peace is achieved by something that emerges within such a federation: the cosmopolitan public sphere. In it, the public opinions of world citizens can be made known and recognized in such a way that even the supreme political authorities of the state cannot avoid acknowledging them. Kant is supported in this hypothesis by current facts of political order that he could not anticipate. To the extent that already-existing states are no longer homogeneous, Kant's implicit principle of "one people, one state" has already become historically irrelevant: the cultural pluralism of most current nation states forces them internally to resemble federations with internally cosmopolitan public spheres. Through these federal associations and through the many other ties that now bind national institutions and their public spheres, "cosmopolitan right" emerges because of, and in public reflection on, the conflicts that political pluralism engenders. In contemporary terms, Kant's "negative substitute" works precisely because pluralistic publics may promote peace by reshaping political institutions in accordance with cosmopolitan right. In some instances, they may even create and then continually reshape new, international institutions based on the principle of interlinked public spheres in which world citizens exercise their sovereignty.

1   The Cosmopolitan Public Sphere as a "Negative Substitute"

The public sphere is meant to be a substitute for the limiting effects of coercive civil law on "lawless liberty" to the extent that a cosmopolitan public sphere can now exercise constraints upon the lawless conditions of constant warfare and political violence. An effective form of international law would thus be the functional equivalent of civil law, to the degree that the political aims of nations would be limited by the coercive power of some higher legal authority. The strategic aims of citizens are limited in just this way by the overwhelming coercive laws of a republican state. Why does Kant search for a "negative" substitute? Surprisingly, international law founders precisely on the issue of its enforcement. Hence, the analogy between the civil state and international law breaks down for want of an authority that is higher, yet more coercive and even more unified than the state power that was able to bring us out of the state of nature with our immediate neighbors.

Because of this disanalogy to the state of nature, Kant is forced to speak only of an "unwritten code" which operates in the global, universal community, a code that least makes "a violation of rights in one part of the world felt everywhere" (p. 108). By this "unwritten code," Kant can only mean that some informal and publicly known equivalent to international law emerges via the nonformal mechanism of world public opinion. It is in the exercise of public reason among the citizens of more powerful and civilized nations that "unwritten" but nonetheless universal rights become a public and political reality, as when del las Casas criticized the Spanish dehumanization of the aboriginal peoples of Mexico. Federalism provides world citizens with the institutional means both to make civil society international and to promote effective public opinion. At the very least, a public forum of nations is needed so that such violations can be publicly acknowledged and the rights and claims of the dispossessed can be recognized and defended.

It is also important to see that Kant does not always limit his discussion of publicity as a substitute for coercive law to the moral persuasion of authority. Publicity has a limiting effect upon all strategic actions, both within states and between states. In the First Appendix to "Toward Perpetual Peace," Kant subjects political strategies to tests of publicity alone: if many maxims of political expediency are publicly acknowledged, they cannot attain their own purpose (p. 128). To the extent that publicity can be an eliminative test for international strategic maxims, an effective world public sphere makes it impossible for nations to use strategies which require secrecy.[3] But Kant goes even further. Under cosmopolitan conditions, the very success of political actions would depend on their public acknowledgment. Kant thus puts his eliminative test positively: whereas some maxims will not succeed if made public, other actions *require* that their maxim be made public in order for the actor to attain his or her ends (p. 130). These are ends that can be attained only by cooperative means, through the harmony of various institutional ends with those of the larger public (in this case the world public sphere of all citizens of all nations). If this positive requirement is fulfilled, it is possible to see why Kant thinks that his negative substitute can produce the functional equivalent of a universal community of all mankind in which power is both limited and generated by the norm of publicity. But in order to serve this function, there must be some institutional and non-institutional locations for both creating and contesting cooperative solutions to common problems.

Such a discussion of the effects of public opinion makes sense in this context only in light of Kant's peculiar interpretation of the norm of "publicity." Publicity here denotes a kind of general comprehensibility and intelligibility in the form of communication. A public is a potential audience of successful communication that is unrestricted in its assumptions, and certainly the cosmopolitan public is the broadest possible audience. Here Kant's odd use of the private and public distinction in "What Is Enlightenment?" turns out to be related to differences in forms of communication in this sense. Kant considers "private" communication directed at a specific and restricted audience.[4] Appeals to nonshared religious beliefs or to specific political authorities are convincing only to those who have accepted such claims already; it is for this reason that religious claims are often nonpublic, and not merely because of metaphysical commitments or conflicting values among different religious groups. Communication on this sort of basis may fail when the audience is not restricted in advance.[5] Notice that publicity does not demand that we surrender our deepest allegiances when communicating in this way; world citizens do not practice what Joseph Raz calls "epistemic abstinence," but rather communicative accountability: they must make their reasons publicly accessible and answerable to others, particularly to those who do not (yet) share their opinions and judgments.[6] Such pluralism must then be built into any account of the public point of view that is adequate to the cosmopolitan ideal. Pluralism entails that we give up convergent agreement as the proximate goal of political association, even if the convergence of all publics is still a regulative ideal of cosmopolitan right.

Kant proposes the public use of reason as an alternative to the limits of authority. As O'Nora O'Neill puts it, "A communication that presupposes some authority other than that of reason may fail to communicate with those who are not subject to that authority; they can interpret it, if at all, only on the hypothesis of some claim that they reject."[7] Publicity is, then, a condition of communicative success without an audience sharing assumptions about who is authorized to make claims. Instead of communicating upon such restrictive presuppositions, the "public use of reason" makes it possible for us to address "the world at large" and to form justifications that anyone may accept. In this way, even the very same reason that is at first put forward as the basis of an arbitrary appeal to authority could indeed be transformed into a public reason, and thus a potentially acceptable one. Publicity here refers to the presuppositions of communication and not its actual scope; a conversation among friends may be just as public and open as the reasoned inquiry of the scientific community. Reasons are public only when the audience to which they are addressed is not arbitrarily restricted. Such an audience is thus more, rather than less, pluralistic and diverse in its opinions.

"Public" reasons are convincing on this account precisely because they are unrestricted in two senses. First, they are directed to an unrestricted and hence inclusive *audience*. Such reasons must be formulated not only to be comprehensible but also to permit all citizens to use their judgment "without let or hindrance," as Kant put it. Second, and more important, such reasons are convincing only if there is no restriction in communication *between* audience and speaker, in the dialogue in which assent and dissent are expressed by free and equal participants. The public use of reason in this stronger sense is not only dialogical but also reflective; its use in communication makes it possible to disclose the limitations and restrictions on both reasons and the reasoning process that cast suspicion on its verdict. This is why Kant argued that publicity and enlightenment were interconnected. The absence of communicative restrictions permits political dialogue to be self-critical. Cosmopolitan deliberators then face new possibilities: they can consider alternative viewpoints and new reasons, they

can reject previously accepted reasons and even entire forms of justification, or they may be able to become aware of the hidden and limiting operation of parochialism and authority over their own public
communication and political discourse.

In relation to judgment, Kant describes public reason in terms of
capacity: as a capacity for consistent and "enlarged thought" or for
"unprejudiced thinking," either of which depends on a capacity "to
think from the standpoint of everyone else" and to revise one's judgments accordingly.[8] In the exercise of these capacities in public
processes of judgment, a stronger standard of publicity can be spelled
out in terms of general rules or "maxims" governing the process. Each
of Kant's "maxims of common human understanding" captures some
necessary condition for the public use of reason: that each individual
abstract from his or her point of view and adopt the viewpoints of
others; that each think consistently in revising shared beliefs in light of
new reasons being offered.[9] Reasons offered in reflective judgments
employing these maxims will be convincing so long as each participant also offers his or her own reason to others, while at the same
time anticipating the collective outcome of such a process as a whole.

A world public sphere demands exactly the sort of unrestricted communication that Kant's ideal of common human understanding requires. But it is also beset with problems that Kant did not consider—
indeed, with difficulties as serious as the ones that make the positive
ideal of a universal republic unrealizable. The cosmopolitan public
sphere will not only be the broadest in scope; it will also be the most
pluralistic and diverse. This same sort of radical pluralism is also increasingly the case for national public spheres, as nation states become increasingly multi-ethnic and culturally diverse. World
citizenship ought not to be simply a matter of all the peoples of the
world finally coming to have enough similar beliefs and goals to enter
into a common republic; rather, it should be a matter of achieving the
conditions under which a plurality of persons can inhabit a common
public space. International law offers the most extreme version of this
problem, with neither a quasi-natural basis for community nor an-
tecedent agreements among world citizens to fall back upon.

A public space can be maintained only if it remains open to many
different perspectives and different viewpoints. These conditions

mean that we must revise Kant's ideas of "thinking from the stand-point of everyone else" to be consistent with such pluralism. With the enlarged capacity of thought, the world public sphere and opinions within it become "many-sided."[10] Impartiality here consists not in the abstraction to some common point of view but in the capacity to make political judgments that reflect this multi-dimensionality. Moreover, impartial agents do not necessarily converge upon a single rational opinion; instead they make use of a many-sided common sense that emerges in the interaction among diverse citizens in the cosmopolitan public sphere. In this public sphere, all citizens have rights of equal access to deliberative forums in which their reasons and goals will be acknowledged to the extent that they are consistent with the norma-tive demands of publicity. Furthermore, the "right to hospitality" is en-sured by "cosmopolitan law" and accords to strangers and noncitizens the right to be heard in national public spheres. Besides the exchange of ideas and goods, universal hospitality makes cross-national associa-tions and cooperation possible, as citizens from other states may min-imally expect that they will be treated civilly when they peaceably use their public reason. On the basis of this emergent international civil society (or "universal community," in Kant's terms), a cosmopolitan public sphere forms within each republic, with transnational relations to many other such spheres.

What will world citizens do in the cosmopolitan public sphere to bring about peace? They will certainly criticize existing forms of power, which is precisely how Kant describes the role of the philoso-pher. They may criticize the state and its authority, all the while being "incapable of forming seditious factions or clubs" (p. 114). The odd and obviously self-justifying "secret article of perpetual peace" is the "silent permission" given by state authorities to criticize their actions and policies (pp. 114–115). The power to criticize goes beyond es-tablished laws and tries to improve them; although authorities need not always give precedence to such universal reason, they must at least give critics a hearing. Philosophers, it seems, are incapable of forming factions against the state, because they speak to a universal audience, and it is the philosopher who represents the activities of the world citizen for Kant in "Toward Perpetual Peace." Citizens, too, are guided by Kant's famous maxim in "What Is Enlightenment?":

"Criticize, but obey!" This maxim is meant to assure authority of any kind that the public will leave its institutional bases of power unchallenged. Moreover, Kant demands that discourse is cosmopolitan to the extent that only the "educated" and literate can participate. This requirement is also an implicit restriction on contestation, since this public is entrenched and privileged enough not to want to use its public reason in dangerous or transformative ways. Citizens still may use their reason critically, in order to reform the laws of the existing state to accord with the emerging norm of publicity of such a universal community.

The criticism of existing law and authority, however, cannot be the only aim of citizens in the world public sphere. They must do more, especially if they take seriously the extreme diversity and plurality of any world federation. For this reason, world citizens must also be able to debate, discuss, and deliberate in such a way as to produce public agreements that would be acceptable from "the point of view of everyone" affected by decisions made within any legitimate political institutions. They must produce "pluralistic consensus" or plural agreements of the sort that would be consistent with the integrity of various political communities, cultures, and forms of life which the institutions of federalism not only permit but also seem to foster. The public of world citizens would not just criticize but also be dynamic enough to reshape the framework of existing political institutions to require acknowledgment of the rights of members of the universal community outside the boundaries of its territory and membership. If Kant is right, the fact that citizens of republics also regard themselves as citizens of the world and acknowledge others as such would already create conditions necessary for a new kind of cosmopolitan politics. Absent in Kant is any mechanism (apart from the teleology of nature) that could plausibly create hospitable civil societies and cosmopolitan public spheres in each republic. I would like to propose an alternative (but still broadly Kantian) model that would supply such a mechanism: the potential for a cosmopolitan public sphere to change and create democratic institutions. I argue that this mechanism is plausible even in view of the problem of the scale and complexity of a global society, which remain the main impediments to conceiving how peace can be created by means of publicity. These problems can be solved by a combination of formal-institutional and informal-public mechanisms.

2   The Cosmopolitan Public Sphere, Civil Society, and Political Institutions

To show how this public sphere is possible on the cosmopolitan scale, let me suggest an alternative to Kant's republic: a well-ordered and pluralistic democracy provides the institutional basis for a much more demanding and potentially transformative cosmopolitan public sphere. In a dynamic public sphere, citizens have to be able to do more than debate the issues of the day and form a public opinion in deliberation. They also have to be able at times to alter the institutional framework that organizes political deliberation. Such periods of change occur when new publics emerge, which in turn alter the relationship of citizens to democratic institutions. The challenge here is to understand how the "societal community" in Parsons's sense (i.e., the core of civil society that can become reflexive about the process of institutionalization) can remain open to new forms of association emerging in everyday life that produce the cultural basis for institutional change. The possibility of an international societal community adds a further challenge: how to organize a cosmopolitan public sphere without the centralized and organizing capacity of large-scale, hierarchical, and coercive institutions.

This interplay between institutions and the public sphere can pull citizens in opposite directions: whereas institutions and their procedures constrain public agendas so as to make timely and effective decisions possible, the public sphere functions to keep debate open and to revise decisions that have already been made. This tension between the public and its organizing institutions is constitutive of a vibrant democracy; it is necessary to its stability and to its capacity for innovation. Certainly, each state can promote the conditions necessary for a well-functioning public sphere. But even with well-ordered democratic institutions, a public can still fail to deliberate well; its citizens may simply not be able to produce publicly acceptable solutions to the problematic situations that initiate their deliberation. Such cognitive failures can be traced back to institutional flaws, as when Kant insists that cosmopolitan right will lead to the reform of some republican constitutions. Nonetheless, it is the citizens alone who ultimately must maintain the democratic character of their own political communication. As part of this process, the public sphere itself will very often be both the terrain and the target of much of their political deliberation. The public's concern for itself becomes cosmopolitan when the network and audience of communication transcends ethnic and political boundaries.

Various historical analyses have shown that public self-reflexivity played a central role in the historical emergence of the public sphere in civil society. The public sphere is not merely a collection of spaces or forums, such as salons, clubs, theaters, union halls, and other meeting places; nor does it consist merely of a set of formal procedures or institutional rules. The constant struggle against state censorship and other coercive limitations on expression shows that a public can be maintained only by being concerned with its inclusive and open character. This concern of the public for the existence of the public sphere defines a public qua public. Furthermore, even the small salons historically shared this concern in the form of an orientation toward a public larger than their own conversation. The participants in discussion did not think of themselves as *the* public or as an exclusive elite of aesthetic experts: "They always understood and found themselves immersed within a more inclusive public of all private persons."[11]

This self-understanding and self-reference affects the structure of discussion within the public sphere: issues discussed were of "common" or general concern, in interest, in importance, and in accessibility. Participants within these publics also discussed the public at large: their topic was, more often than not, the public's own reception of works of art, such as their own behavior in the theater, as well as what was fashionable and popular at the time in the reading, concert-going, and theater-going public. This meant that members of the public wrote about themselves; in coffeehouses, they read about themselves, about their tastes, and about the great issues of the day. In both the United States and Europe in the eighteenth century, newsletters about public opinions and controversies flourished; letters appearing in them addressed the public at large, what members were thinking, or their likes and dislikes. These "public" issues included problems of tolerance, civic virtue, and public morality; the letters and articles were primarily self-critical, as were the reviews of cultural events, and aimed at overcoming "ill-informed judgment," "dogma," and "fashion." Thus, the public "that read and debated these matters read and debated about itself," not only about its own opinions but about itself as a practically reasoning public.[12]

This self-reflexivity has a broader function than merely maintaining the public sphere, limited as it is, in any given historical period. Public activity that is the source of innovation and change begins with essentially self-critical reflection and debate. To be self-critical, such activity must be part of a larger and dynamic public process that involves forming and testing the public's attitudes and beliefs. Becoming accustomed to this sort of self-scrutiny and self-examination is a crucial part of the public culture of democracies. When community-wide biases restrict the scope of such self-scrutiny, usually by leaving relevant problems off the public agenda, a new public emerges to press for public self-scrutiny and sometimes for new rules and institutions. On the model of politics that I am developing here, it is this process that is paradigmatic of the public use of reason. The civil rights movement, rather than the Supreme Court, is the exemplar of the public use of reason that can be extended to cosmopolitan conditions.[13]

This capacity for change and innovation in the societal community is an indication of the effective functioning of the public sphere; it contrasts directly with the effective functioning of current institutions. Political institutions, oriented as they are to solving problems and processing available public input, are not by themselves capable of ensuring flexibility and innovation, particularly in the form of needed cultural innovations and learning. Deliberation within institutions usually aims at solving existing problems and conflicts and thus deals with already-existing materials. Certainly, bargaining and most forms of compromise may involve outcomes like "splitting the difference," and such outcomes more often rearrange than change the available set of feasible alternatives. Similarly, bureaucratic institutions have a built-in bias toward nondecisions—solutions that require neither changing how the organization's resources are used nor coming to an explicit agreement through deliberation.

The public, to the contrary, does not deliberate in this means-ends way. The public thinks and acts self-referentially; it changes the conditions of political deliberation by changing itself. As Dewey puts it in "The Public and Its Problems," the public changes institutions indirectly, by forming a new public with which institutions must interact.[14] In the process, institutions are changed in a variety of ways: in their concerns, in their ongoing interpretation of rules and procedures, in their predominant problem-solving strategies, and so on. Democratic renewal depends on the process of creating new publics, which then organize and are organized by the new deliberative institutions they constitute and create. An emerging cosmopolitan public renews and expands democracy in two ways: via the pluralistic public spheres in each state, and through the informal network of communication among the organizations and associations that constitute an international civil society.

As Kant saw in his more pessimistic moments, such innovation can be blocked or inhibited by current political institutions, especially when they are oriented to and structured by the powerful interests of a specific and limited public. There is a temporal lag between the emerging publics (which seek to reorganize institutions) and the already-existing publics (which have shaped the current set of institutions). For example, the relatively weak state institutions that emerged after the American Revolution reflected a dispersed and decentralized public. Certainly, minimally democratic institutions ensure some stability and continuity; nonetheless, when the existing state loses touch with the dynamic public in complex societies, it no longer fulfills or expresses the public's needs. Dewey saw this tension between stability and innovation as the driving force behind the formation of each new public and each new political form. It is a difficult process: "To form itself the public has to break existing political forms; this is hard to do because these forms are themselves the regular means of instituting change."[15] The new public must not only form itself as a public; it must also change some of the forms of existing institutions, such as their existing channels for public input and decision making. Such changes may require a revolution, since, as Dewey notes, "an adequately flexible and responsive political and legal machinery is so far beyond the wit of man." Institutions that do not remain responsive to new publics lose their legitimacy, and this may become true for political institutions with regard to their increasingly pluralistic and cosmopolitan publics.

These emergent publics create new institutional frameworks, which are often radical and innovative enough to constitute new "constitutional regimes" within the nation state. Such changes alter the possibilities of "normal politics," much as the scientific revolutions discussed above changed the conditions of normal science. In the case of such political changes, the source of many extraordinary periods of democratic lawmaking is the reassertion of popular sovereignty against the resistance of rigid forms of institutionalization and entrenched relations of power. Bruce Ackerman has argued that there have been at least three such "revolutions" in U.S. history, and they have crystallized around paradigmatic historical experiences, such as the founding of the republic, the Civil War and Reconstruction, and the Great Depression and the New Deal. These "revolutions," or democratic renewals, succeed in large part because public actors discover the right political rhetoric and critical discourse to initiate community-wide deliberation about crucial events and historical experiences. A contest for public opinion begins, as is evident from the enormous struggles and conflicts that precede every such transformation. Once public opinion becomes contested, possibilities for public deliberation emerge outside the normal channels of institutions. In a vibrant public sphere with an international civil society, these channels may often be cosmopolitan. It is not unusual for such periods of what Ackerman calls "constitutional politics" to be characterized by moral appeals, which are often said to be "higher" than existing law and which draw attention to existing injustice. In these case, the public declares its sovereignty not simply by influencing existing institutions, but by creating new frameworks in which to organize itself. To make violations of human rights public is precisely to make such a moral appeal that questions the legitimacy and sovereignty of current institutions. In these terms, Kant is postulating something like periods of "cosmopolitan politics" among the enlightened publics of each republic. But, as opposed to Kant's view, such a politics questions the sovereignty of nations, even if such a politics affirms the sovereignty of citizens, now citizens of the world.

If it is to fulfill its innovative role, the public sphere has to be rooted in a healthy civil society in which voluntary associations provide individuals with an arena for experimentation and with potential audiences to whom they can begin to articulate their experiences and needs. Experiments in wider forms of international association require both a plurality of interlocking publics and a civic public sphere that encompasses them all. After formulating their way of looking at the problem in their voluntary associations, world citizens can then address the cosmopolitan public sphere, the broadest possible forum for the exchange of arguments and perspectives. This interchange among publics and institutions means that the public sphere must be relatively free of community-wide biases and serious blockages in communication. The cosmopolitan public organized in world civil society must understand itself as maintaining this openness and inclusiveness in communication; it must be possible for new publics to emerge, to place new themes and issues on the public agenda, and to challenge current public understandings. What does this understanding of the interaction between the public and political institutions suggest about the cosmopolitan public sphere? Isn't the public of world citizens too large and unyielding to perform these innovative functions? The main problem is that we have not yet freed the conception of the public sphere from the intrinsically limited model of the town meeting.

3 The Cosmopolitan Public Sphere: The "Phantom" World Public?

In large-scale, complex societies, the mass media have replaced the reading public of the eighteenth century. Where once writers addressed an educated, reading public, new media have come to play a central role in the dissemination of arguments and information. Even with these effective means of reaching a wide audience, cosmopolitan democracy based on global telecommunication is a technological pipe dream. Nonetheless, it is crucial for the emergence of a cosmopolitan public sphere that the media not be controlled or restricted by powerful social interests, lest the larger public sphere become less receptive to the novel forms of deliberation produced by the emerging challengers within the civil societies of various states. The civic public sphere and the formal deliberative institutions connected to it thus depend on the innovation of smaller associations which emerge around widely perceived problematic situations and which contest the interpretation of crucial events. Citizens replace their current understandings when collective actors, such as social movements, become challengers that contest the dominant way of looking at a problem and create an audience that will listen to them. These new understandings, in turn, define a new public, with its new ordering of concerns and appropriate collective forms of action. Under certain conditions, these publics can cross existing institutional borders and become cosmopolitan.

I have argued that in democracies a pluralistic public sphere plays a crucial role in deliberation, particularly as a source of change and innovation. Its existence is a normative postulate of public discourse: it is the indefinite and unseen gallery toward which one's communication is directed. This public is the collective body of all citizens, but there is no reason why it could not also be the Kantian "world at large," which contains the viewpoint of "everyone else." In this sense, we can speak of world public opinion, and of various ways in which even this largest of publics may be politically organized. But what is this public at large? In complex societies, it may be difficult to see this public as anything more than an abstraction, a place holder, an episodic event (as Hannah Arendt thought) or even a "phantom" (as Walter Lippmann put it). Indeed, Habermas has recently argued that it is only a "structure of communication," an anonymous and subjectless network of communication and discourse.

Certainly, some public at large can form itself into a majority within current institutional arrangements. But the public at large also plays a functional role in the constant interplay between large institutions, such as that between the democratic state and its sovereign citizens—an interplay that has produced changes in political forms such as universal suffrage. If the civic public is a phantom, it is because we have inherited substantialistic ways of thinking about the public that are not appropriate to large nation states. Rather, as Dewey notes, our conceptions of democracy are too often limited to "local town meeting ideas and practices." For Dewey, the public now seems "amorphous and unarticulated . . . as uncertain about its own whereabouts as philosophers since Hume have been about the residence and make-up of the self."[16] In the place of a large and unmanageable assembly, Dewey thinks about the democratic public as a series of local communities within a larger societal community. This is how we ought to conceive of the cosmopolitan public sphere as well, against the background of existing institutional structures that are sufficient for organizing and focusing international civil society around issues of common concern.

Reconceiving the public on a large scale involves the seeming contradiction between the openness of a town meeting and the closed and inaccessible character of large institutions. The problem is that global institutions are international and not cosmopolitan; they are based on negotiating interests among nation states and their representatives, so they are only very indirectly accessible to democratic input. In such meta-institutions, citizens are not sovereign—states are. But not all transnational institutions need to follow this model. The European Parliament already bypasses states in assigning policy decisions to its representatives. Moreover, under proposed ideas of European unity, this parliament can deliberate and set policy. Rather than being an inaccessible bureaucracy, this parliament may become a focus for the organization of collective action in European civil society. When the European Parliament debates farm policy, the civil society concerned with such issues (farmers' associations, ecology groups, and so on) can organize around such debates, attempting to influence not only the representatives in parliament but also the citizenry that elects them. In this case, then, it is possible to see how a cosmopolitan public can begin to be organized by, and in turn reorganize, a deliberative institution. International civil society is not enough; it is too punctual and too divided spatially and temporally to effect decisions. Only the cosmopolitan public sphere can become the location for the public use of reason by international civil society. This public sphere influences the deliberation in existing institutions; but such institutions may not yet exist, or may not exist in a form that could organize public opinion internationally. In this case, it is up to the international associations to engage in the transnational politics of cosmopolitan institution building, much as diverse regional groups formed themselves into the publics of emerging nations.

Once organized around international deliberative institutions, a public sphere of democratically organized international associations could shift the location of sovereignty in the international sphere from nations back to citizens. These citizens would then be world citizens.

In complex societies, public deliberation is mediated not only by the powerful institutions of the state but also by the mass media, which have the capacity to reach a large and indefinite audience. As difficult as it is to separate the idea of democratic participation from the town meeting model, it is also difficult to imagine the public sphere without modeling it on the circulation of printed material.[17] There seems to be little interaction between the public and the media that is analogous to the sort that the constitution guarantees between the public and state institutions. Certainly, there is much less accountability to citizens over the systems of meaning and the purposes that the media embody. This lack of public accountability poses a threat to Kant's negative substitute that he could not possibly have considered: media institutions are the only means powerful enough to achieve a cosmopolitan public sphere, although they are currently not part of it. With some exceptions, these institutions are not concerned about their cosmopolitan publicity, nor do they consider themselves part of international civil society. Nonetheless, such media are conceivable as channels by which to appeal to an indefinitely large audience and by which social movements in civil society may gain and structure international public attention to shared problems.

So what is the answer to Lippmann's question: Where is the "phantom" public in complex, pluralist, cosmopolitan societies? It is certainly the case that the civic public is organized for decision making by political institutions. Transnational institutions must be constructed to fulfill such a function for international civil society. The cosmopolitan public sphere is not merely a structure but an ongoing process: the process by which emerging collective actors address the audience of world citizens and, in so doing, change the institutions that organize the public into majorities. Cosmopolitan social critics and international collective actors may participate in the emergence of new publics, keeping democracy vital and its decision-making organizations flexible. The close connection between the emergence of new publics and processes of change should not be surprising. In order to remain democratic and open to popular renewal, large-scale, and complex societies require institutional learning in open, dynamic, and pluralist forms of public deliberation. Even if innovations begin within international nongovernmental organizations and experimental voluntary associations, they create the communicative networks necessary for a world public sphere in which all citizens participate in global planning and self-governance. Such planning may be the only way to produce cooperative agreements on pressing economic and ecological problems whose interdependencies make it impossible for one set of institutions to solve on its own. These agreements will be forged as the many public spheres of cosmopolitan citizens become linked in moments of transnational yet democratic sovereignty. Only then is the cosmopolitan public not the "phantom," essentially passive and obedient public, which Kant understood as a mere gallery of spectators viewing the passing world spectacle.

Conclusion

One of the main insights of "Toward Perpetual Peace" is that non-intentional but publicly operating mechanisms are making the emergence of an international institutional framework inevitable. The analysis I have just provided substitutes for Kant's natural teleology various social and historical processes of globalization—processes that already make a form of cosmopolitan right a necessary component of multiethnic and multicultural nation states. Two main problems remain for citizens to solve in such a public sphere. The first problem is the potential for conflict that is an unavoidable consequence of cultural pluralism. In such public spheres, citizens do not merely criticize existing forms of power and authority; they try to understand and recognize one another and to peaceably work out solutions to their conflicts. Such solutions must fulfill two main criteria: they must preserve the diversity and plurality necessary for a cosmopolitan order while at the same time making common citizenship and overlapping agreements among plural groups possible on the basis of publicity. In this way, world citizenship can solve the problem of conflict, at least insofar as there is a space in which citizens can come to understand one another, work out their differences, and create new institutions whose deliberations can be influenced by the many cosmopolitan public spheres of international civil society.

The second and perhaps the more difficult problem is how to enact and then practice democratic sovereignty on a cosmopolitan scale. It would seem that such institutions must be invested with powers even greater than those of the nation state if they are to solve international problems such as the current ecological and economic crises. The primary responsibility of federalist institutions is to create the conditions for a world public sphere and to permit an international civil society to flourish. The cosmopolitan public sphere will also be the place for working out the political forms of cooperation needed to solve such problems and for finding the mechanisms for limiting the powerful institutions that may solve international problems only at the price of overwhelming current forms of democratic sovereignty. My argument is that the problem of democratic sovereignty can be solved by international collective actors emerging out of civil society and gaining the attention of the cosmopolitan public.

Viewed ahistorically, the problems of establishing a just set of international institutions and a free and open world public sphere seem intractable and overcomplex. However, such difficulties seem less overwhelming in view of the fact that cosmopolitan public spheres already exist. At a certain scale, and as a consequence of certain historical processes of globalization, all public spheres eventually become so pluralist that they are as a matter of fact already cosmopolitan. The "negative substitute" that Kant proposes can then perform its function in maintaining the peace, once each civic public sees itself as a part of the web of interconnected public spheres that includes all of humanity and begins to reshape itself and its institutions accordingly. The federalism that enables peace is the federation of international societal communities within a cosmopolitan public sphere. In this sense, cosmopolitan democracy is not a mere ideal. It is also a practical way of solving problems of international cooperation while avoiding the dilemmas of universality and particularity that characterize many of the current debates about international law and human rights. Like Kant's proposals in "Toward Perpetual Peace," the frameworks for these actual institutions have been plagued by these dilemmas, mainly because they have never really tried to institutionalize democratic legitimacy as a basic principle of cosmopolitan right. No other standard of legitimacy passes the tests of publicity. Achieving such a democratic basis for international politics still remains the task of the world citizen.

Notes to Chapter 6

1. Immanuel Kant, "Toward Perpetual Peace," in *Kant's Political Writings*, ed. H. Reiss (Cambridge University Press, 1970), p. 123. Page references in the text are to this translation. Because the translation is not consistent in its use of key terms having to do with the nuances of the German word *Recht*, I have revised it significantly in several instances.

2. Richard Falk calls for new forms of "law creation and law application" to emerge out of international civil society. This demand cannot succeed if the current nation-state system is left in place, while a new level of law making that is both cosmopolitan and democratic is simply laid on top. While new forms of law are always possible in the future, they have to resolve persistent enforcement problems at the international level. In this respect, I agree with Kant that a federation is all that can be expected; nonetheless, the federal unity itself can be weak or strong depending on the strength of the connections of international civil society. See Richard Falk, "The World Order Between Inter-State Law and the Law of Humanity: the Role of Civil Society Institutions," in *Cosmopolitan Democracy*, ed. D. Archibugi and D. Held (Polity, 1994).

3. Kant clearly overestimates the effects of publicity here. Consider how strategies such as Mutually Assured Destruction are not only consistent with being made public, but even demand publicity in order to succeed.

4. Kant, "What Is Enlightenment?" in *Kant's Political Writings*, p. 38ff.

5. For a full development of this interpretation of Kantian publicity and its foundational role in the critique of reason, see O'Nora O'Neill, *Constructions of Reason* (Cambridge University Press, 1989), pp. 42–48.

6. Joseph Raz, "Facing Diversity: The Case for Epistemic Abstinence," *Philosophy and Public Affairs* 19 (1990): 3–46.

7. O'Neill, *Constructions of Reason, p. 34.*

8. Kant's maxims are in section 49 of the *Critique of Judgment*. For a clear discussion of the political implication of Kant's notion of universal judgment see Hannah Arendt, *Lectures on Kant's Political Philosophy* (University of Chicago Press, 1982), p. 72ff. For a useful discussion of the themes of communication and the central role of publicity throughout Kant's works, see Hans Saner, *Kant's Political Thought* (University of Chicago Press, 1983).

9. Kant, *Critique of Judgment*, section 49. Seyla Benhabib argues that the capacity for enlarged thought is central to the intersubjective interpretation of Kant; but the maxim of seeing things "from the standpoint of everyone else" is not necessarily intersubjective. Moreover, it is not an account of judgment (but the basis for certain judgments in

common sense) and hence only indirectly related to deliberation. See Benhabib, *Situating the Self* (Routledge, 1992), p. 136ff.

10. Besides Arendt's *Lectures on Kant's Political Philosophy*, where this form of judgment is the main theme, see also her *Life of the Mind: Willing*, volume II (Harcourt Brace and Jovanovich, 1978), p. 242ff.

11. Jürgen Habermas, *The Structural Transformation of the Public Sphere* (MIT Press, 1989), p. 37. For a similar analysis of the North American case (where social equality in the public sphere was less a purely counterfactual assumption than in Europe), see Michael Warner, *The Letters of the Republic* (Harvard University Press, 1990).

12. Ibid., p. 43.

13. On the Supreme Court as such an exemplar within a well-ordered democratic society, see John Rawls, *Political Liberalism* (Columbia University Press, 1993), p. 231ff.

14. John Dewey, "The Public and Its Problems," in *The Later Works of John Dewey, 1925–1953*, volume 2 (Southern Illinois University Press, 1984), pp. 245–246. For an excellent treatment of Dewey's account of the relation of publics to the institutions that organize them, see Robert Westbrook, *John Dewey and American Democracy* (Cornell University Press, 1991), p. 302ff.

15. Dewey, "The Public and Its Problems," p. 255.

16. Ibid., p. 308.

17. Habermas, *Structural Transformation of the Public Sphere, part II.*

7

On the Idea of a Reasonable Law of Peoples

Thomas McCarthy

The central idea in Kant's conception of enlightenment is that of submitting all claims to authority to the free examination of reason: "Reason depends on this freedom for its very existence. For reason has no dictatorial authority; its verdict is always simply the agreement of free citizens, of whom each one must be permitted to express, without let or hindrance, his objection or even his veto."[1] By this means, authority deriving from reasoned agreement among individuals, each relying on his or her own independent judgment, is gradually to displace authority deriving chiefly from tradition, status, office, or might, in both theoretical and practical matters. The form this public encounter takes is critique: "Our age is, in especial degree, the age of criticism [*Kritik*], and to criticism everything must submit. Religion through its sanctity, and law-giving through its majesty, may seek to exempt themselves from it. But they then awaken just suspicion and cannot claim the same respect which reason accords only to that which has been able to sustain the test of free and open examination."[2] "Nothing," insists Kant, "is so important through its usefulness, nothing so sacred, that it may be exempted from this searching examination, which knows no respect for persons."[3]

Behind my remarks here lies a concern with whether this is still a viable conception of enlightenment critique, not in general but in regard to political matters, and more specifically in regard to matters of international justice. This concern has been given a new salience by the recent turn in John Rawls's long path from his starting point in

Kant's practical philosophy: Rawls's second major work, *Political Liberalism* (1993), takes him much further from Kant's enlightenment project than did his first, *A Theory of Justice* (1971).[4] And he is quite clear about the main reason for this, which he calls "the fact of reasonable pluralism." The irreducible plurality of religious, philosophical, and moral views of the meaning and value of human life makes it necessary, in his view, to construct a purely political conception of justice that "stands free" of "comprehensive doctrines" of any sort. In his Oxford Amnesty Lecture, "The Law of Peoples,"[5] Rawls extends this conception to the domain of *Völkerrecht* that Kant dealt with in his essay on "perpetual peace," thereby distancing himself even more from Kantian and neo-Kantian approaches to the theory of justice.

In what follows, I analyze and criticize Rawls's recent turn and suggest a more Kantian strategy for dealing with the problems of pluralism that prompted it. First, however, I will reiterate very briefly what Kant understood by ideas and ideals of reason, as that will figure in my argument.

1

In relation to theoretical inquiry, Kant explained, "ideas of reason" can function only heuristically, as "regulative ideas" that spur us on to ever deeper explanations and ever-broader systematizations. The fundamental error of metaphysics is to understand this drive beyond the conditioned, the partial, the imperfect as if the unconditioned, the totality, the perfect have been or could be achieved—that is, to mistake what is merely regulative for constitutive. This is not to say that ideas of reason are meaningless, but only that we cannot grasp them theoretically or even have determinate knowledge of them. Rather, we have to think of them in relation to practice—here the practice of theoretical inquiry. In this sphere they serve to organize, guide, and constrain our thinking by heuristically projecting a consistent, coherent, systematic unity of knowledge. However, the synthesis of such unity from the multiplicity and diversity of experience and judgment is never simply given [*gegeben*]; it is always and forever a task [*aufgegeben*].

But I am less interested here in the role of reason in the conduct of inquiry than in its role in the conduct of life—that is, in Kant's treatment of ideas of *practical* reason. They too generate principles of systematic unity, only now it is the unity of rational beings under common laws they give to themselves. A major difference here is that these ideas are not merely indirectly practical; they are directly related to action, indicating what we ought to do or aim at. The principles they generate, however, are purely formal; they receive their content only through being situationally applied by moral agents. In this sense, they too are indeterminate: they require filling in with concrete moral experience, deliberation, and judgment in particular moral circumstances. Thus, the idea of persons as ends in themselves, the ideal (i.e., idea *in individuo*) of a kingdom of ends as an association of free and equal rational beings under universal laws they give to themselves, the idea of right as the maximum freedom of each so far as this is compatible with a like freedom for all under general laws, the idea of an original (social) contract as based in the united (general) will of a people, and the idea of a cosmopolitan society in which right and justice are secured internationally all function as general constraints upon and orientations for action in particular circumstances. That is to say, in practice they have to be ongoingly contextualized as changing circumstances demand.

There is no need here to spell out the philosophical problems that have arisen with the conception of reason at the heart of Kant's enlightenment project. In brief, the naturalism, historicism, pragmatism, and pluralism of the last 150 years have made the detranscendentalizing and decentering of Kantian reason unavoidable. The residue of metaphysics in the noumenal/phenomenal split that undergirds it, the dominance of mentalism in the design and execution of its critique, and the subordination of diversity built into its aspiration to unity are no longer tenable. "Pure" reason has had to make fundamental and lasting concessions to the impurities of language and culture, temporality and history, practice and interest, body and desire. More specifically, Kant's notion of using one's own reason, of thinking for oneself, has to be tempered with a recognition of the ineliminable background of what is always already taken for granted in doing so—the preconceptions, prejudgments, preunderstandings, and the like that inform any rational undertaking. His stress on agreement and consensus, especially on the "united will" of a people as the source of the legitimacy of its laws, has to be tempered with an acknowledgment of persistent reasonable disagreements in theory and practice. And his idealized conception of the public use of reason has to be tempered with a heightened awareness of the significance of context and audience in assessing the strength of reasons and the cogency of arguments. It is an appreciation of just such "burdens of reason" or "judgment" that has led Rawls to turn decisively away from Kant in his more recent work.

2

"Reasonable persons," Rawls tells us in a Kantian tone, "desire for its own sake a social world in which they, as free and equal, can cooperate with others on terms all can accept" (*Political Liberalism*, p. 50). But the other defining aspect of the "reasonable," as Rawls understands it, is a "willingness to recognize the burdens of judgment and to accept their consequences for the use of public reason in directing the legitimate exercise of public power in a constitutional regime" (*PL*, p. 54). Recognizing the burdens of judgment means understanding why reasonable disagreements among reasonable persons are not only possible but probable—that is, why they are a normal result of the free use of reason, even in the long run and with all things considered. In light of the many sources or causes of such disagreement, it is unreasonable to expect that "conscientious persons with full powers of reason, even after free discussion, will all [always] arrive at the same conclusions" (*PL*, p. 58). Stylizing somewhat, we might regard these two basic aspects of the reasonable as standing in a tension roughly analogous to that between the two standpoints Kant distinguishes in the *Groundwork* and elsewhere. As rational agents, we want to justify our actions to others on grounds they could all rationally accept. As spectators or observers, however, we note the fact of reasonable pluralism and anticipate that some of the reasons acceptable to us will be unacceptable to others. How are we to combine these two points of view on public justification? Rawls's strategy is to discount for the pluralism in advance, so to speak, by restricting the "political conception of justice" to the ambit of an "overlapping consensus": "Justice as fairness aims at uncovering a public basis of justification on questions of

political justice given the fact of reasonable pluralism. Since the justification is addressed to others, it proceeds from what is, or can be,
held in common; and so we begin from shared fundamental ideas
implicit in the public political culture in the hope of developing from
them a political conception that can gain free and reasoned agreement in judgment, this agreement being stable in virtue of its gaining
the support of an overlapping consensus of reasonable comprehensive doctrines" (*PL*, p. 63). The "practical aim" of attaining a public
basis of justification (*PL*, p. 9) motivates the strategy of beginning
with implicitly shared ideas and working them up via reflective equi-
librium into a political conception that can serve as the focus of an
overlapping consensus and thus enhance stability. And, given the
"practical impossibility" of reaching agreement on the truth of comprehensive doctrines (*PL*, p. 63), it seems to follow that such a conception of public reason will have to be "impartial . . . between the
points of view of reasonable comprehensive doctrines" (*PL*, p. xix).
Thus the pursuit of a practical aim in the face of a practical impossibility dictates the theoretical strategy of *Political Liberalism.*

The same concern with consensus in light of the fact of reasonable pluralism determines the scope of what may count as good reasons in public deliberations on basic issues. "Since many doctrines
are seen to be reasonable, those who insist, when fundamental political questions are at stake, on what they take to be true but others do
not, seem to others simply to insist on their own beliefs. . . . They impose their beliefs because, they say, their beliefs are true, and not because they are their beliefs. But this is a claim all equally could make;
it is also a claim that cannot be made good by anyone to citizens generally. So when we make such claims, others who are themselves reasonable, must count us unreasonable" (*PL*, p. 61) or even "sectarian"
(*PL*, p. 129). That is to say, political agents who "insist" in the public
forum on what they take as true but others do not are being "unreasonable." The political actor's desire to act on publicly justifiable
grounds is, as it were, refracted through the political observer's recognition of the fact of reasonable pluralism and emerges as a desire to
avoid ideological controversy on fundamental matters. In political discourse, this idea of being "reasonable" displaces that of moral truth.
"Within a political conception of justice, we cannot define truth as

given by the beliefs that would stand up even in an idealized consensus, however far extended. . . . Once we accept the fact that reasonable pluralism is a permanent condition of public culture under free institutions, the idea of the reasonable is more suitable as part of the basis of public justification." (*PL*, p. 129) And that idea, which functions more like an updated version of the liberal idea of toleration than like the Kantian idea of reason, serves to define the shape of international justice as well.

3

Like *Political Liberalism*, "The Law of Peoples" (*LP*) is marked by an overriding concern with the "feasibility" or "practicability" of political ideals in the face of cultural and ideological pluralism. Here too "the art of the possible" shapes the construction of a theory of justice. And here too the aim of "stability for the right reasons" signals more than a functional requirement of social order: Rawls wants to assure himself and us that his political conception of international justice could be the focus of an overlapping consensus, because that would mean that it was not just a *modus vivendi* but could gain the (variously) reasoned support of free and equal peoples as rational and reasonable. However, as I shall now argue, the disadvantages of this strategy for constructing "realistic" political ideals become all the more apparent as the range of diversity to be encompassed expands.

The spirit of realism is evident in Rawls's starting point: "Peoples as corporate bodies organized by their governments now exist in some form all over the world. Historically speaking, all principles and standards proposed for the law of peoples must, to be feasible, prove acceptable to the considered and reflective public opinion of peoples and their governments." (*LP*, p. 50)[6] And this means that the specifically liberal-democratic-egalitarian content of his conception of political liberalism will, at the very least, have to be watered down considerably. Although the conception of international justice is to be constructed by way of extending the liberal conception of domestic justice, the mode of extension must be such as to "yield a more general law of peoples without prejudging the case against nonliberal societies" (*LP*, p. 65). For instance, rather than insist on the liberal idea of free and equal citizens having certain basic rights, Rawls seeks to provide an alternative conception of human rights that "could not be rejected as peculiarly liberal or special to our Western tradition" and thus would be in that sense "politically neutral" (*LP*, p. 69). Likewise, by dropping the egalitarian features of justice as fairness he seeks to arrive at an account of justice that has the "greater generality" called for in the international setting (*LP*, p. 51f.). In short, since nonliberal societies cannot "reasonably be expected" to accept liberal principles of justice, even a liberal political conception of international justice would be unreasonable to insist on them (*LP*, p. 75), or rather, especially a liberal conception, for such insistence would violate "liberalism's own principle of toleration for other reasonable ways of ordering society" (*LP*, p. 80).

The idea of the "reasonable" seems to have undergone considerable dilution here; and that, Rawls assures us, is as it should be: "Whenever the scope of toleration is extended, the criteria of reasonableness are relaxed." (*LP*, p. 78) One cannot help but ask, then, what remains of the original idea of the reasonable beyond toleration? In *Political Liberalism* it seemed to cover disagreements that fell within the scope of the burdens of reason or judgment and thus could be expected to result from the *free use of reason under democratic conditions*. Now it seems to cover all political-cultural differences, whether they are due specifically to the burdens of reason or not (that is, whether or not they result from, or could stand up to, the free use of reason). Rawls appeals here to an intermediate category between the "fully reasonable," which allows for full and equal liberty of conscience and freedom of thought, and the "fully unreasonable," which denies them entirely—namely the "not unreasonable," which admits "a measure," even if not a full and equal measure, of them (*LP*, p. 63, p. 225 n.28). And, since "well-ordered hierarchical societies" organized around state religions (which Rawls's law of peoples expressly seeks to accommodate) typically fall into this category, that law would more properly be characterized as pertaining to a society of not-unreasonable peoples, and the corresponding overlapping consensus as obtaining between not-unreasonable comprehensive doctrines. Thus, from *A Theory of Justice* through *Political Liberalism* to "The Law of Peoples" the idea of justice undergoes a progressive weakening in the interest of accommodating the progressively broader range of cultural diversity that Rawls treats as theoretically irreducible.

Let us turn now to some of the details of Rawls's argument in "The Law of Peoples" and analyze just how this transpires. As was mentioned above, Rawls's strategy is to "extend" the political account of justice for a self-sufficient liberal-democratic society to an account of justice for a society of well-ordered societies, only some of which are liberal. This extension takes place in two main "stages": the first develops an ideal theory of justice, which assumes strict compliance and favorable conditions; the second, that of nonideal theory, deals with issues that arise from the noncompliance and unfavorable conditions that mark the real world. "Non-ideal theory asks how the ideal conception of the society of well-ordered peoples might be achieved, or at least worked toward. . . . So conceived, [it] presupposes that ideal theory is already on hand. . . . And although the specific conditions of our world at any given time—the status quo—do not determine the ideal conception . . . , those conditions do affect answers to the question of nonideal theory, [which] are questions of transition." (*LP*, p. 71f.) The Kantian echoes in this statement of Rawls's approach are unmistakable; but, as we shall see, Rawls carries it through in a decidedly un-Kantian fashion, such that features of the status quo get projected into ideal theory itself.

On Rawls's account, ideal theory proceeds in two "steps": first the liberal conception of domestic justice is extended to a law of peoples for liberal societies; then it is further extended to include well-ordered nonliberal societies. Both steps use the "original position" as a device of representation, only now the parties are representatives of societies rather than of individuals. And at each step the parties are situated symmetrically, so as to model fair conditions of deliberation among representatives of peoples, who, *as peoples*, regard themselves as free and equal. Finally, it is, Rawls says, "fundamental" to his account of the law of peoples that "both liberal and hierarchical societies," thus represented as reasonably situated and rational, "accept it" (*LP*, p. 2). This is the crux of the matter: Rawls's strategy requires that the *ideal* political conception of international justice itself be acceptable to all "well-ordered" peoples, whether or not their own conceptions of justice are liberal, democratic, or egalitarian. It follows from this that the focus of an achievable overlapping consensus between liberal and nonliberal, democratic and nondemocratic, egalitarian and non-egalitarian peoples could not itself be specifically liberal-democratic-egalitarian. But why should the common denominator that results from such a strategy be called ideal? And why does Rawls think it would be acceptable to societies which are themselves organized along liberal, democratic, or egalitarian lines? Why should they surrender their basic *political* principles for the sake of reaching agreement with peoples who do not share them? In contrast with overlapping consensus in the domestic case, here not only differences in comprehensive doctrines but also key differences in political conceptions of justice are put out of play.

Rawls tries to reduce this tension by narrowing the gap from both sides: (a) by building into his conception of well-ordered hierarchical societies elements he thinks liberals would regard as minimal requirements of political decency (*LP*, p. 69) and (b) by dropping from his conception of a law of peoples for liberal societies (the first step of ideal theory) elements he thinks some hierarchical societies would find objectionable.

(a) Well-ordered hierarchical societies are characterized (1) as peaceful and not expansionist, (2) as informed by a common good conception of justice and relying on a reasonable consultation hierarchy, so that their regimes are legitimate in the eyes of their own peoples, and (3) as respecting basic human rights.

(b) The law of peoples for a society of liberal societies does not include the specifically egalitarian features of "justice as fairness"—that is, the fair value of the political liberties, fair equality of opportunity, and the difference principle—as these are said to be already unacceptable to other *liberal* societies informed by other, less egalitarian conceptions of justice. Thomas Pogge has effectively questioned the wisdom of this downgrading of concerns with equality in the theory of international justice.[7] I will develop two other points here, relating to political and individual rights.

The central claim of Rawls's entire construction, that well-ordered nonliberal societies "will accept" the same law of peoples as well-ordered liberal societies (*LP*, p. 43), retains whatever plausibility it has only because Rawls silently drops from, or pushes into the background of, the law of peoples for liberal societies (i.e., at the first step of ideal theory) a potential source of major disagreement with nonliberal societies: the *democratic* elements of justice as fairness.[8] His sketch of "principles of justice between free and democratic peoples" (*LP*, pp. 51–59) surprisingly omits any mention of specifically democratic institutions and processes. They are simply not discussed at this step, and so they are not problems at the next step, when nondemocratic peoples are brought into the picture. With the egalitarian features of justice as fairness explicitly dropped and its democratic features tacitly set aside, Rawls's central thesis becomes somewhat more plausible. He still has to deal with the circumstance that well-ordered hierarchical societies organized around state religions will accept only a restricted system of basic individual rights, not the full liberal complement.

Rawls requires of well-ordered hierarchical societies only that they respect "minimum rights" to life, liberty, personal property, equality before the law, and emigration (*LP*, p. 62). They are not required to secure full liberty of conscience and freedom of thought, only "a measure" thereof (*LP*, p. 63); nor need they permit freedom of speech as in liberal societies. They may have an established religion with certain privileges, but no religions are persecuted (*LP*, p. 63). The strategic theoretical advantage of conceiving human rights in this way, according to Rawls, is that they "do not depend on any particular comprehensive moral doctrine . . . such as, for example, that human beings are moral persons and have equal worth"; for that is a doctrine which many hierarchical societies "might reject as liberal or democratic, or in some way distinctive of the Western philosophical tradition and prejudicial to other cultures," whereas his own strategy turns on identifying "politically neutral" requirements for a "minimally decent regime" (*LP*, p. 69). This is, he says, still a liberal strategy, for it begins with political liberalism and "extends" it to the law of peoples; but it does not aim to construct a distinctively liberal idea of international justice. Rather, it probes "the limits of toleration" to find "the bedrock beyond which we [liberals?] cannot go" (*LP*, p. 78f.).

4

There is clearly much to give pause in this sketch of the law of peoples. I will not comment further on its details here, even on such non-minor details as the radical diminution of personal, political, and social rights. I want to focus instead on the theoretical strategy Rawls adopts. Both his terminology and his references suggest that he is consciously revising the Kantian strategy the better to fit a detranscendentalized understanding of reason. Kant still operated with a classically rationalist distinction between conviction and persuasion.[9] Holding something to be true was said to be conviction if it rested on "objective grounds" and was therefore "valid for everyone" possessed of reason. It was said to be persuasion if it had its grounds "only in the special character of the subject." But Kant also acknowledged that in practice the "touchstone" whereby we determine whether holding something for true is a case of conviction or of persuasion is "the possibility of communicating it and finding it to be valid for all human reason." It is only in and through the effort to secure universal agreement, he wrote, that we can "test upon the understanding of others whether those grounds of the judgment which are valid for us have the same effect on the reason of others as on our own." However, the desublimation of our understanding of reason and rationality in the two centuries since Kant propounded these views means that some of the factors he regarded as "subjective" we regard as inevitably figuring in processes of rational communication aimed at reaching reasoned agreements. And this makes it necessary to balance his stress on systematic unity with a correlative recognition of ineliminable diversity.

It is this, among other things, that Rawls is attempting to do with his notions of the burdens of reason, reasonable pluralism, and overlapping consensus. But his way of doing it so dilutes the idea of reasonable agreement that the corresponding idea of objective validity loses much of its reality-transcending ideality. This happens, in large part, because the reasonable pluralism that we would expect to result from "the exercise of human reason under free institutions" (*LP*, p. 82) is, in his construction of a political conception of justice, tacitly replaced by a de facto pluralism of comprehensive doctrines that satisfy the much weaker requirements set by his revised notion of toleration.

This means that in Rawls's construction, as compared to Kant's, the ideas of enlightenment and critique play marginal roles. His "free-standing" theory of justice takes no position on validity claims that do not bear *directly* on the content of the political conception as he understands it.

This becomes clear in the "second stage" of Rawls's sketch of a law of peoples, that of nonideal theory, which considers how the ideal conception might best be advanced in the nonideal circumstances of the real world. The unfavorable conditions he considers include deficiencies in material and technological resources, in human capital and know-how, and in political and cultural traditions. "Many societies with unfavorable conditions do not lack for resources. . . . Rather, the problem is commonly the nature of the public political culture and the religious and philosophical traditions that underlie its institutions." (*LP*, p. 77) If the general interest behind nonideal theory is to assist societies "now burdened by unfavorable conditions . . . toward conditions that make a well-ordered society possible" (*LP*, p. 75), it would seem to follow that among its primary concerns should be the liberalization of such public political cultures and the critique of such traditions—that is, something very like what Kant understood by enlightenment. But Rawls does not take this route, which in his view would amount to another variant of ethnocentrism. Rather, he characterizes the problems of political culture in such "politically neutral" terms as "oppressive government" and "corrupt elites" (*LP*, p. 77). This presumably renders the duty to promote favorable political-cultural conditions compatible with the avoidance of ethnocentrism—with one very interesting exception: "the subjection of women abetted by unreasonable religions" (*LP*, p. 77) is singled out as an unfavorable condition we ought to seek to change. But if Rawls is willing to countenance that not-insignificant bit of enlightenment critique, it is not clear on what grounds he could oppose criticism of "unreasonable religion" and other comprehensive doctrines that justify inequitable treatment of other groups identified by race, ethnicity, class, status, or any other marker—especially since it is difficult to see that the burdens of *reason*, strictly considered, are broad enough to tolerate the elements of traditional worldviews that claim to warrant such subordination.

More generally, Rawls's method of avoidance eliminates any justification *in theory* for criticizing the comprehensive doctrines that serve to underwrite hierarchical social and political structures. Thus it unwittingly runs the risk of placing *ideal* theory on the side of *real* powers that be (ruling elites), provided that they are not oppressive or corrupt, and of depriving it of means of support for indigenous movements of liberalization, democratization, and social justice, which are *also* part of the real world.[10] If an established regime satisfies his three requirements for well-orderedness, there is nothing Rawls's ideal of *political* justice can offer to those seeking to change the reality of illiberal, undemocratic, or inequitable conditions, nothing in it to which reform movements and liberation struggles might appeal to justify even so much as full freedom of speech, thought, and conscience, let alone full equality. This is partly due to Rawls's tendency to see national political cultures as each made from one piece of cloth. Thus liberal-nonliberal differences get represented as "us" versus "them." Rawls remarks, for example, that those holding liberal views may argue that the world would be a better place if all societies were liberal. "But that opinion . . . could have no operative force in what, as a matter of right, they [i.e. we] could do politically . . . [for] to affirm the superiority of a particular comprehensive view is fully compatible with affirming a political conception of justice that does not impose it." (*LP*, p. 81) This remark is evidently directed to "outsiders"; it neglects the *internal* disagreements about such matters that mark nonliberal societies today. But even if, for the sake of argument, we accept this we/they schema, do political theorists have to choose between Rawls's version of "political neutrality" and the "imposition" of liberal views on nonliberal societies? Is there no alternative open to them that is compatible with a recognition of the burdens of reason and the ineliminability of reasonable pluralism?

5

An attempt to construct an alternative might begin by relocating the boundary between ideal and nonideal theory much closer to what Kant understood by idea(l)s of reason. On this theoretical strategy, while the burdens of *reason* and the ineliminability of *reasonable* disagreements would have to be built into ideal theory, for they are features of postmetaphysical and posttranscendental reason itself, the reality of nonliberal, nondemocratic, and nonegalitarian regimes, even of ones that satisfy Rawl's three requirements for well-ordered societies, would be a concern not of ideal but of nonideal theory. Ideal theory could then construct an undiluted idea of a liberal-democratic-egalitarian international order to serve as the final standard of justice and injustice in that domain.

Of course, revising Kant's understanding of reason would affect that construction. If we were to follow Jürgen Habermas's lead, for instance, we would shift the focus of the critique of reason from forms of transcendental consciousness to forms of communicative interaction.[11] Kant's enlightenment project would then turn on cultivating suitable forms of theoretical and practical discourse and establishing institutions and procedures to give them social effect. In regard to practical discourse, it would include criticizing and reforming conditions that impede full public discussion of legal and political matters among free and equal citizens. This strategy would, of course, yield an idea of justice that was unapologetically liberal, democratic, and egalitarian, and thus, in Rawls's view, in danger of being ethnocentric and intolerant. But if "ethnocentric" means here, as it seem to, no more than developing and defending a theory of justice from a point of view that is one's own, then we ought to be, in Rorty's phrase, frank ethnocentrists. This has the advantage of leaving the *ongoing* task of finding common ground to participants themselves rather than ceding it to above-the-battle theorists of overlapping consensus. As there is nothing "unreasonable" about proposing and defending views one regards as well founded, we are not forced to choose between ethnocentrism and accommodation in Rawls's sense. There is also the eminently reasonable option of discussing differences with mutual respect and a willingness to listen and take opposing views seriously, to weigh judiciously the pros and cons, to change our minds accordingly, to compromise where necessary, and so on. This approach is no less capable of accommodating *reasonable* disagreement and *reasonable* pluralism than Rawls's.

But what of the de facto pluralism of political cultures that Rawls seeks to accommodate, within certain limits of minimal decency, in his *ideal* theory? If we leave to *nonideal* theory the question of how to interact with regimes organized around conceptions of justice fundamentally different from our ideal conception, there is no need for intolerance or imposition. That is a practical political question, and it has no one fixed answer. Appropriate policy has to take into account ever-changing circumstances, tendencies, probabilities, and possibilities.

As Thomas Pogge has noted, Rawls seems to forget that, while liberal toleration in the domestic case enjoins leaving room even for nonliberal ways of thinking and living, it does not preclude, and in fact presupposes, the adoption of a liberal basic structure.[12] While a liberal society can tolerate many different worldviews and forms of life, liberal and nonliberal, it can be structured in only one way: along liberal lines. Thus, while liberals must tolerate their fundamentalist neighbors, they must also defend liberal practices and institutions against them. Correspondingly, while liberal theory in the international sphere must leave room for certain kinds of nonliberal societies, it does not preclude and in fact enjoins supporting a liberal law of peoples. More generally, while a just world order might, for the foreseeable future, have to tolerate societies structured in a variety of ways (some liberal and some not, some democratic and some not, some more egalitarian than others), it cannot itself be structured in variety of ways. Accordingly, political theory should unabashedly support liberal-democratic-egalitarian principles of international justice and the sorts of global arrangements they favor. And political practice should seek to promote such arrangements in ways consistent with those principles, in the hope that with their establishment nonliberal, nondemocratic, and nonegalitarian beliefs and practices would gradually change to accommodate them.

This strategy brings us back to Kant's conception of enlightenment as submitting all claims to authority to the "free examination of reason," where each is "permitted to express, without let or hindrance, his objections," so as gradually to displace authority deriving mainly from tradition, status, office, or might with authority based on good reasons. It returns critique to the place of importance Rawls seems to deny it in overprivileging consensus. And it promotes a conception of international right that steers closer to Kant's federation of *republican* peoples than to Rawls's society of well-ordered peoples. But it also steers beyond Kant toward a much stronger conception of cosmopolitan right. In general terms, a cosmopolitan order would require the institutionalization of basic human rights, democracy, and the rule of law at supranational levels.[13] And if that is to happen in a democratic rather than a paternalistic manner, it requires improving the conditions for what we might call "multicultural cosmopolitan discourse." If there are basic differences in beliefs and practices among peoples who nevertheless want to live together cooperatively, and if there is no "view from nowhere" from which to adjudicate those differences, there is no noncoercive alternative to the ongoing search for common ground in public dialogue of various types. But that in turn requires overcoming the profound asymmetries of the global networks within which transnational processes are now situated. It is only in the institutions and practices embodying some such cosmopolitan ideal that Kant's enlightenment project could prove to be more than a Eurocentric illusion.

Notes to Chapter 7

1. Immanuel Kant, *Critique of Pure Reason* (St. Martin's, 1961), cited according to the standard "A" and "B" pagination of the first and second editions (here A738–739/B766–67).

2. Ibid., Axi.

3. Ibid., A738/B776.

4. John Rawls, *A Theory of Justice* (Harvard University Press, 1971), and *Political Liberalism* (Columbia University Press, 1993).

5. John Rawls, "The Law of Peoples," in *On Human Rights: The Oxford Amnesty Lectures 1993*, ed. S. Shute and S. Hurley (Basic Books, 1993).

6. Rawls notes that national boundaries are historically arbitrary (*LP*, p. 223, n. 16), but he does not think this disqualifies them from playing the theoretical role he assigns them. But many theorists of international justice have questioned the advisability of building something as morally arbitrary as the system of nation states, drenched as it is in blood, into the foundations of normative theory. I do not see any justification (i.e. construction) for the significance Rawls accords it within *ideal* theory, but I will not take up that issue here.

7. Thomas W. Pogge, "An Egalitarian Law of Peoples," *Philosophy and Public Affairs* 23 (1994): 195–224. Though he focuses on the distributive aspect of Rawls's sketch, Pogge also notes shortcomings in its human rights component (p. 214f.).

8. This suggests that there is a point to Jürgen Habermas's claim that "private autonomy" is privileged over "public autonomy" (i.e. democratic self-determination) in Rawls's thought. See J. Habermas, "Reconciliation through the Public Use of Reason: Remarks on John Rawls's Political Liberalism," *Journal of Philosophy* 92(1995): 109–131, esp. 126–131, and Rawls's response in the same issue, "Reply to Habermas," pp. 132–180, esp. 153–170.

9. See, for instance, *Critique of Pure Reason*, A820–821/B848–849, from which the passages quoted in this paragraph are taken.

10. As Henry S. Richardson remarked upon the oral presentation of this paper, Rawls would certainly want to support efforts of persuasion and reform in a liberal direction abroad as well as at home. I agree. My only point is that he has left himself with no adequate basis for this in ideal theory; and, since ideal theory guides nonideal theory, it is not clear where the theoretical basis for such efforts could lie in his account.

11. See J. Habermas, *Postmetaphysical Thinking* (MIT Press, 1992), and *Justification and Application* (MIT Press, 1993).

12. Ibid., pp. 216–218.

13. For strong arguments to this effect, see David Held, *Democracy and the Global Order: From the Modern State to Cosmopolitan Governance* (Polity, 1995).

8

Communitarian and Cosmopolitan Challenges to Kant's Conception of World Peace

Kenneth Baynes

In this essay I consider some recent objections to Kant's sketch of a project for international peace that have been raised both by communitarians (or particularists) and by cosmopolitans (or universalists). I argue that, while Kant's theory indeed needs revision and modification, especially in its too unitary or undifferentiated conception of political sovereignty, it nonetheless continues to possess normative relevance.

1   Kant's Republicanism and Conception of World Peace

As is well known, Kant envisioned a condition of international peace in which free and independent nation states would voluntarily agree to a treaty in which each state announced an end not only to a specific war but, indeed, to all war. He dismissed what he described as the otherwise "theoretically correct" idea of a united world state or world republic as practically unattainable and claimed that such a conception would likely give rise to a "soulless despotism" in which citizens no longer felt bound to the laws of their state.[1] Thus, contrary to some interpretations, Kant's sketch of a world order that would secure perpetual peace did not include a single world government, only a very loosely conceived federation—a kind of "international society"[2] of republican nation states based on voluntary acceptance of the rule of law and mutual respect for each other's (internal and external) sovereignty.

At the core of Kant's argument for this conception is his claim that world peace is possible only if states first become republican, since only in a political order in which the rights of individuals are guaranteed through the separation of powers, the rule of law, and representative government is it likely that the bellicose ambitions of monarchs will be sufficiently curbed.[3] Moreover, only a republic in which citizens are free to deliberate and express their opinions about public policy—that is, one that conforms to what Kant calls the "transcendental principle of publicity"—will ensure the sort of internal or domestic conditions necessary for realizing international peace.

However, although a republican form of government that conforms to the principle of publicity is a *necessary* condition for world peace, it cannot alone secure the conditions for its realization. In the "First Supplement" to the Articles on Peace, Kant indulges in a bit of speculative philosophy of history and conjectures that "nature," pursuing a kind of "secret plan," would also work to guarantee peace through the "asocial sociability" of the human species and the development of "a spirit of commerce."[4] Thus, according to Kant, nature or providence works to secure, even against the will of individuals, a condition that all ought to pursue as a moral duty: a federation of independent nation states.

Although a partial analogy can be drawn between Kant's idea of the social contract and the formation of a civil constitution in which individuals give up their "lawless freedom" to form a state, on the one hand, and the moral obligation to leave the international state of nature and pursue a cosmopolitan peace, on the other, Kant (at least in "Toward Perpetual Peace") does not conclude from this that a cosmopolitan state or world republic is required. To be sure, the state is also a "moral person" entitled to freedom or independence, but there is no corresponding obligation (as there is upon individuals) to secure this freedom through the creation of a world state. The international state of nature may not be a Hobbesian state of war, but it is a condition marked by the absence of a supreme authority to settle disputes. Nonetheless, Kant does not conclude that states should quit this condition of freedom in order to make their provisional rights peremptory. Rather, only a voluntary agreement to an international rule of law in which states renounce war is consistent with the principle of sovereignty to which Kant adheres. In short, Kant seems to reject the idea of a world state or world republic precisely because it would have to acquire the same powers of sovereignty that he believes rightly belong only to the nation state as an independent moral-legal person.

In the 200 years since it was put forth, Kant's proposal has been challenged from a variety of different perspectives. Most recently, communitarians and other "particularists" have argued that Kant's procedural liberalism—with its sharp division between the right and the good—is unable to secure the sort of republican spirit that, even on Kant's own terms, is a condition for world peace. Alternatively, stronger cosmopolitans or "universalists" have argued that Kant remains too wedded to the idea of the nation state and thus lacks adequate resources for responding to the resurgence of nationalism or "new tribalism" that impedes the realization of human rights and world peace. I will consider these objections in turn.

2 The Communitarian Critique of "Procedural Liberalism"

In a series of recent essays and books, Charles Taylor has expressed a deep skepticism about liberalism's ability to provide the general conditions necessary for a robust democratic politics or, in his terms, republican self-rule.[5] A "malaise of modernity," which Taylor associates with the rise of atomism and instrumental reason and the "loss of meaning and freedom" in the modern world, has been accompanied by a procedural liberalism and a politics of neutrality that are not capable of producing the requisite loyalties and motivations for a strong democratic or republican politics. Following Kant's own suggestion, one might further claim that the failure to achieve lasting international peace and justice is tied to the failure to realize a genuine republicanism at home. Furthermore, the factors contributing to the modern malaise—e.g., a culture of possessive individualism, unrestrained markets and consumerism, and an unquestioned faith in the benefits of scientific and technological innovation—may also more directly impede the realization of international peace. Procedural liberalism thus tends toward a "soulless despotism" (Kant) at home and is not able to produce the necessary conditions for world peace.

Taylor offers two considerations in support of his position. First, the political liberties and virtues required for republican or "civic humanist" politics require a fairly high degree of individual self-discipline and commitment to "a shared immediate common good."[6] In a nondespotic regime, the only acceptable source of this discipline is the citizen's allegiance or "willing identification with the polis."[7] Taylor refers to this connection between political freedom (or self-rule) and patriotism as the "republican thesis": It is an "essential condition" of a free (nondespotic) regime that citizens have this kind of patriotic identification.[8] According to Taylor, however, it is unlikely that the sort of patriotism required will be found within a liberal or "procedural" republic, since this type of polity does not promote the appropriate political virtues and liberties and does not encourage the requisite "love of the particular" or "common allegiance to a particular historical community."[9]

Second, Taylor claims that liberalism and civic humanism presuppose two "incommensurable" conceptions of citizenship and the citizen's capacities.[10] Liberalism promotes an adversarial model of the citizen who is primarily interested in retrieving his rights and who regards the state primarily as instrument or means for pursuing his own good. The civic humanist, in contrast, defines citizenship in terms of political freedom and the capacity to participate in self-rule.[11] On this model, citizens regard political institutions as an "expression of themselves" and share a deeper "common identification" with it as a particular historical community they are prepared to honor and defend. Once again, only the latter conception of the citizen, with its emphasis on the capacity for self-rule, is likely to generate and sustain the degree of patriotism required for a genuine republican politics.

The first response to Taylor's argument might simply be to ask for a more specific clarification of the political virtues associated with his view of civic humanism and the form of patriotism or "republican solidarity" they produce. Does patriotism entail a broader or more contextually specific set of political virtues than those recently identified by Rawls as necessary conditions for meeting the terms of "fair social cooperation" (e.g., civility, tolerance, reasonableness, and a sense of fairness)?[12] Does it imply more than the respect for basic democratic norms, the mutual respect for basic democratic norms, and the mutual respect associated with the more attractive interpretations of liberal neutrality found in Kant or Rawls? An answer to these questions is obviously required before one can assess Taylor's claim that the two conceptions of the citizen and a citizen's capacities are really "incommensurable" and not simply complementary aspects of one more general concept of citizenship. Toleration and mutual respect, as well as a commitment to fairness, would not seem to preclude the more traditional republican virtues, at least as long as adversaries believe that their claims are pursued fairly and under conditions that ensure equal concern and respect.

However, despite the ambiguity that surrounds Taylor's model of citizenship, there are two reservations that might be raised against it. First, at least in the essay I have been discussing, Taylor advocates an extremely unmediated conception of public life: The citizen's willing identification is directly with the political community as a whole and is not mediated by his or her membership in voluntary or secondary associations. Here the differences between Taylor and Michael Walzer are most striking. In Walzer's model of liberal pluralism, the allegiances of citizens are primarily to the various inherited and voluntary associations to which they belong and only mediately to the political state that protects those associations by promoting the general conditions of mutual respect.[13] Citizenship, on this model, is not seen as an "inestimable good in itself," nor is it held to be a component of an overarching conception of the good life that the state can legitimately seek to promote.[14] Further, patriotism is not defined as the "willing identification" of the citizen with the political community as a whole. Rather, the mark of patriotism, on this liberal model hospitable to pluralism, is whether the citizen can "agree to respect social manyness rather than pledging allegiance to the 'one and indivisible' republic."[15] Finally, while politics is a necessary activity, it is not perceived as a "spiritually sustaining activity," at least for most citizens. Or, perhaps better formulated, on the pluralist model there is a need to consider what is meant by political activity, since most individuals are politically active through their participation in the various secondary associations with which they choose to affiliate. Thus, with respect to each of these issues—citizenship, patriotism, and political activity—liberalism seems capable of accommodating a model of public life and a more abstract or "reflective patriotism" (Tocqueville) in which the political virtues required for mutual respect could be secured without requiring the sort of civic humanism advocated by Taylor.[16]

Second, it is difficult to avoid the conclusion that Taylor places quite demanding moral expectations on his citizens: that citizens share a commitment to a single overarching conception of the good of public life ("the highest political good") and that they be willing to subordinate their own private interests to this common good.[17] In contrast to this position, which ties the conditions of a republican politics almost exclusively to the moral capacities of citizens, one might search for ways in which these expectations can be relieved, and in some cases even replaced, by institutional design.

Elsewhere I have offered some suggestions for an alternative institutional design aimed at a more republican and deliberative politics— including institutions designed to launder or filter preferences, to promote mutual respect among different points of view, and to ensure wider and more public deliberation.[18] In this context, I would like to add that these proposals may also be seen as contributing to what has been called a differentiation of internal sovereignty.[19] It is not only the case, as in Walzer's proposal, that allegiances are distributed within a more general framework for the protection of individual rights, but also that various powers and responsibilities traditionally associated with the political sovereign are shared among other institutions and associations within civil society. Such a differentiation of sovereignty is already implied by the principles of federalism informing the U.S. Constitution, but it can be pursued further in connection with alternative arrangements among various appropriate groups and associations. I have in mind, for example, some proposals for a democratic neo-corporatism proposed by Schmitter, Cohen and Rogers, and others, as well as other proposals that call for alternative models of representation.[20] All these proposals attempt to ensure that all relevant groups have an effective opportunity to participate in the formation (and, in some cases, in the implementation) of policies, and that appropriate channels of accountability be maintained. A strategy of institutional design guided by this concern, however, does not entail a rejection of Kant's liberalism but rather a modification of his underlying conception of sovereignty—a point to which I shall return in a moment.

3 The Cosmopolitan Challenge of a "World State"

A cosmopolitanism or "universalism" more robust than this communitarian or "particularist" challenge to Kant has also questioned the adequacy of Kant's sketch for international peace. Motivated in part by the resurgence of various nationalisms and nationalist movements, these more recent cosmopolitans have questioned the moral value or significance of maintaining or insisting too strongly upon the boundaries of the nation state.[21] For some, Kant's rejection of a world republic simply indicates a failure to be consistent with the deeper motivation of his own moral and political principles. For others, the historical failure of the "balance of powers" and the system of nation states to secure peace and justice and to deal with other pressing international concerns (environmental disaster, etc.) Points to the "obsolescence" of the nation state and the need to bring about a stronger "global constitutionalism."[22] Finally, the emergence of less attractive aspects and forms of nationalism suggest that Kant was too optimistic in his assumption that linguistic and religious diversity could thrive in a balance of power between nation states (see "Toward Perpetual Peace," pp. 113–114) and that he did not confront seriously enough the tendency of nationalist sentiment to undermine the sort of republican conditions he considered necessary for securing a condition of international peace.

The new cosmopolitanism or universalism itself has taken different forms (not all of which are equally inimical to the nation state, though all would challenge its claims to undivided internal and external sovereignty). One form is a renewed insistence on respect for human rights that transcends national boundaries and concerns—reflected, for example, in the revival of interest in theories of international justice.[23] Another form is expressed in the call for a "global constitutionalism" in which power and authority is shared among three systems: nation states, international governmental institutions, and nongovernmental organizations and citizens' associations of various sorts.[24]

Without specifically embracing any one of these proposals over an-other, I would like to explore an alternative way to address some of the deeper concerns that motivate them—one that, while remaining within the spirit of Kantian cosmopolitanism by preserving a role for the nation state, nonetheless questions the conception of sovereignty at work in his theory. In other words, rather than a shift from the na-tion state to a world state in which the underlying conception of sov-ereignty remains unchallenged, I would like to explore the possibility of a more differentiated conception of external sovereignty that par-allels the suggestion made above (in response to the communitarians) for a more differentiated conception of internal sovereignty.

In his discussion of Kant in *Power and the Pursuit of Peace*, Hinsley correctly perceives the centrality of the concept of sovereignty in Kant's argument for international peace: "Kant insisted that some other solution [than a world government] must exist—that interna-tional peace must be based on and obtained through the freedom of the state—because he took the doctrine of state sovereignty and au-tonomy to its logical conclusion."[25] In contrast to Kant's position, I want to consider the possibility of a more differentiated and dispersed conception of sovereignty—one that can retain some element of "legal sovereignty" for states (thus preserving their moral/legal per-sonality) without accepting all the powers and authorities that tradi-tionally have attached to the concept of sovereignty.[26]

As David Held points out in his informative essay "Democracy and the Global System," modern republican theory, including recent de-mocratic theory, generally works with an unquestioned conception of political sovereignty in which the state is conceived as "a circum-scribed structure of power with supreme jurisdiction over a territory accountable to a determinate citizen body."[27] Democratic theory in particular assumes a remarkably unitary conception of sovereignty in its commitment to what Held calls the "symmetrical" and "congru-ent" relationship between political decision makers and the recipi-ents of political decisions: "In fact, symmetry and congruence are assumed at two crucial points: first, between citizen-voters and the decision-makers whom they are, in principle, able to hold to ac-count; and secondly, between the 'output' (decisions, policies, etc.) of decision-makers and their constituents—ultimately, 'the people' in a delimited territory."[28] The concept of political sovereignty presumably strengthens this general conception of democracy both by localizing power and authority in a single agency that can be held accountable to the citizenry and by defining through territorial boundaries the relevant group for whom the sovereign is responsible and to whom it can be held accountable. Internal and external sovereignty thus mesh well with this common interpretation of democracy.

However, as Held (along with many others) points out, this conception of sovereignty is barely recognizable in the contemporary world. Trends toward "global interconnectedness" have both modified and constrained the exercise of sovereignty and called into question its assumptions about symmetry and congruence. Not only have the processes of globalization produced structures of decision making that are less tied to the legal jurisdiction of the nation state and hence also less accountable; at the same time, many of the decisions that are still largely made within the legal framework of the nation state have consequences that go well beyond national territorial borders.

In support of this claim regarding increased constraints not only on the state's de facto autonomy but also on its sovereignty, Held points to structural changes within national political economies, to the growing power and maneuverability of multinational corporations, to recent developments in international law, and to the emergence of hegemonic powers and power blocs (such as NATO and the EU) that make it difficult for independent nation states to pursue policies exclusively on their own terms. Held then concludes: "These processes alone warrant the statement that the operation of states in an ever more complex international system both limits their autonomy and impinges increasingly upon their sovereignty. Any conception of sovereignty which interprets it as an illimitable and indivisible form of public power is undermined. Sovereignty itself has to be conceived today as already divided among a number of agencies—national, regional, and international—and limited by the very nature of this plurality."[29] Following the suggestion of Hedley Bull, Held describes the results of these trends toward globalization as a kind of "neo-medieval international order—a modern and secular counterpart to the kind of political organization that existed in Christian Europe in the Middle

Ages, the essential characteristic of which was 'a system of overlapping authority and multiple loyalty.'"[30] However, in contrast to Bull, whose own position is closer to Kant's, Held suggests that the model of "overlapping authorities and criss-crossing loyalties" may continue to offer some normatively attractive features.

Of course, as Held also points out, these trends have not made the nation state irrelevant or obsolete and these trends are themselves highly ambivalent with regard to the values of global justice, peace, and—perhaps especially—democratic rule. Nonetheless, they indicate, at a normative level, the possibility for thinking creatively about global constitutionalism in ways freed from the unitary conception of external sovereignty assumed by Kant and by much of contemporary democratic theory. For example, although a simultaneous democratization and strengthening of the powers of the United Nations in the post-Cold War world remains an obvious option, the idea of a centralized world government with coercive police powers is not the only alternative to the current system of nation states. Other possibilities for global constitutionalism remain to be explored that would bring together in democratically creative ways the existing system of states, international governmental institutions, and a global civil society comprising a variety of nongovernmental organizations and associations. Of course, such a sketch of global constitutionalism raises difficult questions of accountability and democratic legitimacy. Like the corresponding differentiation of internal sovereignty, the differentiation of external sovereignty would have to proceed in a way that would ensure that the actions of various authorities would remain accountable to the appropriate parties affected by them. Such authorities would also have to be constituted in a way consistent with basic individual rights and principles of democratic legitimacy. I have no particular recommendations to offer in this regard other than to point again to some of the proposals for a democratic neo-corporatism. At a minimum, however, the conception of differentiated internal and external sovereignty would seem to require a corresponding cosmopolitan and pluralist public sphere capable of taking up, in different ways and at various levels, problems and thematic issues bearing on the formation of international policies.

4 Political Identity and Cultural Diversity

This reference to the need for a robust, pluralist, dynamic public sphere as a necessary condition for a genuine republicanism in Kant's sense *and* for a cosmopolitan civil society leads back to the question of the appropriate justification for any binding political authority in such a pluralistic society. More specifically, since in a nondespotic regime such a binding authority can arise only on the basis of freely given consent, what normative orientations must members of a polity share in order for a deliberative politics to be possible? This last question is largely a restatement, at a slightly more abstract level, of the guiding concern behind Taylor's "republican thesis."

Although the recent liberal/communitarian debate has provided a useful context for addressing anew many of the issues that are relevant to these questions, I do not believe that either side has offered an adequate solution. On the one hand, communitarianism can be faulted for its exclusionary and/or assimilationist tendencies.[31] On the other hand, liberalism has often been criticized for not endorsing any conception of community at all and/or for failing to confront seriously enough the "normalizing" effects of the bureaucratization, juridification, and consumerization of everyday life.[32] Although I cannot hope to deal adequately with the many tensions between universalism and particularism posed by these issues, I would nevertheless like to offer three observations that might help to set the stage for further discussion.

First, despite the conceptual and practical difficulties, it is important today to continue to insist upon the distinction between a political community (or polity) and an ethnic or cultural community.[33] Although these two conceptions of community were perhaps not always clearly distinguished in the classical conception of the polis, and although for a time they were again united in the idea of the nation state, they embody ideals and values that are increasingly in conflict with one another.[34] The one conception is committed to universalistic rights and to constitutional principles, while the other is perhaps necessarily particularistic and is defined by the presence of various modes of social exclusion (language, religion, ethnic origin, etc.). In contrast to the arguments of Taylor, MacIntyre, and other communitarians, I have suggested that a republican polity need not require that its members share a commitment to a common cultural tradition or an overarching conception of the good. Rather, what is required above all is what Habermas has called "constitutional patriotism" [*Verfassungspatriotismus*]—that is, a commitment to the more abstract principles and procedures associated with the universalization of democratic norms and human rights.[35]

Second, the idea of "constitutional patriotism" does not mean that there is no need to revise some of the ideas traditionally associated with the liberal constitution. "Constitutional boundaries must be creatively redefined and enlarged through political pressure speaking to new circumstances."[36] Similarly, the "domain of the political" should not be statically defined or unduly constrained by appeals to common sense or to the basic intuitions latent in liberal-bourgeois culture; it should be more dynamically conceived in relation to a reflexive and self-critical application of the idea of a reasonable agreement among free and equal persons. More specifically, it may now be necessary to amend Marshall's threefold schema of the expansion of citizenship rights—civil, political, and social—to include various rights to cultural membership. This would mean not only that citizens have a right to associate freely, but also that "minority cultures" within a political community or polity might be entitled to specific sorts of protections and benefits.[37]

Of course, it is quite possible that the former category of traditionally "civil" rights will conflict at times with the exercise of the latter sort of right (for example, in attempts to preserve the integrity of certain minority cultures). But this tension between universalism and particularism within the domain of citizenship rights does not arise only with respect to the cultural and political identities of individuals. It can emerge wherever the multiple and "overdetermined" identities of a person intersect (e.g., between the public and the nonpublic self, among various nonpublic selves, or among various public selves).[38] Here the liberal must concede that there may not be a possible world without any ethical loss.[39] An analogous problem arises when one moves in the other direction, from citizenship rights to international human rights: although from a universalistic perspective any "national boundaries" seem to be morally arbitrary and contingent, a failure to attach any moral significance to national boundaries would appear to undermine the effectiveness of *any* citizenship rights.[40] Thus, once again, a world with no ethical loss does not seem to be possible.

Finally, neither constitutional patriotism nor a recognition of the value of rights to cultural membership alone can guarantee the sort of political culture that is required in order for a genuine republican and deliberative politics to be effective. Not only a respect for rights and democratic norms but also a cultural recognition of the value of cultural difference is a necessary condition for an effective deliberative politics. Creating and maintaining of this sort of political culture is surely not an easy task. It requires continuously criticizing what Marcuse called the "repressive tolerance" of an "affirmative culture" in the name of a strong form of mutual respect. Kant's reminder that a republican government and a critical public are necessary but not sufficient conditions for world peace is thus also relevant in this context. However, this type of political culture—with its focus on cosmopolitan or world values—is also not merely a utopian ideal; it is already anticipated in everyday forms of communicative practice, and with the assistance of global as well as domestic institutional design based on the ideas of "intelligent self-limitation" and differentiated sovereignty it could become a greater reality within our highly complex, differentiated, and pluralistic societies.[41]

Notes to Chapter 8

1. Kant, "Toward Perpetual Peace," in *Kant's Political Writings*, ed. H. Reiss (Cambridge University Press, 1970), p. 113.

2. See F. H. Hinsley, *Power and the Pursuit of Peace* (Cambridge University Press, 1963), p. 68. For a contrasting interpretation emphasizing Kant's earlier remarks (in "Idea for a Universal History") on world government, see Hedley Bull, *The Anarchical Society* (Columbia University Press 1977), pp. 253 and 262.

3. See Leslie Mulholland, "Kant on War and International Justice," *Kantstudien* 78 (1987): 25–41.

4. For a recent account of Kant's view, see Susan Shell, "Kant's Idea of History," in *History and the Idea of Progress*, ed. A. Melzer et al. (Cornell University Press, 1995).

5. See, e.g., Charles Taylor, "Cross-Purposes: The Liberal-Communitarian Debate," in *Liberalism and the Moral Life*, ed. N. Rosenblum (Harvard University Press, 1989), p. 179.

6. Taylor ("Cross-Purposes," pp. 168–169) distinguishes between a "convergent" common good that individual members happen to share (desire for clean air, military protection, etc.,) and an "immediate" common good that is a feature of a concrete shared or common identity.

7. Ibid, p. 165.

8. Ibid, p. 170.

9. Ibid, p. 176.

10. Ibid, p. 179. For a similar contrast between these two conceptions of the citizen and citizen's capacities, see Taylor, "Alternative Futures: Legitimacy, Identity and Alienation in late Twentieth Century Canada," in *Constitutionalism, Citizenship and Society in Canada*, ed. A. Cairns and C. Williams (University of Toronto Press, 1985), pp. 209–210. In this earlier essay, however, Taylor does not claim that the two models are incommensurable, only that a deep tension exists between them. For an even stronger claim that patriotism requires identification with a particular historical community, see A. MacIntyre, *"Is Patriotism A Virtue?" The Lindley Lecture* (University of Kansas, 1984).

11. Michael Walzer offers a similar contrast between two conceptions of the citizen: the active participant and the passive recipient. Unlike Taylor, however, he does not regard these as "incommensurable"; he regards them as two (ideal-typical) extremes that are perhaps always in tension. See Walzer, "Citizenship," in *Political Innovation and Conceptual Change*, ed. T. Ball et al. (Cambridge University Press, 1989), p. 216; see also "The Problem of Citizenship" in *Obligations* (Harvard University Press, 1970).

12. See Rawls, "The Priority of the Right and Ideas of the Good," *Philosophy and Public Affairs* 17 (1988), p. 263. Insofar as it does not specifically include what he calls "participatory self-rule," Taylor would most likely consider Rawls's list inadequate (see "Cross-Purposes," p. 177). However, this term is itself vague; it may not even refer to a single virtue, as Taylor's identification of it with "patriotism" and "republican solidarity" suggests (see below).

13. Michael Walzer, "The Communitarian Critique of Liberalism," *Political Theory* 18 (1990): 6–23; "What Does It Mean to Be an American?" *Social Research* 57 (1990) : 591–614.

14. Walzer, "What Does It Mean to Be an American?" p. 603.

15. Ibid.

16. See p. 272 of "The Priority of the Right and Ideas of the Good." Also note Walzer's preference for Rawls's position over a stronger civic republicanism ("The Communitarian Critique of Liberalism," pp. 19–20).

17. See "Cross-Purposes," p. 178; "Alternative Futures," p. 213.

18. See my "Liberal Neutrality, Pluralism, and Deliberative Politics," *Praxis International* 12 (1992): 50–69.

19. For the distinction between "internal" and "external" sovereignty, and for an argument for greater differentiation within each, see Charles Beitz, "Sovereignty and

Morality in International Affairs," in *Political Theory Today*, ed. D. Held (Stanford University Press, 1991).

20. See, for example, Joshua Cohen and Joel Rogers, "Secondary Associations and Democratic Governance," *Politics and Society* 20 (1992); Ian McLean, "Forms of Representation and Systems of Voting," in *Political Theory Today*.

21. See, for example, Kai Nielsen, "World Government, Security, and Global Justice," in *Problems of International Justice*, ed. S. Luper-Foy (Westview, 1988); Veit Bader, "Citizenship and Exclusion," *Political Theory* 23 (1995): 211–246.

22. See *The Constitutional Foundations of World Peace*, ed. R. Falk et al. (State University of New York Press, 1993).

23. Charles Beitz, *Political Theory and International Relations* (Princeton University Press, 1979); R. J. Vincent, *Human Rights and International Relations* (Cambridge University Press, 1986).

24. See, especially, the essays in *The Constitutional Foundations of World Peace*.

25. *Power and the Pursuit of Peace*, p. 67.

26. For similar proposals, see Charles Beitz, "Sovereignty and Morality in International Affairs," in *Political Theory Today*; Bader, "Citizenship and Exclusion"; Thomas Pogge, "Cosmopolitanism and Sovereignty, " *Ethics* 103 (1992): 48–75.

27. David Held, "Democracy and the Global System," in *Political Theory Today*, p. 223.

28. Ibid., p. 198.

29. Ibid, p. 222.

30. Ibid, p. 223.

31. See, for example, Amy Gutmann, "Communitarian Critics of Liberalism," *Philosophy and Public Affairs* 14 (1985): 308–322; Don Herzog, "Some Questions for Republicans," *Political Theory* 14 (1986): 473–494; William Connolly, "Identity and Difference in Liberalism," in *Liberalism and the Good*, p. 78.

32. See Connolly, "Identity and Difference in Liberalism," pp. 74–75; *The Ethos of Pluralization* (University of Minnesota Press, 1995).

33. See W. Kymlicka, *Liberalism, Community and Culture* (Oxford University Press, 1989), p. 135. For some of the difficulties involved in drawing the distinction, see Bader, "Citizenship and Exclusion, " pp. 223–224.

34. See, for example, Habermas's remarks in "Historical Consciousness and Post-Traditional Identity," in *The New Conservatism* (MIT Press, 1989), p. 254.

35. Ibid, pp. 261–262. Habermas's conception seems to be close to what Tocqueville called "reflective patriotism"—see Mary Dietz, "Patriotism," in *Political Innovation and Conceptual Change*.

36. Connolly, "Identity and Difference in Liberalism," p. 75.

37. Thomas H. Marshall, *Class, Citizenship and Social Development: Essays* (Greenwood, 1973). Kymlicka argues that the recognition of special group or collective rights for minority cultures (such as aboriginal peoples) is not incompatible with liberalism; see *Liberalism, Community and Culture*, chapters 7–9.

38. This tension is thus analogous to what Connolly calls the "paradox of politics" (and "politics of paradox")—see "Identity and Difference," p. 82.

39. See Rawls, "The Priority of Right and Ideas of the Good," pp. 265–266; see also Isaiah Berlin, *Concepts and Categories* (Oxford University Press, 1980).

40. On this version of the tension between universalism and particularism, see Charles Beitz, "Cosmopolitan Ideals and National Sentiment," *Journal of Philosophy* 80 (1983): 591–600. For some differing views on the moral significance of national boundaries, see David Miller, "The Ethical Significance of Nationality," *Ethics* 98 (1988): 647–662; Robert Goodin, "What Is So Special About Our Fellow Countrymen?" *Ethics* 98 (1988): 663–686; Joseph Carens, "Aliens and Citizens: The Case for Open Borders," *Review of Politics* 49 (1987): 251–273.

41. See Jürgen Habermas, *Moral Consciousness and Communicative Action*, p. 201; Thomas Nagel, "What Makes Political Theory Utopian?" *Social Research* 56 (1989): 903–920.

9

Cosmopolitan Democracy and the Global Order: A New Agenda

David Held

The backdrop of this chapter is the rapid growth in the complex interconnections among states and societies. Section 1 explores the new context of politics in light of the end of the Cold War and the challenges to the nature and efficacy of political communities from processes of globalization. Section 2 discusses the limitations of democratic theory, emphasizing its failure to question whether the nation state can remain at the center of democratic thought and practice. Section 3 explores the terms of the analysis further by examining Kant's understanding of political community, cosmopolitanism, and cosmopolitan law. A critique of Kant's views leads to an alternative conception of the requirement of democracy and the democratic good: cosmopolitan democratic law. Kant's conception of cosmopolitan law is contrasted with the notion of cosmopolitan democratic law; the focus then shifts to institutional differences. Section 4 elaborates an institutional program for a cosmopolitan democracy—a form of democracy, I argue, that can address the limitations of national democracies in a global era and point to some institutional solutions in the short and the long term. In the spirit of Kant, I make the case for a new cosmopolitanism, but with a substantially different understanding of the necessary components of law, order, and accountability than can be found in Kant's writings.

1 The New Constellation of Global Politics

Extraordinary changes have been occurring in international politics since 1989. For almost half a century, a system of geo-governance organized around the bifurcation of East and West dominated the planet. Almost at a stroke, it disintegrated, leaving few clues as to what alternative system might take its place. Now, on the threshold of a new millennium, international relations face new opportunities and new dangers.

In the main, the political opportunities that present themselves are still waiting to be exploited. If for a Pole, a Chilean, a Cambodian, a South African, or a Palestinian the end of the Cold War fosters new hopes for the future, for a Bosnian, a Somali, an Iraqi, a Kurd, or a Rwandan the benefits of the "new world order" are still a long way off. While it is still very early to take stock of the advantages and disadvantages of the termination of the Cold War, three crucial issues can be posed to clarify the nature of the current global order:

i. What are the repercussions for domestic regimes of the end of the Cold War?

ii. What changes are taking place in the structure of inter-state relations?

iii. Which institutions can offer a basis for deliberation over, and action upon, global (i.e., transcontinental and intercontinental) problems?

To clarify the context of this chapter, I will introduce these issues briefly.

i

Among the domestic political changes of recent years has been the remarkable increase in the number of liberal democratic states. In the East, the South, and the North, many states have either restored or newly acquired a democratic system. For the first time in their lives, many millions of people have enjoyed the quintessentially liberal democratic experiences of participating in political discourse without fear of coercion and of voting in free elections. Although the first steps toward domestic democracy have in many cases been tentative and riddled with uncertainties, the first half of the 1990s deserves to be remembered as an era, if not *the* era, of democracy. The desire for democracy has been so strong that some commentators—partly out of optimism, partly out of ignorance of the historical record—have ventured the hypothesis that we are approaching the "end of history" (see Fukuyama 1992; compare Held 1993a,b). Yet, despite the increase in the number of liberal democratic regimes, for millions of people there has been no noticeable improvement—and in some cases there has been a drastic reduction—in the quality of political associations.

Paradoxically, while the number of countries governed on the basis of democratic principles has expanded, civil war has returned to others in which it was believed to have disappeared for good. The events unfolding in the former Yugoslavia, the former Soviet Union, and parts of sub-Saharan Africa reveal just how traumatic the transition from one regime to another can be. The horrifying civil wars in progress are the tip of an iceberg of unrest to which even the most historically consolidated nation states are vulnerable. Ethnic conflict and the reemergence of nationalism in Germany, Italy, Spain, Poland, and elsewhere leave little room for an unqualified optimism about the ability of nation states to keep two of their most important promises: the maintenance of domestic peace and the protection of the safety and property of their citizens.

Viewed from the perspective of domestic politics, the emerging world order is two-faced. It has fostered the extension of democracy; however, it has revealed (and, in some cases, detonated) tensions in nation states. By imposing a form of limited autonomy on the vast majority of states, the Cold War suppressed many forms of domestic conflict—at least in Europe. When the Cold War ended, some of the wounds provoked by domestic discord reopened.

ii

The current historical juncture has posed new problems not only for domestic politics but also for the organization of inter-state relations. When the old, explicitly established hierarchy of states collapsed, dangerous power voids opened up in the management of international affairs. Democratic countries have reacted to this new situation in contradictory ways. On occasion, they have capitalized on their rival bloc's depleted power by acting unlawfully (as, for instance, the United States did when it intervened in Panama). In other cases (most notably in Kuwait and Iraq), they have sought a consensus of principle within the international community and its institutions before undertaking specific actions.

Generally speaking, however, it is striking that the increase in the number of democratic states has not been accompanied by a corresponding increase in democracy *among* states. Policy making in the UN Security Council and the International Monetary Fund, and in less formal settings such as the Group of Seven summits, has changed little since the collapse of the Berlin Wall. National governments, both the powerful and the less powerful ones, have continued to act on the basis of their own reasons of state. The explanation for this has partly to do with uncertainty about the rules, values, and institutions necessary to establish greater accountability among nations. But it has also to do with the reluctance of democracies to extend their model of governance to inter-state relations—that is, with their reluctance to be called to account in matters of security involving foreign and international affairs.

iii

The most conspicuous feature of the new international situation is the emergence of issues that transcend national frontiers. Processes of economic internationalization, the problem of the environment, and the protection of the rights of minorities are, increasingly, matters for the world community as a whole. The limits on national autonomy imposed by the balance of terror have now been supplemented by a much subtler, more structural form of erosion caused by the processes of environmental, social, and economic globalization—that is, by shifts in the transcontinental or inter-regional scale of human social organization and the exercise of social power.

A number of fundamental disjunctures have opened up between democratic politics and the late-twentieth-century world: "disjunctures" in the relations among citizens, individual states, and the economic system at the regional and global levels. There are at least three disjunctures worth noting here (see Held 1991).

First, there is a disjuncture between the formal domain of political authority and the actual economic system of production, distribution, and exchange that, with its many regional and global networks, serves to limit or undermine the actual power of national political authorities. Second, there is a disjuncture between the idea of the state as an independent actor and the vast array of international regimes and organizations that have been established to manage whole areas of transnational activity (trade, the oceans, space, etc.). New forms of multinational politics have been established, and with them new forms of collective decision making involving states, inter-governmental organizations, and a variety of international pressure groups. Third, there is a disjuncture between the idea of membership in a national political community (that is, citizenship), which bestows upon individuals both rights and duties, and the development of regional and international law, which subjects individuals, nongovernmental organizations, and governments to new systems of regulation. International law, moreover, recognizes rights and duties that transcend the claims of nation states. Although such rights and duties may lack coercive powers of enforcement, they have far-reaching consequences.

Democratic politics has traditionally presupposed the idea of a "national community of fate"—a community that rightly governs itself and determines its future. This idea is certainly challenged, if not increasingly undermined, by the pattern of regional and global interconnections. National communities do not exclusively "program the action and decisions of governmental and parliamentary bodies," and the latter by no means simply determine what is right or appropriate for their citizens (Offe 1985, p. 286 ff.).

Of course, there is nothing new about the emergence of global problems. Although their importance has grown considerably, many have existed for decades or longer. Some global challenges were ignored because they were regarded as insoluble during the Cold War. Others have been addressed on the basis of distinctly undemocratic criteria and outside the framework of accountable institutions.

Political and strategic decisions (such as those on nuclear weapons) have been made at US-USSR summits, while economic issues (e.g., interest rates and trade balances) have been considered at G7 meetings. The institutions of the United Nations have generally been marginalized; their function has been more one of discussion and representation than one of effective management of pressing strategic or socioeconomic questions.

Now that the old confrontation between East and West has ended, regional and global problems such as the environment, the spread of AIDS, the debt burden of the so-called Third World, the flow of financial resources that escape national jurisdiction, the drug trade, and international crime have been placed on the international political agenda. Nonetheless, profound ambiguity still reigns as to which institutions should take supranational decisions and according to what criteria.

Political theory's exploration of emerging global and regional problems is still in its infancy. While democratic theory has examined and debated at length the challenges to democracy that emerge from within the boundaries of the nation state, it has not seriously questioned whether the nation state itself can remain at the center of democratic thought. The questions posed by the rapid growth of complex connections and relations between states and societies and by the evident intersection of national and international forces and processes remain largely unexplored.

2 The Limits of Democratic Theory

Throughout the nineteenth and twentieth centuries there has been an assumption at the heart of liberal democratic thought concerning a "symmetric" and "congruent" relationship between political decision makers and the recipients of political decisions. In fact, symmetry and congruence are assumed at two crucial points: between citizen-voters and the decision makers whom they are (in principle) able to hold to account, and between the "output" (decisions, policies, etc.) of decision makers and their constituents (ultimately, "the people" in a delimited territory) (see Held 1991). It has been assumed, in other words, by democratic theorists, orthodox and radical, that "the fate of a national community" is largely in its own hands, and that a satisfactory theory of democracy can be developed by examining the interplay between "actors" and "structures" in the nation state.

At the center of this approach to democratic politics is a taken-for-granted conception of sovereignty and an uncritically appropriated concept of political community. The difficulty here is that political communities have rarely, if ever, existed in isolation as bounded geographical totalities, and they are better thought of as multiple overlapping networks of interaction. These networks of interaction crystallize around different sites and forms of power (economic, political, military, and cultural, among others), producing patterns of activity that do not correspond in any straightforward way to territorial boundaries (see Mann 1986, chapter 1). The spatial reach of the modern nation state did not fix impermeable borders for other networks, the scope and reach of which have been as much local as international or global. Political communities are locked into a variety of processes and structures that range in and through them, linking and fragmenting them in complex constellations. It is no surprise, then, that national communities by no means make and determine decisions and policies exclusively for themselves, and that governments by no means determine what is right or appropriate exclusively for their own citizens.

The assumption that one can understand the nature and possibilities of political community by referring merely to national structures and mechanisms of political power is not justified. While it is a mistake to conclude from the seeming flux of contemporary interaction networks that political communities today are without distinctive degrees of division or cleavage at their "borders," they have been shaped by multiple interaction networks and power systems over time. This leads to questions both about the fate of the idea of the political community and about the appropriate locus for the articulation of democratic political good. If the agent at the heart of modern political discourse (be it a person, a group, or a collectivity) is locked into a variety of overlapping communities, "domestic" and "international," then the proper "home" of politics and democracy becomes a puzzling matter.

3 The Requirement of the Democratic Good: Cosmopolitan Democracy

If freedom is threatened by the behaviors of other nations and states, what is right for a political community, Kant argued, cannot prevail. In contrast, "right" can prevail, Kant held, if the rule of law is sustained in all states as well as in international relations (1970, pp. 107–108; see Reiss 1970, pp. 33–34). Within the terms of the argument presented here, this is an important contention, but it must be recast to meet the conditions of democracy in the context of national, regional, and global interconnectedness. Accordingly, it can be maintained, democracy can prevail in a political community if and only if it is not impeded by threats arising from the action (or nonaction) of other political communities or from the networks of interaction that cut across community boundaries.

Although the threats to freedom derive, in Kant's view, from many forms of violence, they stem primarily from war and the preparation for war. "The greatest evils that affect civilized nations are," he wrote, "brought about by war, and not so much by actual wars in the past or the present as by never-ending and indeed continually increasing preparations for war." (quoted in Reiss 1970, p. 34) A violent abrogation of law and right in one place has serious consequences in many other places and can be experienced everywhere (Kant 1970, pp. 107–108). In Kant's account, the establishment of what is right requires the abolition of war as a means of politics. The "spirits" of commerce and of republicanism provide a clear impetus to this possibility: commerce generates networks of mutual self-interest that become hostile to the disruption caused by war and war efforts, and republicanism creates polities that depend on consent and lead citizens not only to be highly cautious about war (since all its "calamities" fall directly on them) but also to respect others whose republics are also consensual and law-abiding (ibid., pp. 100 and 114).

While the threats to autonomy from war and direct coercion are hard to overestimate, they constitute only one element in the challenge to self-government or self-determination in the political community. Such challenges can come from any of the sources of power and domination—economic, political, cultural, military. Power in any one of these spheres can erode the effective entrenchment of democracy. And challenges to democracy can arise not only from within the power domains of particular communities but also from power domains that cut across communities. Sites of power can be national, transnational, and international. Accordingly, democracy within a political community requires democracy in the international sphere. To put the point somewhat differently: a national democratic state upholding a national democratic public law needs to be buttressed and supported by an international structure of such law, or by what I shall call "cosmopolitan democratic law." By this I mean, in the first instance, a democratic public law—establishing the accountability of power systems—entrenched within and across borders.

Cosmopolitan democratic law is most appropriately conceived as a domain of law different in kind from the law of states and the law made between one state and another (that is, international law). For Kant, the foremost interpreter of the idea of a cosmopolitan law, cosmopolitan law is neither a fantastic nor a utopian way of conceiving law; it is a "necessary complement" to the unwritten code of existing national and international law, and a means of transforming the latter into a public law of humanity (1970, p. 108).[1] Kant limited the form and the scope of cosmopolitan law to the conditions of universal hospitality, by which he meant the right of a stranger or a foreigner "not to be treated with hostility" when arriving in someone else's country (p. 105). He emphasized that this right extended to the circumstances that allow people to enjoy an exchange of ideas and goods with the inhabitants of another country, but that it did not extend as far as the right to be entertained or the right to permanent settlement, let alone the right of citizenship (pp. 105–108). A foreigner ought not to suffer any enmity "so long as he behaves in a peaceful manner," although he can be turned away "if this can be done without causing his death" (pp. 105–106). The right of hospitality is, in short, a right to present oneself and to be heard—the conditions necessary "to *attempt* to enter into relations with the native inhabitants" (p. 106).

Cosmopolitan law, thus understood, transcends the particular claims of nations and states and extends to all in the "universal community." It connotes a right and a duty that must be accepted if people are to learn to tolerate one another's company and to coexist peacefully. In Kant's hands, these arguments also lead to a striking rejection of colonialism as "the *inhospitable* conduct of the civilized states of our continent, especially the commercial states" and "the injustice they display in *visiting* foreign countries and peoples (which in their case is the same as *conquering* them)" (p. 106). For Kant universal hospitality is, therefore, the condition of cooperative relations and of just conduct. But while Kant's opposition to colonialism and arguments for universal hospitality are noteworthy, they do not elaborate adequately the conditions of such hospitality; without conceiving of cosmopolitan law as cosmopolitan *democratic* law, the conditions for the protection of freedom and autonomy for each and all cannot be satisfactorily envisaged.

The pursuit in diverse locales of individual or collective projects, within the context of a commitment to universal "good neighborliness," requires that the anatomy of power and domination be grasped in order that the legitimate boundaries of one's own autonomy and that of others can be appreciated. Universal hospitality must involve, at the minimum, both enjoyment of a certain autonomy and respect for the necessary constraints on autonomy. That is to say, it must comprise mutual acknowledgment of, and respect for, the equal and legitimate rights of others to pursue their own projects and life plans. Moreover, in a highly interconnected world, "others" include not just those found in the immediate community, but all those whose fates are interlocked in networks of economic, political, and environmental interaction. Universal hospitality is not achieved if, for economic, cultural, or other reasons, the quality of the lives of others is shaped and determined in near or far-off lands without their participation, agreement, or consent. The condition of universal hospitality (or, as I would rather put it, of a cosmopolitan orientation) is not cosmopolitan law narrowly conceived—following Kant—but rather a cosmopolitan democratic public law in which power is, in principle, accountable wherever it is located and however far removed its sources are from those whom it significantly affects.

A commitment to this form of cosmopolitanism entails a duty to work toward the establishment of an international community of democratic states and societies committed to upholding democratic public law both within and across their own boundaries: a cosmopolitan democratic community. In Kant's account, the establishment of a cosmopolitan community depends on the creation of a "pacific federation" or "union"—that is, a treaty, among a steadily expanding number of states, to prevent war permanently. Kant distinguished between "pacific unions" based upon federal structures and those based on confederal structures. A federal association is based, "like that of the American States, . . . on a political constitution and is therefore indissoluble," whereas a confederal structure signifies merely "a voluntary gathering of various states which can be *dissolved* at any time" (1970, p. 171). These terms can be refined further by conceiving of federalism as a political union in which there are common financial, foreign, and military policies and no exit clauses for "subfederal" entities; confederalism, in contrast, connotes a union in which nations and states retain separate financial, foreign, and military policies along with exit clauses that can bring to an end negotiated, coordinated relations.

Kant argued firmly on behalf of confederalism in international affairs, on the ground that a single state of all peoples—a state of nations or an international state—is an impractical and potentially dangerous objective. Nonetheless, the idea of a democratic cosmopolitan order is not simply compatible with the idea of confederalism. It is the case that the establishment of a cosmopolitan democracy requires the active consent of peoples and nations: initial membership can only be voluntary. It would be a contradiction of the very idea of democracy if a cosmopolitan democratic order were created nonvoluntarily (that is, coercively). If the inauguration of a democratic international order is to be legitimate, it must be based on consent. Thereafter, however, in circumstances in which individuals are not directly engaged in the process of governance, consent ought to follow from the majority decision of their representatives, so long as the latter—the trustees of the governed—uphold cosmopolitan democratic law and its covenants.

4 The Institutional Program of Cosmopolitan Democracy

Against the background of these arguments, how should democracy be understood? The problem of democracy in our times is to specify how it can be secured in a series of interconnected power and authority centers. Democracy involves not only the implementation of a cluster of civil, political, and social rights (freedom of speech, press, and assembly, the right to vote in free and fair elections, universal education, and so on) but also the pursuit and the enactment of these rights in transnational and inter-governmental power structures. Democracy can only be fully sustained in and through the agencies and organizations that form an element of, and yet cut across, the territorial boundaries of the nation state. The possibility of democracy today must, in short, be linked to an expanding framework of democratic states and agencies bound by and committed to democratic public law. How should this be understood from an institutional point of view? To address this question involves unpacking what I call "the cosmopolitan model of democracy."

To begin with, the cosmopolitan model requires, as a transitional measure, that the UN system actually live up to its charter. Among other things, this would involve pursuing measures to implement key elements of rights conventions, enforcing the prohibition on the discretionary right to use force, and activating the collective security system envisaged in the UN Charter. In addition, if the charter's model were extended (for example, by providing means of redress in the case of human rights violations through a new international human rights court, or by modifying the veto arrangement in the Security Council and rethinking representation on that council to allow for adequate regional accountability), a basis might be established for the UN Charter system to generate political resources of its own and to act as an autonomous decision-making center.

However, while each move in this direction would be significant, particularly in enhancing the prospects of a more enduring peace, it would still represent, at best, a move toward a very partial or incomplete form of democracy in international life. Certainly, each state would come to enjoy greater equality in the UN system, and regional interests would be better represented. But the dynamics and the logic of the inter-state system would still represent an immensely powerful force in global affairs, the massive disparities of power and asymmetries of resources in the global political economy would be left virtually unaddressed, ad hoc responses to pressing international and transnational issues would remain typical, there would be no forum for the pursuit of global questions directly accountable to the sub-jects and agencies of civil societies, and the whole question of the ac-countability of international organizations and global bodies would remain unresolved.

Thus, hand in hand with the changes already described, the cos-mopolitan model of democracy would seek the creation of regional parliaments (for example, in Latin America and Africa) and the en-hancement of the role of such bodies where they already exist (as in Europe) in order that their decisions become recognized, in princi-ple, as legitimate independent sources of law. The model anticipates, in addition, the possibility of general referenda of groups cutting across nations and nation states on issues as diverse as energy policy, the balance between public and private transportation, and the orga-nization of regional authorities, with constituencies defined according to the nature and scope of controversial transnational issues.

Furthermore, alongside these developments, the cosmopolitan model of democracy would seek the entrenchment of a cluster of rights, including civil, political, economic, and social rights, in order to provide shape and limits to democratic decision making.[2] This re-quires that such rights be enshrined within the constitutions of par-liaments and assemblies (at the national and the international level) and that the influence of international courts be extended so that groups and individuals have an effective means of suing political au-thorities for the enactment and enforcement of key rights, within and beyond political associations.

In the final analysis, the formation of an authoritative assembly of all democratic states and agencies—a reformed General Assembly of the United Nations, or a complement to it—would be an objective. Agreement on the terms of reference of an international democratic assembly would be difficult, to say the least. Among the difficulties to be faced would be the rules determining the assembly's representative base. (Should one country get one vote? Could major international functional organizations be represented?) But if its operating rules could be settled—in an international constitutional convention, for example—the new assembly would become an authoritative interna-tional center for the consideration and examination of pressing global issues such as health and disease, food supply and distribution, the debt burden of the Third World, the instability of the hundreds of billions of dollars that circulate the globe daily, ozone depletion, and reducing the risks of nuclear and chemical warfare.

The cosmopolitan model of democracy presents a program of possible transformations with short-term and long-term political implications. It does not present an all-or-nothing choice; rather, it lays down a direction of possible change with clear points of orientation. These include the following changes in the short term:

reform of the UN Security Council (to give developing countries a significant voice)

creation of a second chamber in the UN (after an international constitutional convention)

enhanced political regionalization (the European Union and beyond) and use of transnational referenda

compulsory jurisdiction before the International Court and the creation of a new international Human Rights Court

foundation of a new coordinating economic agency at the regional and global levels

establishment of an effective, accountable, international military force.

For the long term the following changes would be needed:

entrenchment of cosmopolitan democratic law: a new charter of rights and obligations locked into different domains of political, social, and economic power

a global parliament (with limited revenue-raising capacity) connected to regions, nations, and localities

an interconnected global legal system, embracing elements of criminal and civil law, and an international criminal court

separation of political and economic interests through the public funding of deliberative assemblies and electoral processes

establishment of the accountability of international and transnational economic agencies to parliaments and assemblies at the regional and global levels the permanent shift of a growing proportion of nation states' coercive capability to regional and global institutions, with the ultimate aim of demilitarization and the transcendence of the war system.

If the history and practice of democracy has been centered until now on the idea of locality and place—the city state, the community, the nation—is it likely that in the future it will be centered exclusively on the international or global domain, if it is to be centered anywhere at all? To draw this conclusion is to misunderstand the nature of contemporary globalization and the arguments being presented here. Globalization is, to borrow a phrase, a *dialectical* process; local transformation is as much an element of globalization as the lateral extension of social relations across space and time (Giddens 1990, p. 64). New demands for regional and local autonomy are unleashed as groups find themselves buffeted by global forces and by inappropriate or ineffective political regimes. While these circumstances are clearly fraught with danger and with the risk of an intensification of a sectarian politics, they also portend a new possibility: the recovery of an intensive and participatory democracy at local levels as a complement to the deliberative assemblies of the wider global order. That is, they portend a political order of democratic associations, cities, and nations as well as of regions and global networks.

Conclusion

The cosmopolitan conception of democracy is a means of strengthening democracy "within" communities and civil associations by elaborating and reinforcing democracy from "outside" through a network of regional and international agencies and assemblies that cut across spatially delimited locales. The impetus to the pursuit of this network can be found in a number of processes and forces, including the development of transnational grass-roots movements with clear regional or global objectives, such as the protection of natural resources and the environment, and the alleviation of disease and ill health; the elaboration of new legal rights and duties affecting states and individuals in connection with the "common heritage of humankind," the protection of the "global commons," the defense of human rights, and the deployment of force; and the emergence and proliferation in the twentieth century of international institutions to coordinate transnational forces and problems, from the UN and its agencies to regional political networks and organizations (see Falk 1991). Accordingly, it can be argued, a political basis exists upon which to build a more systematic democratic future.

This future ought to be conceived in cosmopolitan terms—a new institutional complex with global scope, given shape and form by reference to a basic democratic law, that takes on the character of government to the extent, and only to the extent, that it promulgates, implements, and enforces this law. But however its institutions are precisely envisaged, it is a future built on the recognition that democracy within a single community and democratic relations among communities are deeply interconnected, and that new organizational and legal mechanisms must be established if democracy is to survive and prosper.[3]

Notes to Chapter 9

1. The exact meaning of Kant's conception of cosmopolitan law has, of course, long been controversial, but this controversy will not be the direct focus here. For a representative range of views see Hinsley 1963, chapter 4; Doyle 1983a,b; Wight 1987; Archibugi 1992.

2. It is beyond the scope of this chapter to set out my particular conception of rights, which I link to the notion of a "common structure of political action": the necessary conditions for people to enjoy free and equal political participation. See pp. 227–235 of Held 1991 and, particularly, part III of Held 1995.

3. The themes presented here are explored at greater length in *Cosmopolitan Democracy: An Agenda for a New World Order*, ed. D. Archibugi and D. Held (Polity, 1995), and in D. Held, *Democracy and the Global Order: From the Modern State to Cosmopolitan Governance* (Polity, 1995).

References for Chapter 9

Archibugi, D. 1992. Models of International Organization in Perpetual Peace Projects. *Review of International Studies* 18: 295–317.

Doyle, M. W. 1983a. Kant, Liberal Legacies and Foreign Affairs, Part I. *Philosophy and Public Affairs* 12, no. 3: 205–235.

Doyle, M. W. 1983b. Kant, Liberal Legacies and Foreign Affairs, Part II. *Philosophy and Public Affairs* 12, no. 4: 323–353.

Falk, R. 1991. Positive Prescriptions for the Near Future. World Order Studies Program Occasional Paper 20, Center For International Studies, Princeton University.

Fukuyama, F. 1992. *The End of History and the Last Man.* Free Press.

Giddens, A. 1990. *The Consequences of Modernity.* Polity.

Held, D. 1991. Democracy, the Nation State and the Global System. In *Political Theory Today*, ed. D. Held. Polity.

Held, D. 1993a. Liberalism, Marxism and Democracy. *Theory and Society* 22: 249–288.

Held, D. 1993b. Anything But A Dog's Life? Further Comments On Fukuyama, Callinicos and Giddens. *Theory and Society* 22: 293–304

Held, D. 1995. *Democracy and the Global Order: From the Modern State to Cosmopolitan Governance.* Polity.

Hinsley, F. 1963. *Power and the Pursuit of Peace.* Cambridge University Press.

Kant, I. 1970. *Kant's Political Writings*, ed. H. Reiss. Cambridge University Press.

Mann, M. 1986. *The Sources of Social Power,* volume 1. Cambridge University Press.

Offe, C. 1985. *Disorganized Capitalism.* MIT Press.

Reiss, H. 1970. Introduction. In *Kant's Political Writings*, ed. H. Reiss. Cambridge University Press.

Wight, M. 1987. An Anatomy of International Thought. *Review of International Studies* 13.

Contributors

Karl-Otto Apel is Professor Emeritus of Philosophy at the University of Frankfurt. He is the author of numerous books, including *Transformation of Philosophy* (Routledge, 1980) and *Selected Essays: Ethics and the Theory of Rationality* (Humanities Press, 1996).

Kenneth Baynes is an Associate Professor of Philosophy at the State University of New York at Stony Brook. He is the author of *The Normative Grounds of Social Criticism: Kant, Rawls, and Habermas* (SUNY Press, 1992).

James Bohman is Danforth Professor of Philosophy at Saint Louis University. He is the author of *Public Deliberation* (MIT Press, 1996) and *New Philosophy of Social Science* (MIT Press, 1991).

Jürgen Habermas is Professor Emeritus of Philosophy and Sociology at the University of Frankfurt. He is the author of numerous books, including *Between Facts and Norms* (MIT Press, 1996).

David Held is Lecturer of Politics at the Open University in London. He is the author of *Models of Democracy* (Stanford University Press, 1987), *Democracy and the Global Order* (Stanford University Press, 1995), and an editor of many collections, including *Cosmopolitan Democracy* with Daniele Archibugi (Polity Press, 1995).

Axel Honneth is a Professor of Philosophy at the University of Frankfurt. He is the author of *Critique of Power* (MIT Press, 1991) and *The Struggle for Recognition* (MIT Press, 1995).

Matthias Lutz-Bachmann is a Professor of Philosophy at the University of Frankfurt. He is the author of *Geschichte und Subjekt: Die Geschichtsphilosophie im Werk von Kant und Marx* (Beck, 1992).

Contributors

Thomas McCarthy is a Professor of Philosophy at Northwestern University. He is the author of *Ideals and Illusions* (MIT Press, 1991) and a co-author, with David Couzens Hoy, *Critical Theory* (Blackwell, 1994).

Martha Nussbaum is Ernst Freund Professor of Law and Ethics at the University of Chicago. She is the author of *The Fragility of Goodness* (Cambridge University Press, 1986) and *The Therapy of Desire* (Princeton University Press, 1994).

Index

Studies in Contemporary German Social Thought
Thomas McCarthy, General Editor

Theodor W. Adorno, *Against Epistemology: A Metacritique*
Theodor W. Adorno, *Hegel: Three Studies*
Theodor W. Adorno, *Prisms*
Karl-Otto Apel, *Understanding and Explanation: A Transcendental-Pragmatic Perspective*
Seyla Benhabib, Wolfgang Bonß, and John McCole, editors, *On Max Horkheimer: New Perspectives*
Seyla Benhabib and Fred Dallmayr, editors, *The Communicative Ethics Controversy*
Richard J. Bernstein, editor, *Habermas and Modernity*
Ernst Bloch, *Natural Law and Human Dignity*
Ernst Bloch, *The Principle of Hope*
Ernst Bloch, *The Utopian Function of Art and Literature: Selected Essays*
Hans Blumenberg, *The Genesis of the Copernican World*
Hans Blumenberg, *The Legitimacy of the Modern Age*
Hans Blumenberg, *Shipwreck with Spectator: Paradigm of a Metaphor for Existence*
Hans Blumenberg, *Work on Myth*
James Bohman, *Public Deliberation: Pluralism, Complexity, and Democracy*
James Bohman and Matthias Lutz-Bachmann, editors, *Perpetual Peace: Essays on Kant's Cosmopolitan Ideal*
Susan Buck-Morss, *The Dialectics of Seeing: Walter Benjamin and the* Arcades Project
Craig Calhoun, editor, *Habermas and the Public Sphere*
Jean Cohen and Andrew Arato, *Civil Society and Political Theory*
Maeve Cooke, *Language and Reason: A Study of Habermas's Pragmatics*
Helmut Dubiel, *Theory and Politics: Studies in the Development of Critical Theory*
John Forester, editor, *Critical Theory and Public Life*
David Frisby, *Fragments of Modernity: Theories of Modernity in the Work of Simmel, Kracauer and Benjamin*
Hans-Georg Gadamer, *Philosophical Apprenticeships*
Hans-Georg Gadamer, *Reason in the Age of Science*
Jürgen Habermas, *Between Facts and Norms: Contributions to a Discourse Theory of Law and Democracy*
Jürgen Habermas, *Justification and Application: Remarks on Discourse Ethics*
Jürgen Habermas, *On the Logic of the Social Sciences*
Jürgen Habermas, *Moral Consciousness and Communicative Action*
Jürgen Habermas, *The New Conservatism: Cultural Criticism and the Historians' Debate*
Jürgen Habermas, *The Philosophical Discourse of Modernity: Twelve Lectures*
Jürgen Habermas, *Philosophical-Political Profiles*
Jürgen Habermas, *Postmetaphysical Thinking: Philosophical Essays*
Jürgen Habermas, *The Structural Transformation of the Public Sphere: An Inquiry into a Category of Bourgeois Society*
Jürgen Habermas, editor, *Observations on "The Spiritual Situation of the Age"*
Axel Honneth, *The Critique of Power: Reflective Stages in a Critical Social Theory*
Axel Honneth, *The Struggle for Recognition: The Moral Grammar of Social Conflicts*
Axel Honneth and Hans Joas, editors, *Communicative Action: Essays on Jürgen Habermas's* The Theory of Communicative Action
Axel Honneth, Thomas McCarthy, Claus Offe, and Albrecht Wellmer, editors, *Cultural-Political Interventions in the Unfinished Project of Enlightenment*
Axel Honneth, Thomas McCarthy, Claus Offe, and Albrecht Wellmer, editors, *Philosophical Interventions in the Unfinished Project of Enlightenment*

Max Horkheimer, *Between Philosophy and Social Science: Selected Early Writings*
Tom Huhn and Lambert Zuidervaart, editors, *The Semblance of Subjectivity: Essays in Adorno's Aesthetic Theory*
Hans Joas, *G. H. Mead: A Contemporary Re-examination of His Thought*
Michael Kelly, editor, *Critique and Power: Recasting the Foucault/Habermas Debate*
Hans Herbert Kögler, *The Power of Dialogue: Critical Hermeneutics after Gadamer and Foucault*
Reinhart Koselleck, *Critique and Crisis: Enlightenment and the Pathogenesis of Modern Society*
Reinhart Koselleck, *Futures Past: On the Semantics of Historical Time*
Harry Liebersohn, *Fate and Utopia in German Sociology, 1887-1923*
Herbert Marcuse, *Hegel's Ontology and the Theory of Historicity*
Larry May and Jerome Kohn, editors, *Hannah Arendt: Twenty Years Later*
Pierre Missac, *Walter Benjamin's Passages*
Shierry Weber Nicholsen, *Exact Imagination, Late Work: On Adorno's Aesthetics*
Gil G. Noam and Thomas E. Wren, editors, *The Moral Self*
Guy Oakes, *Weber and Rickert: Concept Formation in the Cultural Sciences*
Claus Offe, *Contradictions of the Welfare State*
Claus Offe, *Disorganized Capitalism: Contemporary Transformations of Work and Politics*
Claus Offe, *Modernity and the State: East, West*
Claus Offe, *Varieties of Transition: The East European and East German Experience*
Helmut Peukert, *Science, Action, and Fundamental Theology: Toward a Theology of Communicative Action*
Joachim Ritter, *Hegel and the French Revolution: Essays on the* Philosophy of Right
William E. Scheuerman, *Between the Norm and the Exception: The Frankfurt School and the Rule of Law*
Alfred Schmidt, *History and Structure: An Essay on Hegelian-Marxist and Structuralist Theories of History*
Dennis Schmidt, *The Ubiquity of the Finite: Hegel, Heidegger, and the Entitlements of Philosophy*
Carl Schmitt, *The Crisis of Parliamentary Democracy*
Carl Schmitt, *Political Romanticism*
Carl Schmitt, *Political Theology: Four Chapters on the Concept of Sovereignty*
Gary Smith, editor, *On Walter Benjamin: Critical Essays and Recollections*
Michael Theunissen, *The Other: Studies in the Social Ontology of Husserl, Heidegger, Sartre, and Buber*
Ernst Tugendhat, *Self-Consciousness and Self-Determination*
Georgia Warnke, *Justice and Interpretation*
Mark Warren, *Nietzsche and Political Thought*
Albrecht Wellmer, *The Persistence of Modernity: Essays on Aesthetics, Ethics and Postmodernism*
Joel Whitebook, *Perversion and Utopia: A Study in Psychoanalysis and Critical Theory*
Rolf Wiggershaus, *The Frankfurt School: Its History, Theories, and Political Significance*
Thomas E. Wren, editor, *The Moral Domain: Essays in the Ongoing Discussion between Philosophy and the Social Sciences*
Lambert Zuidervaart, *Adorno's Aesthetic Theory: The Redemption of Illusion*